MASTERING
COMMUNITY

MASTERING COMMUNITY

The Surprising Ways Coming Together Moves

Us from Surviving to Thriving

CHRISTINE PORATH

balance

NEW YORK   BOSTON

Balance
Hachette Book Group
1290 Avenue of the Americas, New York, NY 10104
grandcentralpublishing.com
twitter.com/grandcentralpub

First Edition: March 2022

Balance is an imprint of Grand Central Publishing. The Balance name and logo are trademarks of Hachette Book Group, Inc.

The publisher is not responsible for websites (or their content) that are not owned by the publisher.

The Hachette Speakers Bureau provides a wide range of authors for speaking events. To find out more, go to www.hachettespeakersbureau.com or call (866) 376-6591.

Library of Congress Cataloging-in-Publication Data has been applied for.

ISBNs: 9781538736869 (hardcover), 9781538705155 (ebook)

Printed in the United States of America

LSC-C

10 9 8 7 6 5 4 3 2 1

The Mighty Poraths
Mike, Sarah, Annabel, Isaac, Henry, and Noah

CONTENTS

CONTENTS

INTRODUCTION

> A deep sense of love and belonging is an irresistible need of
> all men, women, and children. We are biologically, cognitively,
> physically, and spiritually wired to love, to be loved, and to
> belong. When those needs are not met, we don't function as we
> were meant to. We break. We fall apart. We numb. We ache. We
> hurt others. We get sick.
>
> —Brené Brown

We yearn for connection. But we are disconnected. We find ourselves on platforms, not in communities. It doesn't help that many traditional sources of community have withered. In neighborhoods, kids may gather. Adults, not so much. Droves of people have stopped attending church. And far fewer people are going into a workplace. The very future of the workplace, and the sense of community we felt at work, is at risk.

Despite our deep desire to feel a sense of belonging, many of us struggle to feel a part of a team (or to find a team!). We're on the sidelines. Stuck. The more hours we log there, the tougher it feels—our confidence plummets, our will wanes, our sense of isolation increases. We languish. We break. We numb.

It doesn't have to be that way. We can move from surviving to thriving, together. Someone in my own tribe showed me how.

In 2008, my brother Mike and his wife Sarah had a truly terrible, life-changing day. In the morning, a doctor informed them that their unborn child was missing a kidney and possibly other organs. That afternoon, they returned home to even more devastating news: their two-year-old daughter Annabel had a rare chromosome disorder, dup15q, and her mind would probably not develop beyond that of a five-year-old child.

Feeling lost, scared, and alone, Mike turned to Google. "I wasn't prepared for this very rare disease that we'd never heard of," he said. "I didn't know how to parent a kid like this." Most of the guidance he found online was unhelpful. But then he clicked on a PDF file containing six stories from parents whose children experienced autism, thirty to forty seizures a day, and other disabilities. These were the most powerful stories Mike had ever read, and that's saying a lot given that he had worked as a journalist for ABC News, NBC News, and the *New York Times*. Containing joy and humor, they offered reason for hope. If these parents could cope with these disabilities and even find joy in the process, maybe Mike and his wife could do the same.

Mike grew more optimistic after he and his wife conquered another parenting challenge. Typically, children pick up food and other items by using their forefinger and thumbs in a "pincher grasp." Annabel had trouble with this pincher grasp and couldn't pick up anything, including her favorite food. Mike and Sarah turned to therapists, doctors, and other pediatric specialists, and when nothing helped, Mike again resorted to Google. He posted the pincher grasp question on a message board, and the mother of a dup15q child replied with a solution. Mike and Sarah followed her directions, cutting two tiny holes in a sock—one for Annabel's forefinger, another for her thumb—and placed the sock-glove on her right hand. They put a normal sock on her left hand so she couldn't "cheat" and grasp an item using her two wrists. Every day at mealtime, Annabel's parents equipped her with the sock-gloves and placed some delicious blueberries in her dining tray, knowing how irresistible she found them. Within a month, not only had Annabel activated her pincher grasp—she'd mastered it!

Health solutions, Mike realized, can be simple, and the best ones often reflect lived experience rather than professional expertise. Family and friends are great, Mike told me, but people facing health challenges need a tribe. Instead of asking isolated questions on lone message boards, they need a network, a flesh-and-blood community, and an organized, moderated forum for discussion. He imagined a series of dinner parties, where a diverse mix of doctors, caregivers, researchers, and patients could convene in an intimate, comfortable setting to ask questions or simply seek support. Eventually these dinner parties would morph into something bigger and continuous, like a global network. Such a network had potential for global reach and impact. If well executed, he thought, it could even form a blueprint for the future of healthcare.

In 2014, Mike and Sarah bootstrapped a new venture they called The Mighty, a digital media company connecting people facing disease, disability, and disorders. Since then, The Mighty has grown from a tiny tribe of several dozen to the largest, most engaged healthcare community in the world. The Mighty has attracted millions in venture capital and now hosts over three million members who exchange advice and provide support in seventy-eight different languages. In 2019, after members clamored for in-person meetings, The Mighty orchestrated over one thousand nondigital meetings. Every month, The Mighty stories receive over one hundred million views and the community sends over twenty million emails to members. Many members post questions for others, like the post from a man from Portugal. After asking about his bipolar disorder, the man received feedback the next day from people in fifteen different countries, including developing African nations.

More people today find themselves feeling like Mike on the day he received the devastating diagnoses about his children: alone and disconnected. Our society is increasingly divisive and nasty, lacking the security, support, and warmth of traditional communities. A revealing study showed that the number of "close others" that Americans claimed to have in 1985 was only three. In 2004 this dropped to one, with over 25 percent of Americans saying that they have no one with whom to share a personal problem.[1] Our well-being has declined in turn.

From 2013 to 2016, major depression rose by 33 percent according to data from forty-one million Blue Cross Blue Shield health records.[2] According to the Centers for Disease Control and Prevention, the rate of suicide in the United States increased 28 percent between 1999 and 2016.

Isolation has also damaged business performance. My colleague Tony Schwartz and I asked over twenty thousand people across diverse industries and organizations around the world about their quality of work and life.

The fundamental question we sought to answer was: What stands in the way of being more satisfied and productive at work? This survey was posted on *Harvard Business Review* (and later on *Huffington Post,* where we collected a small proportion of responses). We published results in *Harvard Business Review* and the *New York Times.* Our study found that 65 percent of people don't feel any sense of community at work. Another study found that 76 percent reported difficulty making connections with work teammates.[3] Over 40 percent feel physically or emotionally isolated in the workplace.[4] Lonelier workers reported lower job satisfaction, fewer promotions, more frequent job switching, and a higher likelihood of quitting their current job in the next six months.[5] Lonelier employees also tend to perform worse.[6] As US Surgeon General Vivek Murthy explains, "At work, loneliness reduces task performance, limits creativity, and impairs other aspects of executive function such as reasoning and decision making. For our health and our work, it is imperative that we address the loneliness epidemic quickly."[7]

When people feel a sense of community at work, we found that they are 74 percent more engaged and 81 percent more likely to stay with the organization. They report 83 percent higher thriving at work, an internal sense of being energized, alive, and growing. In another study, Gretchen Spreitzer and I looked across six different organizations from various industries and found that those thriving at work had 16 percent better performance (as reported by their managers).[8] They also were far less burned out, so they missed much less work and reported significantly fewer doctor visits, which meant huge healthcare savings and less lost time for the company.

This research is very personal for me. I find myself—and others—surviving or thriving based on feeling a sense of community and belonging. At the extreme, workplaces may feel void of community, and even toxic. Instead of supportive, energizing connections, a workplace might feel draining from de-energizing ties that suck the life and siphon the spirit from us. I vividly recall walking into a hospital room outside of Cleveland to see my strong, athletic dad with electrodes strapped to his bare chest. What put him there? Work-related stress stemming from two toxic bosses.

At the time, I didn't realize he was inaugurating a family tradition. A couple of years following this medical event, just after I'd graduated from college, I scored what I thought was my dream job, helping a global athletic brand launch a sports academy. Unfortunately, I'd stumbled into an uncivil work culture where bullying, rudeness, and other forms of disrespect ran rampant. Since then I've felt both the joy of working in places that embodied community as well as the sheer disappointment and frustration of working in places that lack community. These experiences inspired me to study workplace culture and how leaders might work together to make their people and organizations thrive.

Creating Tribes That Thrive

I define a community as a group of individuals who share a mutual concern for one another's welfare. I often use tribes to refer to smaller communities, and I call the people who bring tribes together to create a larger community tribal leaders. Communities and tribes are everywhere—they can exist in families, schools, places of worship, and local municipalities. They often include duties or obligations, and members may share ideas, interests, proximity (remote or not), or any other number of things, but a distinguishing factor is caring for one another. Community and tribe are subjective. They reflect an awareness of the bond existing between people.

Unfortunately, community-rooted organizations like The Mighty remain rare in today's business landscape. Organizations consistently underestimate the value of community. Alternately, they focus on areas like employee engagement, retention, and purpose instead of on building community first and allowing these other elements to follow. Our need for affiliation, or connection, is one of our three most fundamental needs, along with autonomy and competence. Of these three, connection is arguably the most important.[9]

I'd like us all to form community-first businesses like Mike's. To that end, I've investigated hundreds of organizations like The Mighty, trying to determine the dynamics underlying successful communities so that we can help create more of them. I've interviewed and surveyed hundreds of thousands of people across six continents in nearly every industry and type of organization, including start-ups, Fortune 500 giants, hospitals, nonprofits, schools, universities, sports teams, religious communities, government agencies, and community, industry, leadership, coaching, and student associations. Consulting with scores of diverse communities around the world, I've discovered that companies and leaders can best build communities by

- sharing information,
- unleashing people,
- creating a respectful environment,
- practicing radical candor,
- providing a sense of meaning, and
- boosting member well-being.

Part 1 of this book details these characteristics in turn, considering how they each help us build the types of communities that bring out the best in employees. I intend this section as a practical guide for leaders and managers seeking to build thriving workplaces, and for anyone trying to become more effective and influential at work. Just because you're not leading an organization doesn't mean you can't make it better for everyone, including yourself. In fact, my research confirms that community matters, and that your kindness, consideration, and respect can have a potent effect, creating a positive dynamic among your colleagues. Through small actions, you can strengthen your community and lift up your organization.

Part 2 of the book reminds us that we as individuals need to control our contributions, bringing our best selves to our tribes. In these chapters, I explore the basics of self-awareness movement, nutrition, recovery, and mindset. Our muscles are like a pharmacy that pump "hope molecules" into our bodily systems, giving us a potential cure to our loneliness and isolation—but only if we get up and move. While a lack of sleep contributes to poor mental and physical health, it also contributes to loneliness. Sleep deprivation is a strong social repellant, complicating our relationships with others and leading to misunderstandings. Pay attention to your mindset and what you're feeding yourself—literally and figuratively. The social media, music, and other entertainment we consume affect not only ourselves but others in our personal and professional tribes. What we ingest from these sources, and our social network, affects our mood and mental health, and we pass our anxiety, depression, and stress on to others.[10]

Introduction

In effect, your body hosts a dynamic and complex inner tribe, comprising over thirty-seven trillion cells. Ask yourself: Am I and my complex inner ecosystem thriving, or am I merely surviving? Don't settle for surviving. Start inching yourself toward thriving. A decade's worth of data, which I've accumulated from tens of thousands of employees across diverse industries and roles, suggests that the vast majority of us are merely surviving. Less than 10 percent of us are managing our inner tribe—our body—well, and only 25 percent are in the reasonable range; 40 percent of us are working at a significant deficit, and nearly 25 percent are in full-fledged crisis. All told, that's 65 percent in the danger zone.

Leaders are most effective when they encourage *and* model respect and care for an inner tribe. When leaders explicitly encourage employees to work in more sustainable ways and when they themselves model a sustainable way of working, their employees are 55 percent more engaged, 53 percent more focused, and much more likely to stay at the company. By creating a culture in which people can thrive, leaders and managers can help us to enjoy happier, healthier, more fulfilling lives so that we in turn can contribute to and enrich our communities.

Too many people today feel like my brother Mike did—disconnected and suffering. As a society, we're not fractured, we're broken. It's time to get back to basics and prioritize human connection. We're not meant to be alone. Community helps support people through challenges and make the good times better. I hope the powerful stories and research in this book inspire and empower you to create a thriving tribe of your own. Organizations and their leaders really do have the power to design groups that strengthen connection. These groups in turn bring out the very best in people, enabling them to elevate additional tribes and communities. Put this book to use, and you'll trigger a ripple effect that will benefit not just your own people, but individuals and organizations across society.

MASTERING COMMUNITY

PART 1

Building Tribes That Thrive

CHAPTER 1

Unite

You can't unlock potential if you cannot unlock people.[1]
—Brené Brown

Phil Jackson coached the Chicago Bulls to six National Basketball Association (NBA) championships, and then came close to repeating that record when he coached the Los Angeles Lakers to five NBA championships. He was legendary as a coach but also won two NBA championships when he played with the New York Knicks. But what set Jackson apart from his peers was something that went beyond his extraordinary ability and skills, according to Steve Kerr, who was one of his players and who is among the very few who can even come close to Jackson's record. An eight-time NBA champion, Kerr won three of his titles as the Golden State Warriors' head coach, and five as a player—three of them with the Chicago Bulls under Coach Jackson. He says that Jackson's success as a coach had much to do with his ability to make his players feel like they were part of a community—a cohesive, mutually supportive community, a band of brothers that was much more than just a sports team.

When Kerr played with the Chicago Bulls, the players started every day with a meeting in Phil's team film room (where they would watch video on their team and opposing teams), which was memorably adorned with a wooden arrow, a tobacco pouch, a bear-claw necklace, an owl feather, a painting that depicted the story of Crazy Horse, and some pictures of a white buffalo calf, the most sacred animal in Sioux lore.[2] These Native

American artifacts were beautiful as decorations, but they were also meant to communicate a message to the players, Kerr explained: "Jackson felt we were a tribe and referred to us as a tribe. That was important to Phil, and he tried to create a sense of a tribe. [Being there] didn't feel like a team meeting. It felt like a gathering spot. And it started to generate conversation. It wasn't about establishing fundamentals that we were going to work on for offense or defense. We were just communicating."[3]

It was on South Dakota's Pine Ridge Reservation, where Jackson and his fellow New York Knicks teammate Bill Bradley had coached a six-year series of basketball clinics, that Jackson was first exposed to Native American tribes and their culture. He was so moved by the Lakota Sioux's practices that he incorporated their values into his leadership and was eventually named Swift Eagle in an official Lakota ceremony. Jackson marshaled his knowledge of Native American culture to promote the idea that for his players, each season should focus on a sacred quest.[4] And just as the Lakota tribe had sacred rites that they practiced, so too did the Chicago Bulls. Before every game they put their hands together for a team chant and invoked their sacred quest—a fourth NBA title was the quest one year.

Central to Jackson's work with his players was the "sense of camaraderie" he provided, according to B. J. Armstrong, who played six seasons for Jackson. This was as important to them as any of his coaching expertise. As Jackson explained to an interviewer, "What we try to do with our group is breathe together, share the same space, find something outside just playing basketball on the court. This 'spiritual stuff' brings an act of community to us."[5] Making sure that everyone on his team felt like they belonged and had a role to play was a critical part of Jackson's overall strategy, and one reason he placed such emphasis on the triangle offense. This is an offense geared toward thinking and moving in unison. What particularly appealed to Jackson about the triangle offense was that it empowered everyone on the team and demanded that they subordinate individual needs to those of the group. It might have seemed like a surprising choice since Jackson had perhaps the greatest NBA basketball player of all time, Michael Jordan, on the team, and most coaches would have designed an offense to key completely off Jordan (as had been the case with the previous coach's system). But Jackson wanted the Bulls to become less of a one-man team fixated on Jordan, to let the ball flow to other players in order to ensure that each player felt his contributions mattered. When he played for the Bulls, Kerr viewed the triangle offense as "part of a whole philosophy of teamwork and connectivity. And I totally felt it when I was playing there. I never felt more important as a player than I did in Chicago."[6]

Jackson developed a culture that demanded and rewarded teamwork, in which everyone felt they were an important part of the team. This applied to the role players, too, those who were not stars or starters. Even those at the very end of the bench were made to feel that they mattered, which encouraged them to remain focused and ready to play anytime they were sent into the game. Player John Salley noted, "On this team you feel like you're worth something even if you're the 12th man."[7] It was that feeling of mattering, of belonging, that unlocked everyone's potential.

Although Jackson's still-unbeaten record of NBA championships coached clearly demonstrates his commitment to winning, he was also committed to the communal spirit that bound the team together, and he understood that winning wasn't the only thing that counted. In 1990, one of Jackson's Chicago Bulls stars, Scottie Pippen, lost his father. Pippen missed a playoff game after the death and was "off" when he returned. Jackson thought it was important for the team to acknowledge Scottie's loss and support him. With Jackson's encouragement, players circled Pippen and said a prayer. "Scottie was clearly moved," Jackson reported, noting that such heartfelt affection was rare in the NBA. Buoyed by his teammates, Pippen lit it up that night, scoring twenty-nine points, with the Bulls finishing off the Philadelphia 76ers to take the playoff series.[8]

By the final game seven of the next series, however, stress had taken its toll on Pippen. He had a migraine that gave him double vision, and his play suffered. Some in the press blamed Scottie for the team's heartbreaking defeat, but Jackson, who was certainly as disappointed as anyone, defended Scottie, as did the men on the team, rallying behind him. That spirit of empathy and camaraderie is the seed from which the championship team was born, according to Jackson.[9]

In one of his books on his coaching experience, *Sacred Hoops* (a play on words that refers both to the hoops on the court and to the Native American metaphor for the loop of life, the "circle of existing things"),[10] Jackson reflects on our society's focus on "rewarding winners at the perilous expense of forsaking community and compassion." He wanted to do things differently, he said—to create a supportive environment for players in which everyone had each other's backs and no one was made to feel that they personally bore the burden of winning. His goal was for the tribe to "heighten the feeling of intimacy, the sense that we were engaged in something sacred and inviolate."[11]

To forge that sense of intimacy and trust, Jackson used the players' daily meeting in the team film room as an opportunity to get them to share their views on topics other than basketball. "Some coaches try to force players to bond with each other by putting them through hellish Marine Corps–style training," he writes. "That's a short-term solution, at best. I've found that the connection will be deeper and last longer if it's built on a foundation of genuine exchange." One of the topics that he focused on for this exchange of views was ethics. Each season, after selecting the twelve-man roster, Jackson would distribute a modern-day reinterpretation of the Ten Commandments and then he'd have one of the players read a section from the book to stimulate team discussion. "Once we had a heated debate about guns after I noticed someone carrying a weapon on the team plane," Jackson writes. Some of the players felt they needed guns for protection, but he challenged them to think about the danger of pulling a gun in a moment of anger. "The Bulls needed to learn that before something tragic happened."[12]

The open dialogue among the players, the willingness to be honest about their thoughts and their feelings, created a deep feeling of trust. "By end of season we had guys crying in front of each other in these meetings," Kerr said. "We had guys toasting one another. It was such an incredible experience. But he set it up by being vulnerable and showing that vulnerability himself and establishing that culture of communication and trust."[13]

All the things that Jackson did to create a supportive community, a tribe, a safe space in which the players felt they could open up and be vulnerable and authentic with each other were critical to the success they enjoyed. And much of what he did to encourage a sense of community is adaptable to all kinds of organizations. In this chapter, I discuss how organizations as diverse as the Chicago Bulls, Cisco, Cleveland Clinic, Spanx, and Google X have created environments that help unlock people's potential, and how you can do so, too.

Shared Patient Experiences: A Rocket Ship for Health

Shared medical appointments (SMAs) may be the medicine of the future. The basic concept works just the way it sounds: A number of patients meet with a single physician, in person or virtually, instead of attending a traditional one-on-one appointment. Dr. Jeffrey Geller, who has been called the godfather of group medicine, started his first groups back when he was still a medical student in 1997, and was one of the earliest practitioners. As a first-year medical resident, Dr. Geller had an epiphany about the potential power of such groups. What he saw among the patients he treated as a resident made him began to wonder: Why did some people exhibit resilience in the face of a medical issue while others completely fell apart? He did some initial research, which showed that people who were lonely were using their health center four to six times more often, and were using the emergency rooms two to three times more often. So he began to view loneliness as a medical issue.

With the help of some grants he received on the basis of his research, and inspired by one of his patients who was doing some informal group work herself, he organized his first couple of groups, both of which focused on diabetes. Dr. Geller, who has been working primarily with underserved areas in Massachusetts and focusing on group work ever since then, sees group work as the antidote to the problem of loneliness. What he discovered was similar to what my brother Mike learned after creating The Mighty, his healthcare organization. The groups under the umbrella of The Mighty were created to address specific health needs, but beyond that they were solving for the fundamental societal problem of isolation.

Explaining how he works with patients in his groups, Geller said that the first visit is really about building rapport, finding out why the patients have come to the group, asking them the one thing they wished they could do if they weren't dealing with whatever problem is making life so hard for them. In a recent diabetes group, he recounted how someone said, "I'm here because I have diabetes and I'm suffering because I have to urinate so often. I can't go to New York City to visit my family. I can't sit on a bus that long." When something like that comes up, someone else in the group will often offer a suggestion—"Hey, I have an idea. Hey, have you tried this medicine? Have you tried eating differently?"—and this kind of exchange bonds people together.[14]

Since then the idea has taken root and spread to many institutions and practices. Dr. Marianne Sumego is the person who pioneered Cleveland Clinic's SMA program in 1999, and she has overseen its development since then. A typical SMA in the Center for Functional Medicine at Cleveland Clinic will bring together ten to twelve patients who share a common diagnosis along with a facilitator who is a registered nurse, and perhaps a nutritionist, or a health coach, advanced practitioners, or experts in whatever field might be most useful to the particular condition being discussed. A physician leads the group and begins by addressing each of the patients individually, soliciting information about their condition, developing a plan for how to tackle it, and then going on to do the same for the next patient until everyone has been heard and everyone has had a chance to ask questions. A physician and health coach work with the group for fourteen of the twenty sessions. A dietitian works with the group independently for six sessions. The process allows the patients to learn from each other as well as from the doctor and helps them to realize that they are not alone in facing their problems. Dr. Sumego told me that these SMAs provide a nonthreatening, supportive environment for patients that is hard to achieve one-on-one.

To illustrate why SMAs can be more effective than individual sessions, Dr. Sumego recounted the story of a patient of hers with a family history of colon cancer who, for many years, had refused to get a colonoscopy. Despite Dr. Sumego's urging, the patient was adamant that she wouldn't do it. This patient later joined an SMA led by Dr. Sumego, and when she revealed to the group her reluctance to go for a colonoscopy, another group member asked her what exactly she was afraid of. It was clear to this group member that the woman didn't grasp the importance of a colonoscopy, so she told her own story. She, too, had been reluctant to have a colonoscopy, she said, but when she finally did, she learned she had cancer. Fortunately, she had caught it at an early enough stage that she was able to seek treatment and enjoy a full recovery. She urged the reluctant patient to go for her test, and rallied her, explaining how she would be able to get through it. Based on this, the woman did finally have the colonoscopy that Dr. Sumego had been recommending for years.

As Dr. Sumego explained, the feeling of community helps patients not to feel so isolated and gives them the advantage of experiences shared by those facing the same issues as they do. Patients will say to one another, "Yeah, you can do it, I know you can meet these hurdles, because I did." That can have a much bigger impact coming from a peer than from a doctor. Patients in SMAs realize they're not the only ones to have these problems, they learn from each other, they get encouragement and reinforcement from their fellow group members, and they celebrate each other's successes. Peer pressure is part of the group dynamic, too, and it also can be more effective than a doctor's recommendations, as the story of Dr. Sumego's patient reveals.

According to bestselling author Dr. Mark Hyman, the founder and director of the UltraWellness Center and the head of strategy and innovation at the Cleveland Clinic Center for Functional Medicine, a communal approach to medicine just might have the potential to revolutionize healthcare. And it may be particularly useful for dealing with the kinds of issues addressed by functional medicine, which is Dr. Hyman's specialty. Functional medicine is focused on the treatment and management of chronic disease through medical as well as behavioral and lifestyle interventions, with a particular focus on nutrition. The many chronic conditions that functional medicine treats range from heart disease to diabetes, autoimmune disorders to obesity, asthma to addiction, arthritis to chronic pain. As of 2020, half of the US population has a chronic condition, and 25 percent has two or more. Chronic disease is the leading cause of death in the US. By 2055, specialists project chronic illness will cost the country $95 trillion.[15]

Dr. Hyman's colleague Tawny Jones has been with Cleveland Clinic for over two decades. She is currently the chief administrator of the Center for Functional Medicine. After the center began taking patients, there was such high demand that it eventually had a waiting list of up to eighteen months. Thinking about how to deal with that challenge, Jones came up with the idea of Functioning for Life, which offers ten-week programs of disease-specific SMAs, from which patients can select the series that is right for them. The programs currently available focus on

- immune/autoimmune disorders, which include conditions such as lupus and psoriasis;
- diabetes, metabolic syndrome, and prediabetes;

- women's health issues, including such conditions as menopause, PCOS, and PMS;
- digestive disorders such as IBD, IBS, GERD/reflux, and gastrointestinal issues;
- weight management; and
- pain management—conditions such as chronic migraine, osteoarthritis, fibromyalgia, and minor back pain.

Each week, the patients interact with a multidisciplinary team of functional medicine providers that may include some combination of physicians, physician assistants, nurse practitioners, dietitians, health coaches, and behavioral health therapists. Patients will also have access to individualized support and ongoing communication with members of their care team throughout the ten-week program.

According to Jones, the patients rate these SMA programs anywhere from one-third to two-thirds higher than one-on-one appointments. Forty percent of patients achieve clinically meaningful changes in mental and physical health, which is remarkable in such a short period of time. And they have an 80 percent retention rate over the course of the ten weeks, which Jones describes as so good that it is "actually shocking." She suspects that these success rates are due partly to the relationships patients develop with each other during the sessions, and partly to how much they learn from one another—often because they end up sharing details about their experience that they wouldn't have thought to mention during a one-on-one appointment. It turns out "getting healthy is a team sport," as Jones puts it. By the end of the ten weeks, they've learned everything they need to know about self-management of their condition, which may include information about diet, the effects of nutritional deficiencies on their health, stress management, relaxation techniques, how to develop healthy sleeping patterns, and the power of movement.

This intimate group model changes the dynamics of honesty. In group settings, once people become comfortable with each other they're often willing to share more than they would with a doctor one-on-one. And the more they share, the more they learn, and the more they understand about how to take care of themselves. Jones explains that often patients don't know how to dial into their own strength; they need to tap into the strength of someone else. But "by the time [people] are halfway through this program, they find their voice, they're empowered, the feelings of loneliness dissipate…and they're encouraging each other to go on."[16] "It's cathartic," she says. "Patients really have a sense of not being in this alone."

One patient whose remarkable success story both Dr. Hyman and Tawny Jones describe was a severely obese sixty-five-year-old woman who was suffering from diabetes, fatty liver, congestive heart failure, kidney failure, and who was in need of both a heart and a kidney transplant. She'd eaten junk food her entire life because that's what her family did. "But in a few weeks of the program," according to Jones, "she was put on an anti-inflammatory whole foods diet, low in sugar and starch, and immediately she saw her levels normalize. She had lost 43 pounds in three months. A year later, she's one of our biggest advocates.…She's lost 116 pounds, and all her conditions are reversed, and she's now medication-free, and saved over $20,000 a year in healthcare costs."

For this woman, who had wanted a one-on-one appointment but went to a group because the waiting list for one-on-ones in the Center for Functional Medicine was so long, the power of the group, of learning about food and self-care from her peers, turned out to be life changing. As Jones says, "Magic happens within the group."[17] Time and again, Jones has witnessed how the openness and extreme honesty of the participants creates a thriving tribe. She views these group visits as a rocket ship for people's health.

The success the Center for Functional Medicine has had with its groups has led to many of the other parts of the Cleveland Clinic organization adopting the group approach and discovering how effective it is. From a total of 385 such appointments at Cleveland Clinic from 2002 to 2004, there were an astonishing 35,000 in 2019 alone. And the variety of medical groups that participate in these SMAs is equally amazing. There are now 260 different types of shared medical groups at Cleveland Clinic. For example, Cleveland Clinic's Minority Men's Health Center partnered with the Center for Functional Medicine, and its founder and former director, Dr. Charles Modlin, who led groups in which there might be five or six men talking openly about health and sexual dysfunction—problems that, as Jones said, "these men are probably not telling their wife or doctor [about] because of shame or embarrassment." But in these groups they are able to "peel back many concerns." And the connections they forge are so strong that some of these men will go on to "meet up separately and support one another for years." Although patients across the Cleveland Clinic SMAs may initially express hesitation as well, they are usually sold after the first shared consult. Approximately 85 percent to 90 percent of patients who attend any SMA at Cleveland Clinic schedule their follow-up appointment as a shared appointment as well.[18] And like the patients who go through the Functioning for Life program, they rate SMAs two to three times higher than the traditional appointments, as Dr. Adrienne Boissy, chief patient experience officer at Cleveland Clinic (and a collaborator of mine), told me.

Not only are patients more satisfied with their experience in the SMAs, but their outcomes are substantially better, too. A Cleveland Clinic study of 2,455 functional medicine patients found that those seen in the SMA program exhibited significantly greater improvements in physical and mental health—and greater weight loss—than patients in individual appointments (at three months). SMAs were also less costly to deliver care than individual appointments.[19] Doctors who see their patients thriving in these SMAs often become the biggest advocates of the programs. Both Mark Hyman and Tawny Jones agree that doctors, after some initial hesitation of their own, have come around, and not just because of how well their patients do, but also because of the way these programs have transformed their own experience. Hyman talks about how SMAs reduce physician burnout by reducing workload pressures, and by making the whole practice of medicine more enjoyable, too. "I feel so much more satisfied because you're connecting with people, you're talking, you're engaging, you're laughing. It's not as exhausting. It actually revives [your] love of medicine. It's really a bi-directional relationship."[20] Another physician reported, "I think that [SMAs] have helped me to be more creative in looking at ways to meet people's needs. Some of that just comes from the patients themselves because they often have some really neat ideas about how to overcome the challenges or difficulties in dealing with diabetes. So, I think that not only have I become more aware but I've also [gotten] some really good tips and ideas. I think there's stuff I learned that I wouldn't have learned if I had done it on an individual basis."[21]

Cleveland Clinic is also looking to partner with other organizations and community groups to bring this shared-experience model to them. For example, the clinic has taken it to over thirty local churches, which offer six-week programs that have helped improve the health of their members as people shed weight and get off medications. Some of the churches are even embedding the idea of getting healthier into their services.

The sense of community SMAs provide is one of their most powerful and promising features. As Dr. Hyman explains, "People are so hungry to connect."[22] Perhaps that's why so many of Dr. Geller's and Dr. Hyman's group members continue to connect with one another, for years and even decades after the groups themselves have disbanded.

Given the increasing demand for healthcare, and the decreasing supply of physicians, SMAs can be a game changer for both patients and doctors. As Dr. Geller, Dr. Hyman, Dr. Sumego, Tawny Jones, and my brother Mike have all witnessed, the groups are important not just because of all the information that patients get in them, but because the interactions among members of the group address the fundamental problem of isolation. Feeling supported by each other and having a sense of belonging tends to produce resilience in the face of health challenges. And what makes this kind of medical practice particularly promising for both the present moment and for the future is that these community bonds translate successfully to the virtual environment, where SMAs have blossomed.

Cisco's Conscious Culture

Cisco has had an award-winning corporate culture for over two decades. It is one of the few companies to land on *Fortune*'s 100 Best Companies to Work For list every year since it was first published in 1998. This is of course an impressive achievement. What makes it all the more impressive is that it managed to remain on the list during a time of great upheaval, when six thousand employees were laid off.[23] And more disruption was yet to come. After Chuck Robbins took over as CEO in 2015, Cisco underwent more change in a matter of three years than it had over the previous three decades, as Robbins steered it from being a predominantly hardware-centric company to a more software-based business.

Change of such magnitude is deeply unsettling. It tends to crush employee morale, and many a firm has sunk under the pressure. Not Cisco. Even as its leaders retooled and replumbed this massive multinational into a business with a different kind of focus, their employees thrived—so much so that in both 2019 and 2020 it ranked number one on *Fortune*'s World's Best Workplaces list as a whopping 95 percent of Cisco's 77,500 employees worldwide reported that they feel proud of their employer and believe it's a great place to work.

There's nothing accidental about Cisco's achievement. Mark Chandler, Cisco's executive vice president and chief legal officer, explains that "historically we've always tried to take the approach of trying to treat all of our stakeholders, our customers, our suppliers, and certainly our whole team, the way we'd want to be treated ourselves."[24] Its previous CEO, John Chambers, had been very focused on creating the kind of collaborative culture for which Cisco became renowned. It was during his regime that one of Cisco's signature employee initiatives, the Our People Deal, got its start. Fran Katsoudas, a twenty-year Cisco veteran who had just been made the chief people officer in 2014, wrote the People Deal Manifesto based on all the input she solicited from employees after she took on her new post. The People Deal set out the goals and values that shape what the employees could expect of their company, and what the company expected of them in return, establishing a shared accountability. A two-way street, the People Deal created an environment in which the employees and the company were beholden to each other.[25]

Then in 2015, when Chuck Robbins became CEO and chairman of the board, he too committed to those values, emphasizing that Cisco's future hinged on its corporate culture.[26] And in the interest of fostering even greater transparency and trust, which are crucial to navigating periods of change, Cisco established Conscious Culture—a culture that is aware and accountable for what's working, what's not, and how the company can improve. According to Fran Katsoudas (now the executive vice president and chief people, policy, and purpose officer), Conscious Culture was an initiative of the company's People Deal Ambassadors—a committee of fifteen employees from around the company who had been chosen in 2018 to help close the gap between the leaders' perception of Cisco and the way the employees experienced it. They're called ambassadors because they represent their fellow employees to management, delivering the tough feedback that employees might be reluctant to voice themselves. Conscious Culture creates an environment in which, as Katsoudas says, "everyone owns it. People are willing to talk about tough things, which leads to those conversations becoming more natural."

Such conversations often involve complaints about bias of different sorts, discrimination, bullying, harassment, etc. If it's determined that valid complaints are serious, they get reported to the board. Each concern is investigated by the employee relations team. Cisco provides details, as necessary, if there are serious allegations. With this information the board of directors can make decisions to ensure that the company is holding true to its commitment to fostering an environment where employees can thrive.

Mark Chandler described how he dealt with one of these complaints, which involved someone who objected to an engineer who had hung a T-shirt from his cube that read "Blockchains Matter." As Chandler recounted, his initial reaction was "Well, in an engineering humor kind of way, I could see why he thought that was funny." But talking to a Black member of his staff helped him see it from another point of view. She said to him, "Stop and think about how a play on Black Lives Matter feels to an employee who has to have the talk with her twelve-year-old son about how to behave with the police, and the fact that she worries every day that he could end up getting hurt... and then decide whether you think that's so funny and we ought to just ignore it." The result of that conversation was that the complaint did get reported to the board. Katsoudas commented that Mark had shared this story at a company meeting to describe his own learning process. As she said, "People may not understand sometimes the impact that they're having," which is why it's important to have an environment in which these things can be talked through honestly. And that's what Conscious Culture makes possible. The learning goes beyond the outcome.[27]

Katsoudas admitted to me that the number of cases reporting problematic behavior in the workplace has gone up. But she sees this as a positive because it says that people feel comfortable speaking up about their concerns.[28]

Love and Loathe is another feedback tool that was created for employees. Instead of doing annual performance reviews, Cisco has a weekly electronic check-in (survey) that allows employees to provide their managers feedback on what they love and what they loathe about their work, their leaders, their teams, and the company. The hope is that by allowing employees to talk about what they loathe, problems can be resolved before they grow. Leaders may catch how an employee is suffering or languishing and be able to offer support or resources quickly. Or, they may pick up on a pattern (for a person, or within a team). Talking about what they love may help their managers to make sure they are using their staff in a way that best utilizes their strengths and their skills. If an employee loathes a task, then that might indicate to the manager that the employee is not in the right role. If an employee loves an aspect of work, what can the manager do to make that a more central part of the employee's work? Because Love and Loathe allows leaders and their employees to get to know each other better, it builds an element of trust and fosters a sense of community. Research shows that small daily interactions matter, and the strongest predictor of retention is the relationship with one's immediate superior. Katsoudas takes advantage of this herself in her weekly report to Chuck Robbins, who is her direct boss. She describes a report she wrote to him late one Friday in which she "loathed" the fact that she had had "a really heavy week." In response, Robbins lined up an 8:00 a.m. Monday meeting in which she could air her concerns. "He was there for me immediately to do a check-in—and that responsive," Fran said.

Another aspect of Cisco's Conscious Culture is its commitment to giving its employees a safe space in which they can talk about concerns that go beyond the workplace. One powerful example of this occurred in the aftermath of the Kate Spade and Anthony Bourdain suicides. Discussing these tragic events and the eye-opening statistics about how many people suffer from mental health issues, Fran and Chuck became concerned about their employees. She remembers Chuck saying, "Wow, I wonder how many people at Cisco at this moment are thinking about ending their lives." The next morning, Robbins sent a heartfelt memo to all employees about the suicides, the gist of which was that no one needs to go it alone, we're here, we're a community, help is available. The response was overwhelming. More than one hundred replies poured in from employees expressing thanks and sharing intimate stories of themselves and their loved ones. It was so powerful that Cisco convened a large meeting at which several people took the stage to tell their stories. In a similar meeting the following year an employee told how one of their children committed suicide; another employee spoke about the experience of childhood abuse. Fran told me that since then storytelling has become a powerful part of their culture. Employees speak with remarkable honesty about their personal struggles in blog posts on the company website, and at the Cisco Beat, a monthly meeting where Cisco encourages people to share their thoughts, their questions, and their challenges.

By breaking the silence on uncomfortable and stigmatized topics like mental illness, leadership wants everyone to know that Cisco is a safe place to be vulnerable. And it keeps offering more resources to its people, like the Safe to Talk community on Cisco's intranet, which includes videos, links to internal and external resources, and employee stories. Cisco trained leaders on how to recognize signs of mental illness and support their teams. Cisco has also improved access to mental healthcare in their employee medical plans and increased the number of free, 24/7, confidential counselor visits per employee to ten a year in the United States, to align with what they were offering globally.

With actions like his suicide memo and his support for programs that offer Cisco's tens of thousands of employees the resources they need to deal with both psychological and professional challenges, Chuck Robbins sets the tone for his entire company.

The result of all Cisco's initiatives: a tighter-knit, healthier, happier community. And a more successful one. According to Katsoudas, Cisco has found that employees who are able to utilize their strengths on a daily basis are 20 percent more productive and creative and six times as engaged at work. Fran told me that the overall metric Cisco uses to gauge progress on culture is percentage of fully engaged employees. The proportion of people who are fully engaged has risen by 14 percent over the last four years. She shared, "The most powerful mechanism we have for creating full engagement is a weekly check-in conversation." The company has seen nearly six million of them in the last four years. Katsoudas noted, "And we have learned the power of asking people about their work experience: employees who are never invited to share their voices are 8.7 times more likely to choose to leave Cisco."

Fear and Failure

Eliminating or at least minimizing fear of failure is another key to creating the feeling of community that comes when people trust one another and have a sense of psychological safety. If they work in a company that tells them not to be afraid to fail, they will feel free to take chances and be honest about when those risks don't work out. In the end, that willingness to fail is what makes employees, and the businesses for which they work, successful—as my colleague Amy Edmondson, the pioneer who has studied psychological safety for decades, has found. Sara Blakely would agree.

Blakely, who in 2012 was named the youngest self-made female billionaire, is the founder of Spanx, an American company that makes shaping briefs and leggings. She attributes her amazing success to the fact that she has never been afraid of failure. This is a mindset that she learned from her father. When she was growing up, he would ask her and her brother what they had failed at that week. And if they couldn't name a failure, he'd be disappointed because it meant they hadn't had the courage to take on something they wanted to do that might have stretched them beyond their abilities, something that really pushed them to the max. So instead of viewing failure as not achieving the right outcome, she viewed it as not being willing to try. And until she found her focus, she had plenty of experience with failure, beginning with a disappointing score on her LSAT—twice—and spending seven years selling fax machines door-to-door, as she has recounted.[29]

Because she believes in failure as the route to success, at Spanx she has instituted what she calls Oops meetings, in which she shares her own mistakes and encourages her employees to do the same. These meetings have become a safe, intimate forum, where people learn from each other and bond as a community over their blunders, which are often told as funny stories that everyone can laugh at. But they have a serious purpose. "If you can create a culture where [your employees] are not terrified to fail or make a mistake, then they're going to be highly productive and more innovative," she says.[30]

In one Oops meeting, Sara described one of her own oops moments. She had been supportive of her active wear department's intention to focus on designing swim garments made out of a waterproof material. Based on her enthusiasm, they started making products with a fabric they thought was right for the job. The problem was that Sara hadn't paid much attention to the particular material they were working with and when they came to her with what they developed, she didn't like it. It didn't feel good on the skin. Unfortunately, based on her initial excitement, the department had raced ahead without checking in with her and had created lots of products using the fabric. By the time they brought what they had created to her attention, they had wasted months of work on something she ultimately rejected. Sara admitted that she made a mistake by not checking in with them more frequently and regularly. She should have asked to see progress, and to test the fabric, which would have allowed them to tweak things earlier. They in turn learned that they needed to be more proactive about giving Sara more information along the way. They had proceeded with such speed because they thought Sara wanted waterproof and chlorine-resistant products. Which she did—just not with the fabric they were using, as it turned out. But that was something she realized only after she felt the fabric. And that happened so far into the process that the department missed some important deadlines. In the Oops meeting, Sara wanted to make it clear to her employees that they should always feel free to check in with her in response to any suggestions they got from her, in order to make sure they understood her intentions. She hadn't meant to drive an inferior product just because she liked the general concept. There should have been more information sharing, more back-and-forth conversation during the development phase. Her willingness to be candid and own responsibility for the failed product line is how she builds a sense of psychological safety in her team, creates the kind of mutual trust and respect that is crucial to thriving and performance.[31]

Another proponent of failure as a necessary step on the way to success is Astro Teller of X (formerly Google X). Teller calls himself the culture engineer of X because what interests him most isn't so much the products that may emerge from their work, he says, but designing a culture that systematizes innovation. He believes that true innovation will be possible only if an acceptance of failure has become so much of a social norm that it becomes embedded in everyone's psyche. The result of creating this as a social norm will be a sense of profound psychological safety around the acknowledgment of mistakes.

At Google's re:Work meeting, which convened a group of top business, HR, academic, and thought leaders to inspire people practices and research collaborations to make work better, Teller told us why accepting failure is critical to advancing the kind of audacious projects he oversees as the head of X, which was set up to be Google's moonshot factory. As the company's website expresses it, moonshot thinking is about pursuing things that sound undoable, but if done, could redefine humanity. X's goals are (1) to identify problems that affect millions or even billions of people in the world; (2) to propose radical, sci-fi-sounding solutions to the problems; and (3) to design the breakthrough technology needed for these solutions. The resulting moonshots include the self-driving car, which seems as though it may be well on the way to becoming a hugely profitable business, and Loon, the balloon-powered internet, which has the potential to connect billions of people to high-speed internet.

Among the moonshots that they've abandoned are Google Glass, the head-mounted wearable computer that looked like a pair of glasses and was ridiculed when it came out; clean fuel created from seawater, which, while viable, couldn't quite compete with the cost of gasoline; and airborne wind turbines. This was an attempt to create an entirely new kind of wind energy technology, which X and its parent company Alphabet have now deemed too long range a project for them to continue to support.

That's the cost of moonshots—some of them don't work out. But encouraging teams to take on only the most ambitious projects while allowing them to fail at them is what leads to profoundly amazing things, which is why "embrace failure as learning" is one of Teller's ten key tips for unleashing radical creativity.[32]

Team members at X are the Navy SEALs of innovation. And since X's projects are so high risk, it's a given that some teams will hit walls, will see from their pilot test results that their idea is not working, and will have to conclude that their precious prototype just might not be worth it. That's inevitable, and at X it may also be very expensive, as some of these projects require tens or even hundreds of millions of dollars of investment. Failure can seem particularly daunting when the stakes are so high. That's where their "kill metrics"—data points or other milestones that a team agrees on when the project starts—are crucial. If the project team isn't hitting the milestones within the time frame, it's a sign that they should walk away from the project. Teller insists that his teams admit failure openly and honestly. This can be a hard lesson to learn, since most of us have been conditioned from childhood not to fail. But not failing means not taking risks, and risk taking is what Teller requires; it's part of his company's DNA. As he says, "At X, our breakthrough idea isn't a technology. It's our people. It's about engineering a culture and designing an organization that can overcome the powerful forces that cause humans to retreat to the comfortable and conventional."[33]

To illustrate how he has designed this culture, Teller describes how he'll celebrate teams that have thrown in the towel on their projects once they realized the projects were good but not great. This often happens at X's all-company meeting every two weeks in Moonshot Factory's auditorium—the transformative central atrium, a large open industrial space with high ceilings and exposed concrete and steel—in Mountain View, California, situated about a half mile away from Google's main campus. If a team has decided to wind down their project, they'll share their reasons and what they've learned with the whole company. When teams do this, Teller stands them up onstage and tells Moonshot Factory employees that by admitting failure, they did more to move innovation forward at X than anything that any of the people in the audience did. Then he gives a bonus to those who just punted their projects. Teller even tells the folding teams to take a vacation—to relax a little bit. He wants to give them time to think about what to do next. Maybe they want to jump onto a team to elevate an existing project, or maybe they want to start a new project. He leaves it up to them.

Teller knows that for people who are just getting used to X's ways, this celebration of failure can seem really messed up. And they're likely to be resentful: "I'm working my ass off, and these people are calling it a day, but they're getting a bonus and I'm not. How's that fair?" Teller also knows that the first few times people watch these ceremonies they'll probably think he's crazy. Yet Teller is confident in his approach—he knows it works. By the fifth time employees see one of these celebrations, the lesson gets through: Admitting failure is okay. It's more than just okay—teams get standing ovations at X for having killed their projects! They get high-fived. They get promoted.

Another X ritual that promotes the social norms Teller wants to embed in the culture is the Audacious Goals Award. An audacious goal, he explains, is something that has only a 10 percent chance of happening. Competition for these awards is extremely stiff, and getting one is so highly valued that at one of the presentation ceremonies, the team that won the award—a team of patent lawyers—had tears streaming down their faces when they went onstage to collect it. The Audacious Goals Award is given quarterly, but one year they postponed giving it. The next quarter X had three possible winners and couldn't decide which team was the most audacious.[34] When X finally made their decision and it was time to celebrate the winner, Teller welcomed the team onstage to claim the trophy. Their team representative, Grant, sauntered up onstage and said, "Thank you very much but we don't think we've been audacious enough." They really appreciated it, he said, but they wanted to win it for the right reason. And then Grant handed the trophy back to Teller and left the stage.

Teller was stunned, and at first he felt terrible—like he'd whiffed! Then he realized, "No, no, they're one-upping me on the things I'm trying to get Google to be like." Instead of feeling he'd blown it, he felt a huge sense of pride at the realization that he'd truly engineered a culture in which people felt so safe that they could admit to falling short of their own goals, could say before an audience of hundreds of their colleagues that they hadn't been quite audacious enough. Teller has worked very hard to create that space of psychological safety, and he was thrilled to see he'd succeeded.

Whether you're leading a company or a small tribe, consider what you might do to surface failures and make them acceptable, to help people see them as just part of the process of getting things done. Kim Scott, author of *Radical Candor*, created a weekly "whoops-a-daisy" exercise for her team when she worked at Google. To create a safe place for admitting mistakes, she'd bring a plush daisy into a meeting with her team where they would have a conversation about who had screwed up that week. To set the tone, and model vulnerability, Kim, as the leader, would start. Then the team members jumped in, taking turns, revealing their biggest mistake of the week, and Kim would award the daisy to whoever had screwed up worst. Moments like these create a sense of intimacy among the group, plant seeds for trust to take root, and establish a foundation for relationships to grow stronger.

Solidarity Forged in Crisis

Times of great adversity can also be community builders, uniting even previously divided tribes and communities. Rebecca Solnit's book *A Paradise Built in Hell* recounts the stories of communities in crisis, people who survived earthquakes, volcanoes, hurricanes, and other catastrophes. She found that they often looked back at those events as being the most meaningful of their lives (and remarkably joyful) because of having gone through them with others. The shared experience of danger, loss, or deprivation had provided the opportunity for intimate connection with others, explains sociologist Charles Fritz in Solnit's book. Their time of trial gave them "a feeling of belonging and a sense of unity rarely achieved under normal circumstances."

At times of crisis, leaders can use the challenges facing their communities to tether a tribe more tightly together and to help them develop newfound resolve and strengths. This was what Ralph Boyd was able to do during the yearlong acute crisis his organization endured.

Boyd has a remarkable résumé, having worked—among other jobs—as an assistant US attorney in the Major Crimes Unit of the Boston US Attorney's Office; a partner at a major Boston law firm; assistant attorney general of the United States heading the Department of Justice's Civil Rights Division under President George W. Bush; EVP and general counsel of Freddie Mac, and chairman, president, and CEO of the Freddie Mac Foundation; and most recently as president and CEO of SOME, Inc. (So Others Might Eat), a major affordable housing and human services provider in Washington, DC.

It was during his stint at Freddie Mac, one of the two huge home-mortgage government-sponsored entities (GSEs), that he faced one of the biggest challenges of his career. Ralph had the first inkling of trouble when he walked into his office on a Monday morning in early September 2008. He had spent the prior week traveling for business. It was during the height of the crisis in the global capital markets resulting from the imploding housing bubble. Arriving at work early, he found a woman he didn't know making herself at home in his office. Startled, he asked, "Can I help you?" Without missing a beat, the woman responded, "Aren't you expecting me?" Puzzled, Ralph inquired, "And who might you be?" Looking somewhat surprised herself, the woman disclosed that she was an official from the Federal Housing Finance Agency (FHFA), Freddie Mac's principal regulator. Two days earlier, the Freddie Mac and Fannie Mae (the other home mortgage GSE) boards of directors had voted to accede to the Treasury Department's plan to stabilize the two GSEs by placing them into federal conservatorship, but somehow there had been a communications lapse and Ralph hadn't been told. The FHFA official had been sent to oversee Ralph's activities as a Freddie Mac senior executive, acting effectively as his "chaperone" during the initial stages of conservatorship.

This was the beginning of an incredibly stressful time for Freddie Mac and its employees. And Ralph Boyd now had a watchdog who'd been sent to shadow him full-time. He quickly learned she wasn't kidding. She hovered around him during every phone call and attended every meeting, positioning herself within arm's length of him, reminding him constantly of her presence. She even went so far as to monitor his casual hallway conversations and interactions. Ralph joked, "The only place I could shake her was when I went to the men's room, and even then I wasn't entirely sure she wouldn't follow me inside!"

Ralph Boyd is the kind of person who radiates unbelievable positivity, even under pressure—actually, especially under pressure. He'd had plenty of experience with it during his time in the Major Crimes Unit, investigating and prosecuting drug dealing, firearms trafficking, homicides, gang violence, and bombings, and receiving death threats that were serious enough at one point that US Marshals monitored his home and his children's school bus routes. He also had to go into crisis mode after 9/11, when he was serving as assistant US attorney general and had to help manage several aspects of America's response to the terrorist attacks.

So dealing with crises was not new to Ralph, and his "shadow" did not rattle him. But he sensed that the constant surveillance was having a negative effect on some of his community and that he needed to help them deal with this new challenge. Observing that the FHFA official adhered to a strict nine-to-five schedule, he called a town hall meeting for his employees after hours, in the early evening. When he addressed them, Boyd framed their current situation as a gut check—a test of their resolve and self-belief. He acknowledged how anxious they were about all the media noise, scrutiny, and accusations that were directed at the GSEs. But he reminded them of their excellence, and specifically of all the efforts they had made in the preceding months to optimize how they conducted business. With their regulator as their witness, they now had not just a challenge but a great opportunity to demonstrate all the improvements they had put into practice in key aspects of their operations.

As he explained to me, "We had already analyzed our investment port-folio to assure ourselves of the accuracy of our calculations; and during the years immediately preceding conservatorship, we had also enhanced the rigor of our grant-making processes so that the process as a whole was more transparent and analytically grounded, both quantitatively and qualitatively." These advances in their practices touched on key elements of the criticism of the foundation and of Freddie Mac more broadly. "We just haven't had an opportunity to rebut this criticism, but our regulator can," Ralph said to his employees. "We can tell people they're wrong and that we're doing things the right way, but it's way better if our overseers actually see us do it and then *they* tell the world."

This really *was* an opportunity, and he wanted to make sure his employees saw it that way. The FHFA official sent to scrutinize them shouldn't be feared but rather embraced, he told them. In fact, she was their best chance at being appreciated for their true worth. Once she saw how good their work was, she could be their best advocate to the FHFA—and the world. So Ralph urged his team to make the most of the challenge. As the father of a soccer-playing daughter and as someone who had been a soccer referee himself, Ralph knew that too often even the most elite player would tighten up when she saw the ball headed her way. So just as Pia Sundhage, the former US women's Olympic soccer team coach, used to scream "Enjoy!" when she saw one of her players panicking as she was about to receive a line drive or a tough pass—the message being that she was lucky to get the ball and the chance to act on it—Ralph had a similar message for his team.

Once his shadow, the FHFA official, got outside the sensationalist media bubble with its relentless "Freddie Mac and Fannie Mae suck" narrative, and saw, firsthand, how the foundation actually operated, Ralph's tribe won her over. "She was more of a fair and objective advocate for us than she ever was our jailor," Boyd said. "And I believe that she materially influenced how the FHFA portrayed us... in their interactions with both Congress and the media.... It was decisive with respect to the FHFA's abandonment of its reported plan to shut down the foundation immediately." Instead of redirecting $220 million in assets to Treasury, "the foundation continued to operate unabated into the next decade, providing financial support and technical assistance to nonprofits providing housing, supportive human services, and academic enrichment, education, and job training for vulnerable adults and children in its chosen investment areas." As Freddie Mac's regulator, she and the FHFA were more likely to be persuasive than Ralph Boyd or Freddie Mac's corporate CEO ever could have been. "So we made a little bit of lemonade out of a truckload of lemons," Boyd joked.

Boyd knew how to use an incredibly stressful time to make his community stronger and more effective. As he said to me by way of summing up his experience at Freddie Mac, "Never waste a good crisis"—one of the many excellent lessons that the people in this chapter offer us.

If you want to unlock your community's potential, create a safe space for everyone where they all feel connected to each other and supportive of one another, as Phil Jackson did. People desperately want to feel a sense of belonging, membership in a united tribe that goes through challenges and hardships together. If you create a sense of community among your employees or members, you increase your chances of having a thriving tribe—and a very successful business—as Chuck Robbins at Cisco recognized. By consciously crafting a culture marked by transparency and trust, caring, and sharing, which he and Fran Katsoudas and many others at Cisco did, they ensured that their employees felt invested in the success of the company and were proud to work there. Embrace failure as Sara Blakely, Kim Scott, and Astro Teller did. Let your tribe know that you—and other members—will pick them up, if needed. Surface fears as Ralph Boyd did, and address them directly. Encourage your community to make the most of their opportunities—and to enjoy them!

CHAPTER 2

Unleash

Control leads to compliance; autonomy leads to engagement.
—Daniel Pink

One day Becky Kanis Margiotta, the director of the 100,000 Homes Campaign, received a very surprising email from her communications director. It said that a community organization in Hilo, Hawaii, had just done a registry week. For the 100,000 Homes Campaign, registry week was a five-day process that participating cities used to support the long-term goal of housing one hundred thousand Americans, and it was deployed in a very systematic way. On the Monday of registry week, volunteers would come together to be trained on how to use the vulnerability index (VI) to identify the people at greatest health risk in order to prioritize those who were most immediately in need of permanent housing. Early Tuesday, Wednesday, and Thursday mornings the volunteers were sent out to put VI to work by surveying every single person they could find who was sleeping outside between four and six o'clock. On Friday, Becky's team would use the data the volunteers had entered and the photos they had taken to give a PowerPoint presentation to key players in the community—area residents, city council members, mayors, and others. They wanted to put names and faces to the raw data to help the community understand the urgency of the problem, to show them who was at risk of dying if they didn't do something about it.

Registry week was a critical tool in the 100,000 Homes campaign, and it was proprietary, too. Margiotta herself had pioneered the registry, along with the VI, during 2003–2008, the period when she was working to address homelessness in Times Square. For a while she had personally driven the twenty blocks surrounding Times Square throughout the night, engaging the homeless—getting to know their names, faces, homelessness history, and vulnerability factors. Eventually she developed the registry week to do a more systematic job of collecting and recording data on homeless people, and she and Beth Sandor, another employee of Common Ground, the parent organization of 100,000 Homes, began to travel throughout the country, conducting registry week workshops to teach people who had signed on to the campaign how to do the homeless surveys. It had become a signature element of the 100,000 Homes Campaign. So Becky was puzzled to learn that people in Hilo had used it, because Hilo was not one of the participating cities. How could people in Hilo, Hawaii, of all places, have completed a registry week?

When Margiotta examined the information Hilo had gotten from its registry week, she was surprised again. "It was textbook, a perfect registry week!" she told me as she recounted what she found. Feeling the need to understand how this had come about, and also to be able to exercise control over a process that had somehow spun off her own organization without her knowing about it, she spent two weeks trying to contact the Hilo group's director, Brandee, calling her every day, but the Hilo people kept blowing her off. Looking back on these events, she described how "indignant" she was at the time, and admitted thinking, "I am the director of the 100,000 Homes Campaign! You're doing my thing." And if they *were* going to do it, she wanted to get them involved in 100,000 Homes.

When she eventually reached Brandee, she began by telling her that her registry week was "really good." Then she asked, "How did you learn how to do it?" Brandee said that Sophia in Honolulu had given her a registry week binder—which detailed all the steps involved—and they had followed it. Margiotta was both surprised and amused to hear this, since she recalled that two years earlier, at a boot camp her team had conducted in Albuquerque, New Mexico, to train people from six different cities on how to conduct their own registry week, the people from Honolulu had been so exhausted by jet lag that they seemed to have slept through the entire boot camp. "Their heads were on the desks...I didn't want to wake them up."

But apparently the registry week binder was informative and clear enough that even someone who had slept through the presentation could put it to use. Moreover, it was so good that she could then hand it off to someone else, who hadn't been there at all, who could also use it effectively. Reflecting on what she learned from this, Margiotta acknowledged that until then she had thought that her own presence was key. "How arrogant was I to think that for it to be any good, I had to be there personally for it?" She realized that "you could go through the whole training, and not meet me, or care about me—someone who slept through the training could hand someone else the notebook and it would be just fine....It was a lesson in humility. And in making good binders."

Once she thought about it, Margiotta went from the fear of having lost control to thinking that what had happened was great. "Isn't that something? I wake up and people are doing my thing and I don't even know who the heck they are! I remember when I was all tired out from doing all these things myself thinking only I can do it....Well good job! I guess you don't need me anymore!"

What happened with the people in Hilo was an inadvertent "unleashing"— a term coined by the Billions Institute, founded by Joe McCannon, an expert in scaling up efforts in the social sector, and Becky Margiotta. When Margiotta's team did the training in Albuquerque, it was precisely because of the need to scale up. They'd gotten too big to be able to do the registry work themselves, so they were training people in participating cities how to conduct their own registry work. They had arrived at the stage where the unleashing that McCannon and Margiotta have conceptualized could start to occur. This meant that they were clear about what they were trying to achieve; they had developed a handbook—their registry week binder—for the steps involved in getting there; and they had enlisted thousands of deeply engaged people willing to devote significant amounts of time to making their goal a reality. Soon they would be working with McCannon and learning more about the unleashing process they had accidentally set in motion—how to make it intentional, and how to maximize its effectiveness.

A veteran of a number of social change initiatives, in the government as well as the nonprofit world, co-founder of the Billions Institute and founder of Shared Nation, both of which focus on bringing together those who are trying to effect large-scale change, Joe McCannon has advised organizations and movements in the US and many other countries. He defines unleashing as the intentional loss of control of thousands of creative people who are moving in the direction of a desired goal. The process always has to begin with a well-defined goal—a goal that taps into people's deepest motivations, taps into their values. "In a transformative community," McCannon explained to me, "you need to get people to agree on the mission, align it with their values, but then you have to let them accomplish it their way—honor the fact that they're the experts, and support them."

According to McCannon, unleashing people who are engaged in movements that have an ambitious aim involves creating ground rules for them, providing tools and support to help them move forward, and then seeing what they do within that framework, how they adapt it to their own purposes. He told me unleashing requires shifting from asking, "How can I get all these people to do what I want?" to "How can I help all these people do what *they* want to do?" Once you make that mindset shift, you've set the stage for how this wonderful unleashing can happen, he said. As he sees it, giving up control is critical to the process.[1] It's a bit of a paradox because although it's orchestrated by leaders, their goal is to intentionally lose control of a tribe that is heading in the right direction but needs to find its own way there. The community takes responsibility for driving the work forward, but the leaders have defined the goal they are trying to achieve and provided the infrastructure of support they need to take them there.

Successful unleashing may be uncomfortable for leaders, especially initially, because it's not what they learn about how to manage people. Margiotta remembers thinking, "It's almost as if I had done something wrong because I had lost control." Like McCannon, Margiotta described unleashing as paradoxical,[2] because, as she explained, "Most of what we're taught in the management literature—leftover stuff from factories—is how to control people, right? But the truth is [it's only when you lose control] that you are actually beginning to do something right."[3]

Playing the Backbone Role

Losing control in the context of unleashing doesn't mean just walking away—quite the opposite. As McCannon makes clear, and as Rosanne Haggerty, who is head of Common Ground and the founder of the 100,000 Homes Campaign (and a winner of the prestigious MacArthur Fellowship), also explains, leaders play a crucial role in successful unleashing. While leaders cede a lot of decision-making discretion to the community, playing the backbone role requires them to bring people together in the first place, create the connections among them, provide the data they need to act effectively, and support the group's learning, communicating, and organizing.

That's how it happened in the 100,000 Homes Campaign, when communities that had a shared sense of mission and purpose partnered with the campaign leadership, which provided them with feedback, data, and tools. A successful collaborative campaign culture, as McCannon sees it, must be based on trust, continual learning, and *not* requiring consensus at every step.[4] His aphorism: "Consensus kills." What works, he says, is to create an environment where you trust that everyone in your tribe is so locked in on the same goal that they will be inspired to come up with new ideas, breakthroughs, and innovations that you could never have imagined.

Ultimately, unleashing achieves the desired results; along the way it drives collaboration and creates a sense of fulfillment among community members. The more people feel they have a say in how things get done, the greater their energy and motivation. Confidence surges when they feel trusted to own the issue—and the solution. With greater discretion, members are less inhibited and more likely to bring their full selves to the community, leveraging their experiences and local knowledge to solve problems in much more effective and innovative ways. And, if community members are allowed to take ownership of their decisions, when they make a mistake, they are more likely to look for opportunities to learn from that mistake rather than try to cover it up or blame it on someone else.

The examples of successful unleashing described in this chapter show how the staff of several organizations have fulfilled the backbone role through facilitating connections, providing and analyzing data, communicating learning and best practices, and supporting the community's communication and organizing efforts.

From Hundreds of Homes to 100,000

How did Becky Margiotta, Rosanne Haggerty, who founded the campaign, and the 100,000 Homes team learn about unleashing and get comfortable with being uncomfortable? Let's travel back to the early days and how this unique campaign unfolded. In 1990, at the age of twenty-nine, her calling having crystallized after her years volunteering in various homeless shelters, Rosanne Haggerty formed Common Ground Community, a nonprofit to provide permanent and transitional housing for homeless people. When the landlord of the notorious single-room-occupancy Times Square Hotel in Midtown Manhattan was booted out of the building because of the terrible conditions there, Common Ground was given the opportunity (and funding from city and federal sources) to renovate the building and turn it into a source of housing for homeless as well as low-income people.[5] When it opened its doors in 1994, it was the largest supportive housing community in the country, offering a range of social services to those in need. Half of the 650 residents were low-income working people, some of whom worked in shops and restaurants at the bottom of the building; the other half were people who had been homeless.

Despite the success of this effort, Rosanne Haggerty was surprised at the number of homeless people she continued to see on New York City's streets, and wondered why there were so many who still had no home. Haggerty sent staffers to interview homeless people to learn more about their needs, and she quickly learned that housing the homeless was a "bureaucratic nightmare" that no person, agency, or nonprofit body really oversaw or "owned." While there were thirteen agencies officially charged with combating homelessness in her area, which contained the highest density of the homeless in New York City, none were connected with each other and there was no concerted, collaborative effort to do anything about the problem. While all tried to offer something to make the homeless a little more comfortable, none actually provided homes for them. Nor was housing them a goal they were even expected to achieve. Instead, the agencies were given incentives simply to make various kinds of contact with the homeless, like giving them a sandwich or a blanket.

Determined to own more of the process, Haggerty created the Street to Home initiative and hired West Point graduate and Army veteran officer Becky Margiotta to lead it.[6] Haggerty figured that because of her background in the military, Margiotta would have the skills and qualities Haggerty was looking for—"someone who was dauntless, a good team builder, knew how to use data, was unafraid to work without a map, learn his or her way"—to achieve the initiative's mission: reduce the number of street homeless in Midtown by two-thirds within three years.

In 2003, Margiotta kicked off their initiative in Times Square. Within three years, it was able to reduce homelessness by a stunning 87 percent in their target area, and by 43 percent in the surrounding Midtown area. They also helped inspire New York City to revamp its homeless outreach program. As word of their success reached advocates of the homeless in other cities, Margiotta began developing tools they could use to teach other organizations how to tackle similar problems. Out of that need came registry week and the vulnerability index, both adaptations of tools she had created for her own use in the Times Square project. By 2008 Rosanne Haggerty and Becky Margiotta wanted to figure out how to scale up their efforts to bring a much larger group of people into their network. Then they learned about the Institute for Healthcare Improvement (IHI), which had created the 100,000 Lives Campaign to teach hospital personnel policies and practices that would save lives by reducing medical errors. Over three thousand US hospitals had signed on to the campaign, which spread simple, proven practices that ranged from urging healthcare providers to wash their hands in order to stop the spread of infections to reminding everyone who comes in contact with a patient on a respirator that the bed ought to be elevated at least forty-five degrees, which reduces the risk of pneumonia. The result: 122,300 fewer preventable deaths in US hospitals over eighteen months. Hospitals also institutionalized new standards of care that continued to save lives and improve health outcomes.

Inspired, Margiotta wondered, "Could we do this?" with homelessness. In 2009, Margiotta contacted Joe McCannon, who had been the campaign manager for 100,000 Lives. After a meeting with the Street to Home people,

McCannon was ready to sign on with them as a consultant. "I just remember leaving and saying, you know, I've got to work on that. I don't care if I have to do it on nights and weekends, I have to help with that."[7] He could tell from talking to them that what they were trying to do wasn't just "vapor" (as he had seen in other groups that had contacted him for help). They had a deep understanding of the problem they were trying to solve, had spent years refining their goals and their strategies, and now they were truly ready to take it to the next step. In 2010, they launched the 100,000 Homes Campaign, with a goal of placing one hundred thousand people in permanent housing by 2013.

Of the many lessons Joe McCannon imparted, the importance of decisive action was central. Instead of holding endless meetings and spending countless hours debating the perfect plan and imagining every possible problem and contingency, get into the field to do the work as soon as possible—because every minute you're debating what to do next is time taken away from actually helping people. Margiotta did just that. Living with her two dogs in her car, she traveled from city to city doing registry weeks. As she went, she solicited input from the various communities piloting the Street to Home initiative to learn what was working and what wasn't and to listen to any suggestions.

During his time with 100,000 Homes, McCannon went out into the field, too. He recounted going into an abandoned house in Charlotte and trying to do the VI with the homeless man he found there. "I remember him so vividly," McCannon said. "He was initially quite threatening and then we got talking and his story was amazing. . . . It was one of those experiences where you wake up and say 'Oh my gosh, these are not nameless, faceless people, these are people with stories.'" And that was when he understood the power of the tools Becky had developed and was spreading to the dozens of communities that signed on to the 100,000 Homes Campaign. As he told her, "What you did so masterfully is you reminded us that these are human beings with their own dreams and their own aspirations. And we can't just look at them as statistics."[8]

The unleashing McCannon urged occurred at many different stages along the way. In 2010, Rosanne Haggerty founded a new organization, Community Solutions, that spun off from Common Ground to manage the campaign. And in 2011 it launched its first boot camps in Los Angeles and New York, partnering with local leaders and organizations to plan processes for placing people into permanent homes. Their team asked the leaders to sit down, and on a map resembling a Chutes and Ladders game board, use magnets to trace the process of housing people in their communities. It took teams an average of three hours and twenty minutes to figure out the path for a single homeless person! These logjams were indicative of the average of 245 days that it took to secure housing for a single homeless individual—and even that happened only if they didn't just give up because it seemed impossible. Rosanne told me that until that point, she hadn't realized that these community members felt constrained by the long, narrow, winding path on the "Chutes and Ladders board" and thought they needed approval from the campaign to deviate from it. Community members weren't even bothering to look for ladders. They were marching in lockstep rather than bringing their full selves and resources to the issue because, like so many of us, they were used to following the path and staying within the lines. So the leaders of the 100,000 Homes Campaign gave these teams permission to take out steps—to remove the logjams where people would get stuck in the system, or where a particular issue, such as health, employment, or sobriety caused them to walk away from the problem (and the person). Instead of forcing them to march forward in lockstep along the Chutes and Ladders board, the campaign team unleashed them to design a frictionless process. They wanted community members to be bolder—to find ladders to expedite the housing process for people—to think outside the box rather than robotically wind their way along the long path. Playing the backbone role, campaign leaders sketched out the ideal process as well as an acceptable middle ground that fell within existing rules and regulations. As McCannon told me, the backbone role "does all the setup. It clarifies aim, and makes safe space collective."

Successful unleashing led to all kinds of innovation. In Nashville, there was a flood and the city received FEMA vouchers. Margiotta said that she learned the leaders there said, "You know what, we're going to use some of those to house some people." She said, "The opportunism, the invention, the innovation, the desire to do better, it was electric, and just fantastic."[9] This is what McCannon says they refer to as "playing jazz." It's about being opportunistic and improvisational in the way Nashville was. It's a sign of being unleashed.

Yet there were setbacks along the way, and at one point a study they commissioned revealed that they were not going to make their deadline of housing one hundred thousand people by July 2013. As Becky recalled, "That was a really, really bad day." And she was going to have to look at a very visible representation of their failure on her own body, in the form of a 10,000 tattoo she had gotten when they had housed their first ten thousand people. "I got a tattoo with the last zero missing as like a down payment on the one hundred thousand and a sign of my commitment." Now Becky feared she'd be looking at that tattoo with the missing zero for the rest of her life. They had to devise new strategies with a heavier reliance on data and on ambitious but achievable intermediate goals, and had to extend their deadline by a year. But finally there came a day when Becky got a call from a team member announcing that the campaign had hit the one hundred thousand homes goal. "That was one of the best moments," she said. At last she was able to add that final zero to her tattoo of the 100,000 Homes logo.[10] On June 10, 2014, the 100,000 Homes Campaign officially announced that it had reached its goal. It had housed 101,628 homeless people. An independent analysis estimated total taxpayer savings from housing one hundred thousand chronically homeless Americans at more than $1.3 billion annually.[11]

How to Unleash

Unleashing unlocks your community's potential, yet as Becky Margiotta pointed out, leaders still tend to default to control, to constrain rather than unleash. Why? Most of it boils down to fear. What will happen if they're not in charge? What if the tribe screws up? Both she and Rosanne Haggerty struggled with this discomfort. They're not alone! Following are some ideas from executives at a number of companies about how to let go—successfully.

Southwest

Southwest Airlines, the fifty-year-old company that is now the world's largest low-cost air carrier, has a long history of empowering its people. It all begins with the way the company hires and trains employees. It recruits for attitude, to ensure that its employees are genuinely compatible with the company culture, and it trains for both skill and values. Southwest is intentional in how it instills employees with a sense of what the company stands for. And what it stands for comes directly from the co-founder himself, Herb Kelleher, whose philosophy was embodied in the oft-quoted statement that "a company is stronger if it is bound by love rather than by fear";[12] whose golden rule was that it is okay to break the rules; and who viewed their work as a cause—a cause to serve the public by making flying affordable, giving ordinary people without big bank accounts the freedom to have adventures, to go to new places and experience new things, and to connect with family and friends.

During training, new hires attend Fly Class, which is a day and a half of a deep dive into the company's values and its expectations of employees. At the end of the class, one of the top executives comes to speak with them and answer questions. Ryan Martinez, who is now Southwest's managing director of investor relations, was a new hire fourteen years ago, and he can still remember what a big impression it made on him when Colleen Barrett, then president and chief operating officer, came to their class, because having her there allowed employees to "see and feel the values from the beginning." Meeting Barrett reinforced that "people at the very top walk the talk and live the values." The values are posted all over the place, but for him, "seeing is believing," and Barrett seemed to personify those values.

Ginger Hardage, who was hired in 1990 as director of public relations, had a similar experience. As part of the orientation she attended, CEO Herb Kelleher himself gave a talk to the group of new hires. When Ginger walked into the room for the presentation, she expected him to be behind the podium. But he wasn't. He was serving food to the employees. Not enough waitstaff had shown up. "What did that immediately challenge me to do?" Hardage recounted. "I grabbed two plates of food and started serving food as well.... [I learned that] as leaders we can never forget that how we act always trumps what we say."[13]

Many years later, when I spoke at an event at Southwest's headquarters in Dallas, Texas, I observed that employees were instilled with Kelleher's philosophy, which has been at the heart of their culture for many decades now. "When you join Southwest you join a cause," CEO Gary Kelly was explaining to employees. "Your duty is to serve customers and take care of people," he told them, in language just like Herb Kelleher's. He stressed how Southwest's values were part of their belief system and would serve as a guardrail, ensuring that Southwest employees would not go off track even when given discretion. Implicit in this was the idea that he and senior leaders expected employees to do the right thing—for both their fellow employees and for their customers—but also that on occasion they would have to figure out what the right thing *was*, in line with the values they were absorbing.

After the training Southwest employees go through, which arms them with plenty of information as well as steeping them in the company's values, the goal is to set them free to deliver on the expectations that have been instilled in them. In short, Southwest wants to unleash its employees, but to unleash them to do things the Southwest way. Hardage describes this as freedom within a framework, because Southwest has discovered that it pays to give their employees the freedom to exercise their own judgment. A minor but telling example of this, which you may have experienced if you've ever flown Southwest, is the way many of the flight attendants deliver the standard FAA in-flight safety briefing about seat belts and emergency exits and oxygen masks. It's a message that flight attendants on every airline have to give, but attendants on Southwest have figured out how to do it so that people actually listen to it instead of automatically tuning it out, which is what usually happens. Some Southwest attendants sing it, others rap it, and many insert jokes into the announcement, and as people laugh and enjoy the performance, they are absorbing the information that they might otherwise have ignored.

This is one of the many ways that Southwest reaps the advantage of unleashing employees to express their individuality. Again it's Southwest's founder, Herb Kelleher, who first instilled this belief in his company's employees. "We've never thought that you should have to come to work and...look like you're a bunch of little lead soldiers stamped out of a mold," he said. "We give people license to be themselves." Kelleher believed that having a degree of autonomy was essential to the imagination, improvisation, and innovation Southwest desires from its people.[14]

Ryan Martinez particularly values this emphasis on autonomy and creativity—in fact it was why he joined the company. Before he went to Southwest, Martinez had been working in an accounting firm where he knew his place in the hierarchy and was expected to just fit into that slot and not show any kind of individuality. Although he wasn't trying to "buck the trend at work," he became envious of his wife, a Southwest employee. Watching her, he realized, "She was so able to be herself." He could see from her experience that at Southwest, "you don't have to change to fit in." But more than that, you are not supposed to. You are expected to bring all of yourself into your work, because Southwest views that as key to the thriving of the community. Best of all, at Southwest, "you always have the latitude to do what you think is right." Martinez and others rattled off multiple examples of employees living the Southwest values in service of the customer, without fear of being penalized for making decisions that deviated from the standard practices, even when those decisions ended up costing the company money.

There was the pilot who noticed the distress of a shabby-looking customer at a ticket counter when he was told that he couldn't board the plane with his dog unless he had the approved travel carrier. The pilot could tell the customer didn't have the money for the carrier, so he paid for it himself before going on his way. Southwest later received a letter of profuse thanks from the brother of this customer, saying that the pilot could not have had any idea how important what he did was for their family. The writer of the letter explained that his brother, who was homeless and had been estranged from the family, would never have boarded that flight and returned to them without his only possession, his pet.

Another example: Jessica Chatellier accompanied her husband to the airport for a flight on Southwest Airlines when he was being deployed to Kuwait for six months. After she and her young children reached security, they watched him proceed through the gate and turn to wave goodbye to them. Unbeknownst to her, Kelli Evans, a Southwest customer service agent who was observing their farewell, noticed that Jessica's husband was in uniform. She approached him and asked him if he was being deployed. When he said yes, she asked Jessica if she and the children would like to go to the gate with him. Shocked and delighted, they said yes and were able to wait with him until it was time for him to board the plane. After they hugged him goodbye, they stayed to watch his plane take off. At that point another Southwest employee, operations agent Felix Joseph, came over, tapped her on the shoulder, and told her he wanted to do something for her. Her first thought was "What could you possibly do to make things any better right now?" But Joseph had realized that there were a few minutes before the plane's scheduled departure time, so he made a quick phone call, and the next things she knew, he told her that she and her kids should get on the plane. As Jessica remembers it, "The kids ran down the tunnel. When we got to the end of the tunnel, a flight attendant called out on the intercom asking if there was a John Chatellier on the flight and we saw my husband's hand go up in the air and the kids were able to run to him and give him one last hug." It was such a touching moment, Joseph recounted that "all the passengers started clapping and everyone was tearing up." When Jessica spoke with her husband after he landed in Kuwait, he said that the "whole experience made him realize that people were going to be watching out for us, watching out for him and just taking care of us."

In another instance, an elderly woman's son was supposed to drive from Tucson, Arizona, to meet his mother's Southwest flight in Phoenix. But he was seriously hurt in a car crash on his way there. When the woman landed in Phoenix, a Southwest employee tried to book her on a different airline to Tucson since Southwest doesn't fly there. He couldn't find her a seat. "He didn't call headquarters and ask what to do," former CEO James Parker said. "He just went to the employee parking lot, got his car, and drove her to Tucson"—about one hundred miles away.[15]

"Warrior spirit" is a term used often at Southwest. It's the spirit employees are expected to embody in the face of serious challenges. What happened after the downing of the World Trade Center towers and the attack on the Pentagon on 9/11, when all flights were grounded, showed just how deeply their employees had absorbed that spirit. Many Southwest employees had stories to tell me about what their colleagues did to take care of passengers that terrible day. There were flight attendants who ordered food for all the stranded passengers. A pilot paid for hotel rooms for passengers whose flights had been diverted. These actions were taken with personal credit cards, and without corporate approval. Southwest refunded employees for all these expenses.

Another pilot who had to make a forced landing on 9/11 was told that he would have to wait four hours on the tarmac before unloading passengers because there was no off-ramp available. The Southwest crew decided to grab an idle luggage loader and use it to improvise a ramp to escort passengers to the ground. Those crew members also arranged for buses to take passengers to the Amtrak station and paid for their train tickets home.[16]

One thing is clear from all these stories: Southwest employees tend to act swiftly and with confidence, demonstrating the spirit of caring that has been instilled in them, and also the entrepreneurialism that is their version of unleashing. "I'd like to believe that we get it right 99.9 percent of the time," Martinez said. "As long as it's best for the customer, and holds with our values." Perhaps my favorite (and certainly the funniest) example of their entrepreneurialism is the Southwest manager who escorted a belligerent passenger to another airline's counter, where she bought him a ticket to fly the competitor![17]

Southwest provides the guardrails—but trusts its employees to make the correct decisions within them. Like 100,000 Homes, Southwest encourages its employees to remove logjams whenever possible. James Parker, who was general counsel at Southwest for sixteen years before serving as CEO from 2001 to 2004, believes a company like Southwest succeeds partly because its employees work together toward a big-picture goal of serving customers and have the flexibility to do it as they think best, even when it means doing things that might not be considered part of their job descriptions.[18]

As dedicated as Southwest is to serving its customers, Herb Kelleher believed that it should also serve its employees. In fact, he "believed that employees should be treated like customers and celebrated for going above and beyond the call of duty." Sounding very much like J. Willard Marriott, the founder of the Marriott hotel chain, whom you'll meet in chapter 6, he explained, "If you treat them well, then they treat the customers well, and that means your customers come back and your shareholders are happy."[19] Perhaps this is why Southwest has done profit sharing with its employees from its very early years.

Celebrating employees for going above and beyond the call of duty— unleashing them—means that the company will also be willing to go beyond the bounds of typical corporate responsibility to support its employees when they *are* unleashed. Whitney Eichinger, managing director of culture and engagement at Southwest, gave me the example of how the company helped employees who wanted to find a way to fund various charitable causes. This involved forming an LLC, a new structure within the corporation, in order to adhere to legal requirements. In addition to making it possible to donate to charities outside the company, the LLC also allowed employees to donate to a catastrophic fund for their fellow employees—to take care of their "family," as I've heard CEO Gary Kelly refer to the Southwest community. If a tornado hit an employee's house, for example, these funds could be used to help with the necessary rebuilding. Creating the LLC required Southwest to do a lot of extra legwork, and to incur substantial legal fees. Instead of objecting because it cost too much or was outside the scope of its obligations to its employees, however, Southwest listened to them and empowered them to fund causes near and dear to them.

Supporting its employees in these ways, costly as some of them are, is worth it. Southwest has been the most profitable airline this half century.[20] The Department of Transportation, which tracks the number of customer complaints about airlines, reveals that in twenty-six out of twenty-nine years of rankings, Southwest has had the lowest number of complaints. It's also racked up a slew of other awards, and is known for having one of the most highly motivated and productive workforces in the industry. In other words, unleashing pays.

GoDaddy, The Mighty, etc.

CLARIFY WHAT'S ESSENTIAL.

Before unleashing, get clear on what part of your path to your purpose is nonnegotiable, and what could or even should be adapted to different contexts and circumstances to get you to your goal. Imparting this lesson, Joe McCannon uses the analogy of making a turkey sandwich. For him a turkey sandwich should be made with rye bread, Swiss cheese, lettuce, tomato, mustard, and onion. But he recognizes that other people might opt for other ingredients—a bagel, cream cheese, pickles, cucumber, mayonnaise, ketchup, horseradish, whatever. If it's got turkey on some kind of bread, it's still a turkey sandwich. But the turkey and the bread are sacrosanct. "If you take away the bread or the turkey, however, we have a problem." In the 100,000 Homes Campaign, Becky Margiotta noted that her turkey sandwich included the vulnerability index as the meat and the registry week as the bread—and that was it. Otherwise, she was flexible about adaptations. Community leaders could add or adjust so long as those essentials remained.

Mike Porath has his own sense of what is essential to The Mighty and what can be altered as necessary. "We may say we're The Mighty community but really it's The Mighty communities or tribes, and they each have their own practices, priorities, and sometimes taboos. For example, in some tribes, members would never share intimate information about something like weight. But in others—those focused on issues like dieting or diabetes for example—that would be a focus of conversation. We had to learn to hand control to our teams and say, 'Run with it.'" Not always easy, but that's what unleashing entails.

No Playbooks.

Michael Nixon, vice president and advisor to the CEO at GoDaddy, an internet domain registrar and web hosting company, shared how he learned "Don't do a playbook." Many years ago, he lived through a merger and acquisition where a large consulting firm "came in on day three wearing blue suits, red ties, white shirts, with a four-inch binder detailing how they were going to transform us in thirteen months." Nixon told me, "It was rigorous. And, they were right, we were transformed in thirteen months. It was mind-blowing." He paused, and with a deep sigh said, "But it was the most dehumanizing thirteen months of my career." The framework was so rigid that "it sucked the life from people."

Michael and his CEO, Aman Bhutani, with whom he worked for many years at Expedia and other places before they both joined GoDaddy in September 2019, do things very differently. They create a framework, but it's a flexible one, a work in progress that is based on a willingness to learn, understand, and adjust as they go. According to Nixon, "That flexibility and willingness to learn goes back to Aman's scientific method—his belief that you test hypotheses. You're always willing to learn and improve." Aman Bhutani is known for establishing a data-driven, "test and learn" culture that valued experimentation when he was at Expedia, and he has brought the same kind of culture to GoDaddy.[21]

BE READY FOR CHANGE.

A forty-four-year-old native of New Delhi known for being a wise but humble leader with a good sense of humor and endless energy, Aman Bhutani applies something he learned decades ago from his father, who would often ask, " 'How do you ride a tiger?' " The answer, he learned, is: "You ride a tiger on its neck. And the reason is that if you ride the tiger on its tail, when it goes right, you go left, and when it goes left, you go right. So there's a whiplash every time. But if you ride the tiger on the neck, you're always aligned with where the tiger is going. And it doesn't matter how the tiger moves or how quickly the tiger turns, you turn at that same moment. And the fact is that change is like the tiger, so you need to ride it the right way." Because we live in a time of such rapid and massive change, Bhutani's father's advice has never been more important, and Bhutani himself knows how to ride the tiger, to be ceaselessly open to adapting to change— and to allowing his employees to ride the tiger to wherever it takes them.[22]

The philosophy seems to be working: In 2020, which has certainly seen a record number of changes of all kinds, GoDaddy experienced significant growth—adding four hundred thousand new customers in the second quarter and again in the third quarter. "They're the biggest quarters we've ever had," Bhutani said.[23]

BELIEVE IN YOUR PEOPLE.

Bhutani's recipe for unleashing them and making (or allowing) them successful is simple: (1) believe in the person, (2) give the person an opportunity, and (3) if he or she fails, forgive. You can coach the person. Having seen the results Bhutani has gotten with this formula, in all sorts of contexts, and through major structural changes, Nixon echoed him: "How can you bring out the best in people if you don't believe in people? You need to bet that they're good."

Jen O'Twomney, vice president of strategic initiatives at GoDaddy, who has worked with both Bhutani and Nixon for many years and followed Bhutani from Expedia, told me that she's learned this the hard way. She remembers that when they were at Expedia, Bhutani had wanted a certain person who worked at Expedia to join their mergers and acquisitions (M&A) team, but O'Twomney doubted this man. She was skeptical of his abilities and let Bhutani know it. Bhutani pushed her, telling her that she would get extremely high performance from him if only she believed in him.

The person failed. Bhutani's take on what had happened: "He failed because you failed him." O'Twomney told me, "It was true. I didn't believe in him." Reflecting on what went wrong, she realized that although she was actively involved in the other team members' day-to-day work activities, actively coaching and mentoring them, she didn't spend time with this man the way she did with the others on the team. She failed to shake her skepticism about him, his competence, and his fit on her team. "It was my lack of interest in helping him succeed that contributed to his failing," she admitted. Looking back, she saw that her perspective was so biased at the time that she could see only the shortcomings in his work, not any of the positives. It was the self-fulfilling prophecy—if you expect the worst in others, you bring out the worst in them. She believes that even her nonverbal communication and body language were so negative that they discouraged him from seeking guidance and learning from the team.

"After this experience," she said, "I consciously chose to believe in my people, and the results were such a contrast." Although "not everyone has wild success" when she puts in the effort to help them, some do. "And for those who don't, they still achieve more than had I not put that force of belief behind them. I've now seen this play out enough times to have conviction in the practice of belief," she told me.

USE DATA!

Data don't just come in the form of numbers and statistics; they encompass all kinds of evidence, lived and observed as well as measured. Aman Bhutani is a big believer in using such evidence to test the workability of ideas and hypotheses. He jokes about how he even uses it in his personal life, as when his older brother said, "We should live together. It's been fifteen years since we've done that." They were both married, with two children, so this was quite a bold departure from the usual, at least in this country. But Aman and his brother decided that they'd try it for a while, as something of a social experiment. If it worked, they would layer in their parents, too, to have a three-generational household. That was in 2014. It's worked well ever since then.

Joe McCannon is also a big believer in using data to determine what works and what doesn't. One of the invaluable things that the 100,000 Homes Campaign took from McCannon was how to use data once you unleash. That was the point of the Chutes and Ladders exercise. McCannon said you have to test a lot of potential ladders while you're in the middle of the Chutes and Ladders board to find out which will be the long ladders you need to make progress and move ahead, and which turn out to be chutes. By giving the participants in the campaign the freedom to figure out which steps could be removed to facilitate the progress toward the goal, the campaign leaders were unleashing them.

McCannon views data as something you use for the purpose of learning, not judging. He asks leaders, "What are your priorities when it comes to data and measurement?" The goal as he sees it is to use data, about both successes and failures, so that it's useful to those on the front lines, the people who are trying out things in the hope of changing outcomes. In his 100,000 Lives Campaign McCannon asked: How can physicians and nurses use the data to improve patient care? And in the 100,000 Homes Campaign, he asked: How can the local community use this information to house more of their homeless population? All too often, however, as McCannon recognizes, data is used as a club, as in "Why didn't you meet your goals?" rather than as a learning tool.[24]

USE STORYTELLING.

Few things move people as much as stories do. Storytelling is a phenomenal way to teach people about your culture and the behaviors you desire. Look for opportunities to reinforce and celebrate when employees or members of your community live the values, improvising or innovating. Southwest CEO

Gary Kelly records a message every week to employees updating them about the previous week's events and what is scheduled for the upcoming week. Employees can listen to the audio or read a transcribed message online or via email. At the end of the message, Kelly always includes a shout-out to a specific employee who's really living the "Southwest Way." This tactic shows employees "what type of behavior is valued and widens their view of how far they might go to deliver great customer service," says Hardage.[25] And from the pride in the voices of the employees who told me so many wonderful stories about their colleagues' efforts, it's clear that storytelling has become a critical part of advancing the values Southwest wants its people to live by.

FRAME MISTAKES AS LEARNING OPPORTUNITIES.

To reduce fear across your community, frame mistakes as just part of the game. Google has a postmortem process in place to share information so employees can learn from their most important mistakes. Googlers work together to create a written record for what happened, why, its impact, how the issue was mitigated or resolved, and what they will do to prevent the incident from recurring. They suggest asking:

- What went well?
- What didn't go well?
- Where did we get lucky?
- What can we do differently next time?

Importantly, they focus on learning and growth—not blame. This is crucial to fostering psychological safety—repositioning failure as an opportunity for growth and development rather than as a setback.[26] As we saw in chapter 1, creating a culture in which failure is accepted, or even—as at X with Astro Teller and at Spanx with Sara Blakely—celebrated, is the way to unleash your employees.

LEARN TO FUNNEL.

Leaders may fear that unleashing will result in too many inferior initiatives that siphon energy and resources from the best ideas. Try *funneling*. At Southwest, true to its tradition of empowering its employees, enthusiastic employees generate loads of interesting ideas, but not all are worth pursuing. So Southwest uses its President's Council, a committee with members from all levels of the organization, to see to it that only the potentially viable ones get through to the testing stage.[27] Since the council comprises such a diverse group of employees with such different kinds of expertise—pilots, operations agents, ticket and gate agents, flight attendants, and others—it means that they are open to hearing many voices. But their discussions do a good job of prioritizing which ideas should have resources of time, energy, and money devoted to them, and which won't make it through the funnel. Southwest's unique numbered boarding process began as an idea that worked its way through this committee.

EMBRACE YOUR TEAM'S INNOVATIONS.

Rebecca Onie, founder and CEO of Health Leads and a winner of the MacArthur Fellowship, believes that the primary fear related to unleashing is not that others on the team won't do it as well, but that they're going to do it better than we have. It's quite possible. Becky Margiotta and Beth Sandor of 100,000 Homes had to learn that other people could do registry weeks just as effectively as they did. But once they saw what they had unleashed, they got over their defensiveness. And when a team in San Diego found ways to improve the materials and presentation in their binder, a binder they had spent years pounding away at until they thought it was perfect, they were delighted. In fact, Margiotta and her team negotiated a contract to have the San Diego organizer codify the material and create a training notebook for the campaign. Six weeks later, she said they had "a beautiful standardized binder and a CD-ROM with everything downloaded."

Leaders might also fear getting into risky ventures if they unleash. Bhutani says, "Let go lightly," to managers struggling with this. In other words, see what happens with some initial slack on that chain. Try experimenting—unleash a bit and see how it goes, then a bit more. Or begin with a slightly shorter leash. Ease your way into comfort with the process by carefully monitoring the results and tightening up on the leash, or loosening it, as necessary.

Although for many leaders, unleashing takes them out of their comfort zone, the results speak for themselves. In embracing the discomfort, Rosanne Haggerty has housed well over 235,000 people in the US, and more in Canada and other countries. She's poised to house many more. In 2021, Community Solutions won 100&Change—MacArthur's global competition to fund a single proposal that promises real and measurable progress in solving a critical problem of our time a $100 million grant to accelerate an end to homelessness in seventy-five US communities.[28] Haggerty attributed her greatest learnings to unleashing and the backbone role, and, specifically, the need to be uncomfortable through it all. Joe McCannon believes that unleashing not only drives innovation and therefore better results, but helps create an attitude and spirit among your tribes that will carry them through many difficulties and challenges. Empower people like Southwest Airlines does.

Unleashing applies to all sorts of teams and communities, and is practiced by many outstanding leaders, even if they don't use the same language to describe what they do. As coach Phil Jackson of the Chicago Bulls put it, he was always striving to be an invisible leader. His goal: to give his players increasing responsibility to shape their roles. Help people connect with their role.

What can you do to unleash your tribe?

CHAPTER **3**

Respect

*Every action done in company ought to be done with some sign
of respect to those that are present.*
—*The Rules of Civility and Decent Behaviour in Company and
Conversation*

At seven thirty one morning, Jeremy Andrus drove into the parking lot of his office at Traeger, an Oregon-based company specializing in wood pellet outdoor cooking grills. As soon as he arrived, he saw that it was surrounded by fire trucks and policemen. After getting out of his car, he saw that one of Traeger's eighteen-wheel big-rig trucks was on fire and had been burned almost to the ground. Though he didn't know who was responsible, he felt sure it was arson. The newly minted CEO of the company, he'd recently announced that Traeger would outsource its warehouse and trucking operations to UPS. Traeger had offered the several dozen employees who were affected generous severance and outplace assistance, which included the option to work for UPS. But the news had not gone over well, and Andrus was aware that many of his employees were unhappy.[1]

When Andrus was recruited for the job at Traeger, it was at a time in his life when he was looking for a new venture. He wanted to find a company he could buy and run himself. Before he decided to accept the job, he had weighed many options and looked at a number of other companies, but he was won over by the enormous growth potential he saw in Traeger, believing they had not yet scratched the surface of their market. When he joined the company in early 2014, the private equity (PE) firm that had approached him about the job held a minority stake, and he invested his own money to become another minority shareholder. Although Traeger's headquarters were in Portland, Oregon, the company also had a small sales office in Springville, Utah, and an office in China. Andrus lived in Utah and decided to commute between there and the Oregon headquarters.[2]

Unfortunately, problems arose early on. The majority owner of the company was a serial entrepreneur who lived in Florida. During this man's eight-year tenure as leader, he'd hired seven CEOs, each of whom had departed. Andrus was the eighth. As he later discovered, employees were referring to him as Ocho (eight in Spanish) behind his back, assuming that just like his predecessors he wouldn't last long. Many treated him like he was already on his way out. When he asked for data, they ignored him. When he'd ask people to collaborate on projects, they'd refuse. When he visited the headquarters, Andrus asked the CFO—a man who reported to him—to meet with him. The CFO first said he couldn't find time in his schedule, though he did eventually grant him thirty minutes of his valuable time.

These were all problems at the employee level. But it was soon apparent that the problems came from the top. Andrus found that the majority owner was very abrasive in meetings and other interactions. Initially this didn't bother him. However, a mere thirty days into his new job, Andrus saw clearly that the owner's aggressive, abusive style had rubbed off on many of the employees, and created a company-wide atmosphere that was filled with fear.[3] Everyone was afraid of this owner—including Andrus himself.[4] As he described it, "Every time the phone rang and it was him, my stomach sank. And every conversation was hard." It became a struggle just to go to the office every day. He felt the hostility was affecting his performance.[5] He "started thinking if I feel sick to my stomach, chances are other people probably do too."

In hopes of changing the culture, Andrus soon brought in four executives—good friends from his previous job as CEO of Skullcandy. But much to his surprise, this seemed only to make things worse, creating an us-versus-them situation, with him and his new team on one side, the owner and long-term employees on the other.[6]

Just five months into his role, the need for a change became clearer than ever at a board meeting. Perhaps the first sign was the majority owner refusing an open seat next to Andrus. Over the next four hours, as Andrus gave a ninety-eight-slide PowerPoint presentation detailing his vision for the company, the owner never said a word. But the steam coming out of his ears was practically visible. At end of the presentation, he angrily pounded his fist, "spitting across the table" at Andrus, and shouting, "I disagree with every f——— thing, and every f——— slide."[7] At that point Andrus figured it was either him or the majority owner.[8] He called his PE partner and told him that life was too short to continue like this: "Either buy this thing, or let me help you find another CEO." The PE firm acted quickly, buying the owner out (with Andrus) on June 20, 2014.

Once the former owner was out of the way, Andrus was free to turn his attention to various problems, and initiated several strategic and operational changes in the way Traeger did business. He also spent a lot of time meeting with his top thirty to forty employees to assess their willingness to change, and did a cultural survey that allowed for anonymous feedback in order to get ideas for how to create a more positive, collaborative culture. Andrus and his leadership team formulated a new mission and five values that were meant to drive the company forward, but no matter how hard he worked to communicate and reinforce them, nothing seemed to change. Many of the employees had been working there for a long time—some were even second generation—and they seemed to have little motivation to do things differently or create the kind of community Andrus envisioned. He wondered if the fact that he spent most of his time commuting to Oregon was holding these efforts back, and briefly considered moving his family from Utah so that he could be there full-time and try to shape the community through role modeling and daily practices. But he doubted this would fix the culture.[9]

The day he saw the eighteen-wheeler on fire in the company parking lot was the day he decided he had to do something radical to effect change. During a meeting he convened with his executive team to discuss how to handle the truck fire, a longtime employee came in and announced that he had heard that something big was going to go down that day. Someone else had just relayed the news that a disgruntled employee in an office in Alabama had shot and killed two colleagues. Andrus said that this was the first time he ever felt physically unsafe at work. Nothing in his past had prepared him for the toxic culture he faced. He decided that the only way to change it was to completely dismantle it and build a new one from scratch.

Although most employees in toxic workplaces aren't literally burning company assets, the damage they do to an organization's bottom line and reputation is very real, and it has to be stopped, which sometimes requires drastic action. It's a "near impossibility [to] transform a legacy culture in which negative attitudes were so deeply ingrained,"[10] Andrus says, in explaining his decision. "You can fix strategy and operations, but the only way to fix culture is to start over." Which is what he did. He decided to close the Oregon headquarters, since that was where most of the employees who were blocking his efforts to create a more positive, collaborative culture worked. This was a costly and painful move but a necessary one. Traeger paid severance to people they let go, and retention bonuses to key people who remained in Oregon until the new headquarters was set up.

In deciding whom to invite to make the move to Utah, Traeger assessed each of the remaining ninety employees on both competency and cultural fit. People were graded as positive cultural leaders, neutral, or cultural detractors. No matter how competent the many cultural detractors were, Andrus decided Traeger didn't want them. Andrus knew that, as research shows, toxicity is like a virus, and they had to make sure not to bring in anyone who would infect the Utah office. Of the twelve to fifteen employees who ranked as neutral or positive, most of whom were relatively new employees who hadn't been indoctrinated in the old toxic ways, five made the move. About fifteen employees came from the Springville, Utah, office to the new headquarters in Salt Lake City.

The Utah headquarters opened in September of 2015, and Traeger said goodbye to its last employee in Oregon in 2016. As of 2021, it had 720 employees globally. Andrus now spends time with every job applicant to make sure he or she has the right kind of values and skills before any job offer is made. Andrus has also worked with architects to create a positive physical environment for his employees and has made a point of having the employees cook breakfast together every Monday morning, and lunch on Tuesday through Friday. He feels that preparing food together is an important way to show that they care about one another, and is also a way of reminding everyone that their brand is based on a cooking and food-related product.

It took Traeger twenty-six years to get to $70 million in revenue. In seven years with Andrus as CEO, Traeger has grown ten times—to $700 million in revenue. He credits culture: "Because we're still selling a wood pellet grill. We're selling a better one, but we didn't come in here and say we've got to completely change what we're doing. We're still positioned the same way in the market. The only variable was the team and culture. And I think it mattered." Andrus describes the mood at headquarters as being noticeably different from what it was before, and feels that has been communicated to Traeger's retail partners and to the larger community as well, which is another factor in burnishing the company's reputation and driving business.[11] Employees seem to agree, as in 2020, they rated Traeger's culture a 9 out of 10 (average), with 91 percent feeling connected to the company's vision, mission, and values in pulse (short) surveys. (The industry average was 48 percent, and benchmark across companies 46 percent.)[i]

Andrus pointed to something else. "Unlike any moment in my career, I have received hundreds of appreciative notes from people. . . . I think people sense when you're not only doing the right thing, but you're doing the right thing for the right reasons. I think it's because people have fun at Traeger, and people almost never leave. It's a place that—we stretch them, we push people really hard, and we're competitive and we want to win, but when you learn that's not mutually exclusive with building an environment that makes people feel like they're growing, they're accomplishing, they're connected. It's been nice to figure out how you do these in a symbiotic way, where one reinforces another."

The powerful story Andrus told me of the corporate upheaval and rebound he led at Traeger reveals something similar to what I've seen in my research. If you want to drive performance, you have to make your employees feel respected. If instead they feel devalued and are living in a culture shaped by fear and negativity, they will not achieve their full potential. Andrus

---

i   For perspective, the industry average was 48 percent, and benchmark across companies 46 percent.

experienced that quite viscerally himself, in the very pit of his stomach. The toxic culture the owner had created made him dread his dealings with the man, and undermined his ability to do his job.

Incivility is not just unpleasant. But as my research has shown time and again, it is costly to the bottom line. *Mastering Civility* documents many of these costs and shows how you can enhance your influence and effectiveness with simple acts of civility. This chapter explores the dynamics of civility, revealing how critical a role it plays in the success of any community. And it shows how to use the Cycle to Civility® tool I have developed in the consulting work I do with various companies—to build respectful communities that allow employees to flourish.

Breakdown of Community: The Costs of Incivility

As Jeremy Andrus's experience with Traeger reveals, disrespect, disregard, and incivility erode people's sense of belonging, fracture a sense of connection, and can leave members of the workplace community feeling isolated, alone, betrayed and belittled. When the social fabric of the community is damaged, there are real and measurable effects on performance.

Within workplace communities where life-and-death decisions sometimes have to be made, rude interactions affect performance in a way that could have potentially lethal effects. A doctor described to me how on one occasion a supervising doctor belittled a medical team on duty. Soon after, the team accidentally administered the wrong treatment to a patient, having failed to read vital information that had been right there on the chart. As a result, the patient died. An isolated incident? Not at all. In a survey of 4,500 doctors and nurses, 71 percent saw a link between disruptive behavior (defined as "abusive personal conduct," including condescending, insulting, or rude behavior) and medical errors they knew of, and 27 percent connected such behavior to actual deaths among their patients.[12] Physicians exposed to rudeness tend to get stuck on an initial incorrect diagnosis, leading to medical errors.[13]

In a study of how incivility can play out in medical settings, twenty-four medical teams from four neonatal intensive care units in Israel were invited to a training designed to improve quality of care. As part of this training, the teams needed to treat a premature infant whose condition suddenly deteriorated due to a serious intestinal illness. (This was only a simulation; no infant's health was endangered.) Staff had to identify and diagnose the condition and administer proper treatment, including CPR. Teams were told that an expert from the United States would be watching them remotely and would occasionally comment and advise them. That "expert" was a member of the research team. Half the teams received neutral messages from the expert, who spoke about the importance of training and practice using simulations but did not comment on their work quality. The other half received insulting messages about their performance and the "poor quality" of Israeli medical care.

Researchers filmed these simulations, and objective judges evaluated the results. The teams exposed to rudeness displayed lower capabilities on all metrics of diagnostic and procedural performance, markedly diminishing the infant's chances of survival. This was mainly because teams exposed to rudeness didn't share information as readily and because they stopped seeking help from their teammates.[14] They also failed to share the workload.

I frequently see results like these in my research into incivility: Lacking a sense of psychological safety (or trust and respect), people shut down, often without realizing it. They are less likely to seek or accept feedback. They're also less likely to experiment, to discuss errors, and to speak up about potential or actual problems.[15] Even without an intimidator in the room, they work in a cloud of negativity and are unable to do their best. Other community members, who catch this virus or who are left picking up the slack, also feel these effects.

As a mathematical model developed by Yale psychologists Adam Bear and David Rand showed, people who are typically surrounded by jerks learn intuitively to be selfish and also not to deliberate over their actions. They wind up acting selfishly even when cooperating would pay off, precisely because they don't stop to think.[16] Our community rubs off on us, and if our community is toxic, we can expect to stay somewhat sick and to pass the virus on to others. Customers, clients, patients, and other community members may be affected more than we think. In our research, Debbie MacInnis, Valerie Folkes, and I learned that simply witnessing employee disrespect repels customers!

Several colleagues and I did a study of the effects of de-energizing relationships in the workplace—which we define as relationships characterized by "an enduring, recurring set of negative judgments, feelings, and behavioral intentions toward another person." The relationship of the owner of Traeger to his CEO, Jeremy Andrus, could be described as de-energizing. Employees at an engineering firm who perceived more people as de-energizing were twice as likely to voluntarily leave the organization. But what is particularly alarming is that it's the top talent that is most likely to leave when having to deal with de-energizing relationships. High performers with an above-average number of de-energizing ties were *thirteen times* more likely to leave than low and average performers with the same number of de-energizing ties.[17] The Society for Human Resources Management estimates turnover costs at $3,500 per employee. It estimates departures of lower-level employees cost organizations 30–50 percent of employees' yearly salaries. For middle-level employees, the figure climbs to an estimated 150 percent of each departing employee's annual salary. For high-level employees, the figure can balloon to over 400 percent of annual salary.[18] These figures can quickly multiply when other community members happily follow these talented folks to greener pastures (often to the same organizations, which may be competitors). When you recognize that communities stand to lose their most valuable members if they are exposed to such relationships, it becomes imperative to do something about them, as Andrus did. But as I've seen in my own research, there are many ways of intervening to improve workplace interactions, and they don't always require getting rid of the de-energizers.

Civility Creates Stronger, Higher Performing Communities

After years of trying to stamp out incivility, disrespect, and negativity in communities, I wanted to show that it pays to go beyond neutral. And my research has confirmed that: It's not enough just to eliminate the negative; finding ways to introduce positive behaviors into the community has an even bigger payoff. Even small actions matter—thanking people, listening attentively, humbly asking questions, acknowledging others, sharing credit, smiling or other nonverbal behaviors—not only with respect to well-being and happiness, but also with respect to the success of a business.

Civility is a magnet. Civility makes community members more likable, enjoyable, and attractive. People are also more likely to view civil individuals as having greater integrity (and garner greater status and power) than uncivil individuals.[19] As a community, you're likely to attract and retain members based on respect.

You're also likely to garner commitment, engagement, and performance from these members. In our study of twenty-thousand employees around the world conducted by Tony Schwartz published in *Harvard Business Review*, no other leader behavior had a bigger effect on employees across the outcomes we measured than respect. Being treated with respect was more important to employees than recognition and appreciation, communicating an inspiring vision, providing useful feedback—even opportunities for learning, growth, and development.[20]

Those who get respect from their leaders reported 56 percent better health and well-being, 1.72 times more trust and safety, 89 percent greater enjoyment and satisfaction with their jobs, and 92 percent greater focus. Those who feel respected by their leaders were also 1.1 times more likely to stay with their organizations than those who didn't. Respect also had a clear impact on engagement. The more leaders give, the higher the level of employee engagement: People who said leaders treated them with respect were 55 percent more engaged.

Our research found that respect spurs positive energy and eagerness to participate and contribute to communities. Civility increases performance, collaboration, creativity, individual initiative, and the detection of mistakes. Such actions have positive multiplier effects in the community, rippling through our social network.

In a study of all employees from a research and development department of a biotechnology firm, we found that employees seen as civil were more likely to be sought for information, and twice as likely to be viewed as leaders. Respect paid off: The civil performed 13 percent better. Digging deeper, we conducted an experiment to learn more about *why* civility paid. We found that people were 59 percent more willing to share information with and 71 percent more motivated to work harder for a civil person compared to an uncivil person, largely because they saw civil people as a powerful and unique combination of warm *and* competent.[21]

We were curious about how these benefits might ripple in communities. In a study in a biotech company, my colleagues and I found that when people are civil in small ways, their behavior is likely to be reciprocated and passed forward.

The positive and inspiring feelings that can arise from our interactions with others lead to what my brother Mike refers to as "The Mighty Magic." Respect has an almost magical effect on tribes. In a study of 180 of its active teams, Google found that who was on a team mattered less than how team members interacted, structured their work, and viewed their contributions. Employees on teams with more psychological safety—a sense of trust and respect—were more likely to make use of their teammates' ideas and less likely to leave Google. Those on teams that had this feeling of respect and safety also generated more revenue for the company and were rated as "effective" twice as often by executives.[22]

Civility is the foundation community members need in order to feel comfortable speaking up and sharing ideas. In one experiment, I found that psychological safety increased by 35 percent when a person received a suggestion civilly (i.e., was thanked) compared with uncivilly (i.e., inconsiderately interrupted). Small moments matter. Especially if you're a leader.

When Aman Bhutani (whom you met in chapter 2) was growing up in India, his parents told him a story of a mango tree, which helped to teach him about humility. It was particularly helpful, because very early on a leader told him that humility is not a strength for a leader (in the West). He had to redefine humility for himself, and found himself returning to the lesson his parents taught him twenty years before about the mango tree. A little background helps to understand the humility tree. Aman explained, "Mango is the king of fruits in India—it's fibrous, it's juicy, there's a hundred varieties. To grow this king of fruit you put a seed in ground, and it takes about five years for the tree to produce the big and heavy mangoes." Bhutani described how the more fruit it has, the more the branches bend to the ground. A key lesson about humility is to start with the idea that every human being has gifts. He explained, "We have tremendous amount of gifts and those gifts are like mangoes on the mango tree. Your job is to make those gifts easier for others to take from you, which is what the mango tree does. It brings the fruit closer to the ground so more animals can consume it. And in the moment, in the moment where you take that gift and you give it to somebody, your best idea, your gift [to] somebody else, what you want to do is bow. Just like the tree bows. If you find in that moment that you're bowing or sharing your gifts, you've found humility." Bhutani went on to note how when you've found humility, it produces a lot of positive outcomes for leaders. People are willing to speak up to you, and even give you tough feedback. He said, "Everybody else around you is going to tell you how you can do it better because they will be in your corner. I've had the most random of people give me advice when I most needed it."[23] Bhutani now uses this to teach his community (as humility is one of its norms).

As this story and that of Jeremy Andrus and numerous other examples throughout this book will reveal, leaders set the tone. A medical resident told me about a surgery in which the anesthesiologist was seconds away from administering anesthesia to the patient. A nurse suddenly piped up, proclaiming, "This is a mistake!" The surgeon who was in charge instantly stopped and, bewildered, asked, "Why?" The nurse explained that the information on the chart must be wrong. It was too high a dosage and could kill the patient based on his weight. Although skeptical, the surgeon asked the team to double-check the information and crunch the numbers again. The team quickly found a mistake and made the necessary dosage adjustment. After successfully completing the operation, the surgeon, who was highly esteemed among his colleagues and well liked, wrote up the nurse, nominating her for an award with MedStar Health, a 120-entities system, which she won. Instead of burying the incident, the doctor used it to highlight the type of responsible behavior that the hospital wanted from its staff. By doing so, he reinforced a culture in which everyone on staff, including lower-level employees who in other hospitals might have been too intimidated to question a superior's actions, was encouraged to speak up. This meant that potential risks and safety concerns could be addressed immediately.

Stories like this get passed on within communities. They perpetuate the values of the institution and say far more about what's truly desired and rewarded than a list of abstractions slapped on the walls or bullet pointed on a website. Such lists all tend to look remarkably similar and are never very convincing.

Cycle to Civility

Companies that want to "civilize" their cultures can use the four-step Cycle to Civility® plan I've introduced into dozens of the businesses I've consulted for. The plan covers the entire employee life cycle: recruiting, coaching (training), scoring (evaluation and rewards), and practicing (improvement, termination, and exit). Although focusing on any of these steps individually will help, you will move your tribe or community's culture toward civility faster if you work on more than one at a time. The more you do, the more apparent it becomes that the impact of civility and respect really does run deep. Emphasis on these qualities signals that you care about the development and well-being of your tribe and community.

Recruit: Hire for Civility

Fostering a feeling of community begins with whom you hire. One founder and CEO told me he was ready to make a key hire for a top, pivotal executive position. He was delighted that his selection, an extremely successful entrepreneur and top executive with a technology company worth several hundred billion dollars, was interested in working with their small, but growing, company. The founder met with this acclaimed individual several times and was excited. It was almost too good to be true. Before making an offer, however, the CEO checked with a trusted advisor, who happened to be the firm's biggest investor, who in turn offered to call the prospect's former CEO.

"Don't do it," the advisor counseled after talking to the man's former boss and pursuing a long trail of information. "He's toxic." He explained to the CEO that Silicon Valley and potential investors would look down on this budding firm and question the wisdom of a CEO who would hire such a person. The CEO nonetheless remained tempted. After all, the "toxic person" had worked for only a short time for the man who gave him the negative report. But after more digging, the CEO concluded that there was too much damaging information about this potential hire's effect on people.

The CEO was lucky. He had an investor who cared deeply and was willing to do the due diligence required to get a true assessment of someone's reputation. Most people, like this potential hire, can supply several good references. But that shouldn't be the end of your background checks. Especially in the case of key hires, it's imperative that you do your homework. Collect feedback from those above, across, and below, because toxic people tend to present different personas to different hierarchical levels—the "kiss up, kick down" syndrome. Reach out to as many of your industry and organizational contacts as possible. Former United States deputy secretary of labor Chris Lu simply picks up the phone and calls people who know the candidate. Chris says it never fails; he gets great information on almost all candidates from his trusted network. Let your contacts know that you want to hear the good, but also the bad and the ugly if there's anything that needs to be said. Better to get that information before hiring than afterward, when the new employee can infect your workplace like a contagion and cause long-term harm.

Andrus has interviewed almost every single one of his employees. "Part of it is I want to make sure that I'm the screen of the culture fit of who comes into the community, but the other is I think it starts the partnership and friendship off on the right foot. And I hear this almost every single time, usually from someone multiple levels removed from me. They say they 'can't believe that I took the time to meet with them.' And I say, 'This is important, this matters to us more than anything, and every single person matters in this organization.'" Andrus is committed "to the first experience that someone has with us," and wants the person "to believe that we actually care about our people."

Even the most careful of employers occasionally make bad choices, of course. And even when they don't, when a company acquires another, the employees from the acquisition may bring with them a culture of values that is not compatible with that of their new workplace. In that case, it's best to intervene and resolve any issues related to incivility as soon as possible.

Coach: Training for Civility

If you are a leader, it pays to think of yourself as a coach. Review the fundamentals with employees.

One way an organization can **communicate its expectations** is by making civility part of its mission statement. Clear norms established by a founder or the leaders of a tribe and embodied in the mission statement can set the right tone and inspire a more positive culture.

As we kicked off a Southwest event at its headquarters (mentioned in chapter 2), Raquel Daniels, director of diversity and inclusion, got up on the stage and, music blaring, sang Black Eyed Peas' "Be Nice." She ushered employees into the act, belting out, "Be different / Be nice. / Just smile. I promise it'll change your life." People began singing their little hearts out. As Raquel swayed and clapped, we stood up, raised our arms, and followed along.

Southwest Airlines' mission statement proclaims the following: "Employees will be provided the same concern, respect, and caring attitude within the organization that they are expected to share externally with every Southwest Customer." CEO Gary Kelly believes such behavior is even more important today, a time when "we see more examples of civil discord than ever." He adds, "If I had to boil it down, I'd say: Do the right thing, treat people right, and do it in a way that goes beyond just being polite. We are here to serve others. If we can do that in a genuine way by demonstrating a desire to listen, to understand, and to be tolerant of different points of view, every Coheart [the name for Southwest employees] and every Customer will feel respected. We are all responsible for making a difference in the world and at Southwest Airlines." The Southwest brand, "One Team. All Heart," says it very well.

Sometimes small interactions inspire Cohearts. A flight attendant learned of a passenger who had forgotten his suit for the bar exam out of state. It was 11:00 p.m. when the flight arrived out of town—too late for the passenger to buy one from a store. An employee realized he was about the same size as "Joe," a Coheart who lived in this city. She contacted Joe, who brought his suit to the hotel for the passenger. This passenger sported Joe's suit to the bar exam, which went well.[24]

Kelly closed our session with the idea that while Southwest tolerates a wide range of opinions, views, and beliefs, it tolerates a small range of behaviors. In other words, Southwest holds people accountable if they're not respectful.

Train employees. Go beyond educating them on the norms. Coaching employees requires helping them to listen fully, give and receive feedback (positive and corrective), work across differences, and deal with difficult people. Learning how to deal with others respectfully can involve any and all of the following: empathy, negotiation skills, stress management, giving and receiving feedback, an understanding of how to participate in difficult conversations, and mindfulness.

Get employees into the act. When I work with organizations, I like to take them through an exercise I call "Who do you want to be?" in which they define the norms that they want to shape their work identity. I ran this at the Irvine, California, office of law firm Bryan Cave, whose managing partner at the time was Stuart Price. We asked employees to name norms for which they were willing to hold one another accountable. In just over an hour, they generated and agreed upon ten norms.[25] The firm embraced these norms and bound them into a "civility code" that they prominently display in their lobby—in granite! According to Price, it's the civility code that was directly responsible for the firm being ranked number one among Orange County's best places to work.[26]

Encourage community members to hold one another accountable. People's spirits sink and they can become cynical if norms are just words that don't result in the behaviors that are deemed desirable. In one training session at an organization in which leaders had created ten principles of civility, a blue-collar employee proudly told me, "We just call each other out on these now...we say, "Seven, dude, seven," or "Five, man, five!" Their civility principles had become so ingrained in the workers that a simple numerical reference was all that was needed. Employees living the norms and holding one another accountable protect the values and minimize the likelihood of disrespectful behavior escalating. And, if you can get people to do it in the informal, fun-loving way that employee described—"Seven, dude!"—all the better.

Case Study: Coaching at Cleveland Clinic

Some of the most successful civility training I've seen has been done at Cleveland Clinic. The specific form of civility that the clinic aspires to is empathy.

When Adrienne Boissy was hired as the chief patient experience officer (CXO) at Cleveland Clinic in 2007—the first major medical institution to make improving patient experience a strategic goal—she quickly homed in on empathy as a means of delivering great patient care.[27] As a neurologist, she knew the neuroscience of empathy, understood how its effects worked in the brains of those on both the giving and receiving end of empathy, and wanted her staff to learn how powerful a force it can be in healing. Empathy as she defines it is the ability to imagine what someone else is feeling, to feel it oneself, and then to do something about it. Physicians who want to cultivate empathy for their patients will ask about their insights and feelings, reflect what they hear back to them, and act in a way that acknowledges what they have heard.

Boissy believed that empathy would not just help patients but doctors, too. Most doctors get into the profession because they care about people, but too much of the way modern medicine operates—the time pressures, the paperwork involved in filing insurance claims, the threat of malpractice suits, etc.—is destructive to the human connection between doctor and patient. Empathy training can help restore that connection and in doing so can decrease burnout among physicians, which is widespread. Nearly half of physicians face burnout,[28] which costs the US economy $4.6 billion a year and results in anxiety, depression, self-harm (including the very high rates of suicide among doctors), and malpractice claims.[29]

Boissy believed that active listening and empathy could be doctors' greatest tools in reducing physical and emotional harm—and financial harm, too. The number one reason patients file malpractice claims isn't inappropriate medical management, but a lack of human connection. This lack of connection can quickly translate into millions of dollars in claims.

Yet Boissy recognized the challenges. Physicians have an inherently stressful job. They bear a tremendous responsibility for their patients' health, they must field questions for which they often have no answers, they are under pressure for time, which predisposes them to interrupt patients and fail to listen to them, and particularly during their internship and residency they often suffer from sleep deprivation. Research has shown that physician empathy levels decline throughout training, and rise again only later in a doctor's career. Boissy believed that empathy training, which very few physicians receive, could alleviate some of the stress that doctors feel and alter their behavior—though she also knew that there would be a lot of resistance to it, because the doctors would see it as a "soft fluffy" thing, not a critical tool.

When Boissy spearheaded the communication training program she designed to teach listening and empathy skills to the physicians at Cleveland Clinic, she had a clear, tactical vision for whom she wanted to teach in the program. When she started out, she chose people who had been at Cleveland Clinic for thirty or forty years—specifically surgeons—because 60 percent of the doctors on staff were surgeons. Beginning at the top, she reached out to the chair of neurosurgery, who responded, "That's very nice. I appreciate that you thought of me. There's a young woman who recently joined our practice. I think she might be better. I think this would be perfect for her." But Boissy knew she needed someone who was a node of power in the institution, not a new young hire—and not a woman, either. Going to the institute chair for support, she explained, "I'm being very strategic about who has organizational influence here, and I think [the chair of neurosurgery] is the right person." In the end he did agree to teach in the program, which had a big impact on people's willingness to take it. "People often come to me and say, 'I wouldn't have come to the course, except I heard what you did....You got Dr. So-and-So to teach [it].'" Word of mouth had a very powerful effect. "You can't underestimate that power of one person who is... [a] sphere of influence."[30]

Cleveland Clinic's program started out with about one thousand people who came by invitation, but eventually it was scaled to the entire enterprise, which included about four thousand physicians, including residents and fellows. The eight-hour course became an expected requirement of all physicians. By now some forty thousand caregivers in total have received the training at Cleveland Clinic.[31]

There were two different agendas in the course, Boissy explained. "One was to teach content, to be an informative course on effective communication skills. But the second was more transformative, which is this idea that you're changing thinking and attitudes and belief. And much of that was about this context of relationships. What would your language sound like if you were trying to build a relationship with someone, as opposed to just trying to get them to take their medicine?"[32]

In order to explore that question, physicians role-played scenarios about how to have better conversations with patients.

Boissy shared how this works by relaying a typical doctor-patient conversation:

Doctor: We need to talk about quitting smoking. We talked about this last time and there hasn't been much progress.
Patient: It's been really hard since my mom died.
Doctor: Well, if you don't quit, you're going to have another heart attack and get that lung cancer that you were worried about getting.

Boissy said that in the training, she will intervene and dissect such a conversation in order to find more effective ways to communicate the no-smoking goal:

Boissy: Tell me what your intention was.
Doctor: I want the patient to quit smoking.
Boissy: Okay, tell me *why* you want the patient to quit smoking.
Doctor: It's going to hurt their lungs.
Boissy: Tell me why you care.
Doctor: Because I care about them.
Boissy: Can you just say that?[33]

By showing how to express concern in a way that patients can hear, you help both the physician and the patient. The magic, Adrienne Boissy explained, is that, "you are literally teaching physicians to express their intention of care." As she and other trainers see again and again in these role-playing scenarios, the physicians simply forget to say, "I care about you," "I'm in this with you," and "We're going to figure this out together." That's what patients need and want to hear. The purpose of these sessions, as she says, is to create "a platform to attend to [the patient] as a human being and that became the secret...that became the power of the training."[34]

Cleveland Clinic learned that being empathetic is self-perpetuating. The more you do it, the more you are able to and want to do it. According to research by Nicholas Christakis, who studies the dynamics of social contagion, empathy can also be contagious. If I'm empathetic to you, you'll be empathetic to the next person, and so on.

In a study of 1,500 physicians who participated in Cleveland Clinic's empathy and communication skills training, there was a statistically significant and positive impact on patient experience, capacity for empathy among physicians, and burnout.[35] In particular, there was a decrease in the emotional exhaustion of the physicians, a decrease that persisted for three months after the completion of the course (when the study ended). At Cleveland Clinic, burned-out physicians are twice as likely to leave as those who remain engaged and satisfied, and it takes significant time, energy, and dollars to replace them.[36] So in addition to all the other benefits, the increase in physician retention yielded financial dividends, too.

No matter how long the physicians had been in practice, their specialty, or what their skill level was when they started the program, everyone improved their communication skills after completing the course, according to Boissy. "And I think that's an important lesson. That all of us have something to learn." This was true despite the fact that everyone who walked into the training was skeptical about whether the training would change anything. Nearly everyone walked out thinking it had been helpful, which was borne out by the fact that both the self-ratings *and* the patient ratings of empathy increased. Boissy told me that her meta-observation was that "this wasn't about a communication course. What happened was a life-changing, aha lesson. The communication skills platform was just a platform to attend to be seen, heard, and valued. The same skills used with patients were the very same skills they began using with colleagues. Once these participants learned what it felt like to receive—and deliver—empathy and respect, people changed their words." Boissy and her program had unlocked these caregivers, and it set off positive effects for their community.

Score: Evaluating and Rewarding Civility

If you value civility (and I'm hoping you do now!), then you should show how much it matters to you and your organization. And the best, most compelling way to send that message is to **recognize and reward civility**. What's your current system of performance metrics like? Performance metrics need to be designed to account for what people are actually doing to propel their tribe forward. Does your performance management system help foster the civil behaviors you're trying to encourage? Are you promoting behaviors like collaborating well with others? If not, then this chapter suggests a few key things you can do to start.

Performance evaluation systems should score and reward employees who are living the community's values. At one Fortune 50 technology firm, bosses downgrade the employee performance if he or she falls short on the how. They did this with a superstar who was great at the what, but "left dead bodies in the wake." At law and consulting firms we have worked with, uncivil partners refused to change their behavior until it hit their pocketbook (through reduced shares).[37] For the most potent impact, evaluations must be tied to meaningful financial incentives and career progression decisions.

Cleveland Clinic evaluates all caregivers on how well they deliver respect and care. In advance of the annual review, the caregivers being evaluated are invited to provide their own narrative of their performance. Then a member of the Board of Governors, which is composed of physician colleagues, meets with the caregivers to discuss their performance, patient safety metrics, and patient satisfaction, as well as ways in which they can grow. They also have a discussion about what patients have said about the caregivers. Boissy described it to me as a "beautiful opportunity to support people...and a huge effort."

Expressing gratitude to employees for the contributions they make is crucial but something we too often fail to do. Thank people. It's simple but powerful. We take a deeper dive into this in the next chapter.

Practice: Improvement and Accountability

What do you do if your evaluation or scoring system uncovers tribe members who are behaving uncivilly? You have two options: **Work with them or show them the door.** Most companies I consult with decide to expend at least some effort working with offenders—and rightfully so. The vast majority of employees who behave rudely can improve their behavior if they are helped to become aware of it. As one CEO put it to me, they can be "recycled." This means working with the employee to improve behavior, and following up (or closing the feedback loop) to track improvement and make adjustments as needed.

In our study of de-energizing relationships, it became clear that de-energizers aren't necessarily that way because of any inherent defects in their personality or character. They may have lost interest in their job for one reason or another, or may be in a job for which they don't have the necessary skills. Timely intervention by management may be able to change the dynamic, as we saw when one man, who had been promoted into a managerial position supervising a dozen other employees who found him a disruptive force, was given the additional training he needed and the problem was resolved.

Some community members may not be recyclable, however, and that has to be acknowledged and acted on because the costs of incivility to the culture of the community, and to its bottom line, are too high. As Jeremy Andrus said, allowing cultural detractors to stay "is one of the worst things that you can do in a business."

At a dinner the night before a leadership conference, the CEO of a hospital told me about being in a meeting in which a very talented senior physician unleashed on a high-potential young physician with a string of aggressive, belittling, and demeaning comments as he was presenting. The CEO said it had made him very uncomfortable, yet he did nothing. He knew he should have stepped in and managed the situation. Instead, he sat frozen. But once he reflected on the incident, he did speak to the senior physician and made it clear that his behavior had been unacceptable. In this case the intervention was not effective. The man persisted in the same kind of behavior, which he had a reputation for and had been allowed to engage in for too long. Ultimately, he had to be let go.

The day after our conversation, in front of nearly a thousand top physicians and staff, this CEO addressed the leadership conference, telling them about his failure to act in a timely fashion and detailing how he should have tackled the situation. He encouraged employees to extract themselves from any interaction in which they feel they are being treated disrespectfully. If there is something that makes them uncomfortable, he said, it's acceptable to simply get up and leave. Since then I've heard employees using this suggestion to guide their behavior—and to teach it to others in their tribe.

Unfortunately, most incidents of incivility go unreported, often because employees believe no action will be taken. Less than half of the people we've surveyed bother to report incivility, largely because they assume that nothing will be done in response. To combat this problem, leaders must set the norms of acceptable behavior and then act when they are not adhered to. They can encourage people to speak up about such violations as well as holding themselves accountable for being respectful.

Danny Meyer, the owner of twenty New York City–based restaurants and founder of Shake Shack, says he preaches civility and tolerates nothing less. Bad behavior, even from an exceptional chef, must be corrected quickly, and if the behavior does not improve, the chef is let go. Meyer is convinced customers can *taste* incivility in their food.

Sometimes circumstances prevent getting rid of someone, at least in the short term. Even if you can't get rid of a toxin, you can isolate it so the effects don't spread. You might put some physical distance between the offender and the rest of the team by reassigning projects, rearranging the office layout, scheduling fewer all-hands meetings, or encouraging people to work from home, as needed.[38] One Fortune 100 firm had acquired a talented but toxic employee who was crucial to the development of a key technology. They opted to create a lab for him—in large part, to keep him isolated from others. The fewer people he touched, the better! An easier fix is if the toxic employee is able to work remotely. And, the more independently the toxin can work, the more you will limit the negative effects.[39]

Some of the world's finest sports teams practice zero tolerance as well. Norway's ski team dominated the 2018 Olympics again and had three racers in the top four of the World Cup overall standings. Team members are expected to enact a mix of humility, egalitarianism, and basic respect in their daily lives.

"We believe there is no good explanation or justification for why you have to be a jerk to be a good athlete," Kjetil Jansrud, the defending Olympic super-G champion, says. "So we just won't have that kind of thing on our team. You have to get along with everyone." His teammate Aksel Svindal echoes this sentiment: "We have a saying. There is almost no skill or ability you can have that is so good it allows you to ruin the social qualities of the team." Referring to the roughly 250 days the teammates spend eating, training, and living together, Svindal says, "Across 250 days together, your life off the snow has to be really good."[40]

Creating a culture of respect requires attention and care, but it pays off. You'll unlock people's potential by providing an environment where they feel a sense of belonging, where they know they matter and are encouraged to do their best work. Even those who witness civility feel a boost, and as positive emotions build, so too do motivation and performance. Organizations like Traeger offer hope that even in extreme circumstances, leaders have an opportunity to hit "reset"—they can reboot. As Jeremy Andrus explained, "As a leader you have to protect culture with your life. There is nothing more important you do than protecting your culture."[41] Incivility is a virus, and it spreads quickly. But the good news is that civility is contagious, too.

What can you do to lift people up and kick-start a positive cycle in your community?

CHAPTER 4

Practice Radical Candor

People don't care how much you know until they know how much you care.

—Theodore Roosevelt

As Matt Dailey, a software engineer for a data management company, watched a video of Kim Scott giving a talk on her concept of radical candor, he realized how eloquently it spoke to him. Its goals—to solicit honest feedback, offer specific praise, and give criticism helpfully and kindly—would be valuable in both his professional life and his intimate relationships, and Matt felt he needed help in both those areas. Soon afterward, a good friend mentioned that Kim was working on a start-up and suggested Matt might be interested in joining her. Matt reached out to Kim, and she emailed him an early copy of what became a *New York Times* bestseller, *Radical Candor: Be a Kick-Ass Boss Without Losing Your Humanity*.

Matt dove into it, devouring its message, and he was sold. He jumped ship to take a job as a software engineer with the executive education company Kim was starting, which would develop programs for workplaces of all sizes, around the world, to help them put into practice her ideas about effective feedback loops. For Matt, it was more than a career move. After suffering a personal loss, the importance of human connection was salient. Matt felt like we could use a tool kit to help us in our personal and professional relationships. He believed that radical candor was a useful tool.

In her talk, Kim said, "Unfortunately, the Beatles got it wrong." When it comes to our relationships, she explained, "love is not all you need. You also need the other dimension, you also need the 'challenge directly' dimension of radical candor. Figuring out how to be willing to say the thing that might upset the other person because they need to hear it, because you do care about them is the essence of radical candor."[1]

As a young manager, Matt felt he would have benefitted from radical candor. He managed a team with an engineer who didn't report directly to him. At one point, this engineer wasn't performing well. This was clear to Matt—and to the employee. Yet Matt said he "wasn't bridging the gap of how to make the situation better." His team missed their deadline. Matt realized part of the problem was his inability to provide the kind of feedback this employee and their team needed. He explained, "I just didn't have the tool set to do it—to have the conversation—at that point."

It didn't help that Matt worked in a culture of ruinous empathy—the state Kim described, which occurs because you want to spare someone's short-term feelings, so you don't tell them something they need to know about themselves. Matt wasn't getting the necessary feedback from his boss, or the person who worked with Matt's boss. Matt's professional network lacked the tools that would have clarified structure, deadlines, and competencies directly. When he learned of radical candor, it seemed really valuable—not only to their team's performance, but also to grow stronger relationships.

Matt was drawn to Kim Scott since she clearly cared about these values. Once on board with Kim's company, Matt helped to develop a radical candor feedback app, Candor Coach, for managers to practice giving and asking for feedback with their team. It would have you import your team and then provide a sequence of suggestions to practice different aspects of effective feedback with different team members. For example, on Monday it might ask you to practice humble criticism, and then on Wednesday it might suggest practicing specific praise.

Before it was completed, Kim realized that "if the purpose of radical candor is to put the phone away and have a conversation, then the app was a value-subtracting round trip."[2] The only way to get these feedback skills, Kim eventually recognized, was through practice. No matter how many books you read about what to do, no matter how many scripts you memorize with words that might be appropriate to use, change is not going to happen without the back-and-forth of real human exchanges. But what kind of practice would be helpful?

In 2019, in what was certainly an original move, Kim Scott formed a partnership with Kelly Leonard, executive vice president of the Second City, a world-renowned theater troupe whose fame was rooted in its groundbreaking improvisational games. In a typical Second City sketch, one of the improv actors is given a description of a situation he finds himself in—say, a guest at a wedding or dinner party—and starts acting it out, and the sketch develops as the other actors try to play off the first actor and each other, all of it unscripted. Founded in 1959 in Chicago, this small cabaret theater grew to become the most influential and prolific comedy empire in the world. Second City alumni include Alan Arkin, Dan Aykroyd, John Belushi, John Candy, Steve Carell, Stephen Colbert, Tina Fey, Bill Murray, Amy Poehler, and countless other stars.

The partnership with Second City was born of Scott's realization that the skills involved in improv might have something to teach her clients about how to bring authenticity to the act of giving feedback. Shortly after the publication of her book, Kim was on a podcast Leonard hosts, and they spoke about how improv can really help people develop the practice of radical candor. They admitted that nobody likes to role-play, even though it would make great practice. Kim explained, "In some ways a role play is like asking somebody to play in a symphony before they've learned the instrument; or to play in a scrimmage before you've learned how to throw the ball. And so it became clear that improv has a bunch of drills that can help you learn the discrete skills that you need in order to be radically candid." Kim shared that one of the things that resonated with people is to listen with the intent to understand, not to respond. She says that one of the things that improv does in addition to teaching you to be very funny is to listen with enormous compassion.

The success of any given Second City sketch depends on the actors' ability to read each other's cues and build a little world—a community—that they share. They have to pay deep attention to each other so that they can keep moving forward in sync, and they have to be constantly on the alert for changes in the mood of the audience—their larger "community"—so that they can adapt accordingly.

Kelly explains, "Improvisation is like yoga for your social skills because it teaches you to see what someone else maybe isn't noticing in the room because you're picking up on gesture." Are the other people leaning back or leaning forward? Are they checking their email? What do their eyes tell you? What does their body language say? Are you getting through to them or losing them? Kelly described how, in improvisation, "you build something out of nothing, so you learn how to pay attention to the environment you're in."[3] Matt concurs with Kelly's yoga analogy. He also extends that analogy by noting that in radical candor, "there's moments where you're out of balance—that you learn from...and still fail." Any good yoga teacher will offer positive feedback to a student who falls out of a pose, because falling indicates a willingness to go further into the pose, to take a risk, to be willing to fail.

Another way in which the yoga analogy is relevant is that yoga is a practice. It's not something you do because you're trying to achieve perfection in the various movements and poses—it's something you do over and over, always learning from it, always finding new ways to tune into your mind and your body. Improvising radical candor is also, as Matt says, "100 percent practice," because it, too, is always asking you to pay attention—not to yourself, but to those who are part of your community.

As a leader, learning how to read and interact with the members of your tribe increases your influence and effectiveness. So does the ability to give and receive appropriate feedback. That is the key to your tribe's development. If you do so with radical candor, which requires that you show that you care before you offer a critique—Kim's shorthand for this is "Caring Personally while Challenging Directly"—you maximize the potential of everyone in your community. A community that practices radical candor tends to perform better and be more innovative. The people in the community also tend to build stronger, more authentic relationships.

Perhaps one reason the partnership between Radical Candor and Second City makes so much sense is that comedy is a very powerful and memorable way to get messages across, even tough messages that might otherwise be hard to hear. "Comedy is a safe way to hold a mirror up to reality and when you do that as management, you gain enormous credibility," according to Kelly.[4] As Anne Libera, Director of Comedy Studies at Columbia College Chicago, a collaboration with the Second City, says, "We learn when we laugh."

This has been true for Second City as an organization, too. Second City has a holiday party each year in which the staff puts on a show. Standard practice at these parties is to make fun of all the executives. One year the waitstaff wrote a song that they sang directly to the owner, where they said to him, "You can dress up a pair of jeans, but why do, why does the staff not have health insurance?" Kelly said, "I was just sinking in my chair. Like, they're going to get fired. I'm gonna get fired." But that didn't happen. The next day the owner brought the executive team in and said, "How do we get them insurance?" The staff got insurance. Kelly explained that this would not have happened if there weren't a format.[5]

What radical candor does, according to Leonard, is create the structures within which truth can be spoken to power. Communities that practice radical candor allow people to deliver tough messages without fear of retribution. As the Second City holiday party demonstrated, the organization's members had the freedom to speak directly to those over them, about a matter that affected the greater good of all, and from that freedom, real change was able to occur.

Why Feedback—both Positive and Negative— Fosters Community

Kim Scott now refers to radical candor as **compassionate candor**. She believes that both positive and negative feedback can be compassionate, and describes the kind of honesty she's talking about as empathy in action. The community member who receives such feedback stands to benefit by becoming more competent. This typically leads to improved decision-making and collaboration, as well as increased productivity and performance. And this benefits not just the individual, but the community as a whole because they will have the advantage of a stronger contributor. The snowballing of these benefits, from individual to community, can have huge consequences. In our study of over twenty thousand people across industries and organizations, we found that higher levels of feedback are associated with 89 percent greater thriving at work, 63 percent more engagement, and 79 percent higher job satisfaction. People who receive more feedback are also 1.2 times more likely to stay with the organization.

Feedback that comes in the form of recognition of the contributions of individual tribe members is one of the best ways to boost morale, especially when the entire community makes it a habit. It's also a way to make members feel a part of the community, which affects the likelihood of their staying with the organization. Workhuman, a company that creates social recognition software designed to encourage employees to recognize each other's positive performance and behaviors, has demonstrated through its clients' experience that community building through recognition works. For example, data from JetBlue revealed that for every 10 percent increase in the number of people who reported that they felt recognized, the company saw a 3 percent increase in employee retention and a 2 percent increase in engagement. A study by IBM Smarter Workforce Institute and Workhuman found that organizations that deliver a positive experience outperform their cohorts threefold for return on assets and twofold on return on sales.[6] Their survey showed that the engagement level of employees who receive recognition is almost three times higher than the engagement level of those who do not.

At BP, data showed that after the company launched Energize!, the global peer-to-peer reward and recognition solution designed by Workhuman, employee turnover was reduced. New hires who felt recognized had a 50 percent lower turnover rate than their unrecognized peers. In Hungary, among BP employees who received just three rewards, turnover was cut by 66 percent. And after LinkedIn launched its Workhuman-designed Bravo! recognition and rewards program, the data showed not only the ripple effect that occurs in terms of performance (54 percent of employees who received three-plus awards showed a year-over-year increase on their performance rating), but the transformation of praise recipients into praise providers. As people became happier and more engaged, they became part of the process of making their colleagues more positive and engaged, too. This is how a community is built.

Giving each other honest, careful feedback creates deeper, more fulfilling relationships. When radical candor becomes the norm, it leads to a culture of guidance and coaching. As members of the tribe help one another improve and hold each other accountable, they create a community feedback loop in which each person both gets and provides useful feedback. The more this happens, the stronger the connections among them, with tribe members who receive this feedback feeling that those who provide it are partners or coaches who have a personal stake in their development. The community thus becomes an incubator, a safe, protected space, within which its members can grow stronger. Ideally, other members of the community, or its leaders, will check in with the receiver of the feedback to see how the person feels about the feedback, and how the tribe can further support him. All of these actions minimize feelings of isolation, strengthen bonds, and contribute to the overall social fabric of the tribe. This is much like the Chicago Bulls environment Steve Kerr described in chapter 1.

Positive feedback, or recognition, makes community members feel valued, reduces power and status differences between tribe members, and may increase everybody's sense of belonging. Although recognition costs virtually nothing, it's one of the tools that is most underutilized by leaders and their organizations. A mere 42 percent of the over twenty thousand people we surveyed believed that their manager recognized and appreciated their work.

Tony Schwartz, who has co-authored a number of studies with me, is the founder of the Energy Project, which focuses on corporate wellness. When his organization interviewed heart surgeons and their intensive care nurses at a large, well-known hospital where understaffing, long hours, and burnout were widespread, they learned a vivid lesson about what matters most to workers. They asked dozens of nurses what the biggest challenge was they faced at work. Given the intense demands on these nurses, Tony's team assumed the answer would have something to do with exhaustion, or how little time they had to unwind, relax, and catch their breath. Instead, the nurses said it was insufficient appreciation from the surgeons whose patients they served with such devotion.

Tony and his team then went to the surgeons. They were far better compensated than the nurses, but they, too, worked under difficult, high-stress conditions, while facing large quotas for the number of surgeries they were expected to perform. What was their biggest challenge? Again they were surprised. The most common answer? Lack of appreciation from the hospital administrators. "I save lives every day, but I sometimes feel like I'm working in a factory," one surgeon told them, echoing several of his colleagues.

Being on the receiving end of praise typically results in the release of dopamine, a transmitter associated with well-being and pleasure. That is the reason praise feels so good. It gives us a social boost, too, as it fulfills the human need to feel that we matter, that we are valued. With an increase in people feeling so disconnected, isolated, and lonely, recognition is less available and much more necessary. The benefits of recognition in such an environment may pay even more! When we're recognized by members of a community, it makes us feel a tighter tie to that tribe.

That's why Jeremy Andrus recognizes someone acknowledged by a peer in every Monday morning meeting at Traeger. "It's one thing for a leader to recognize someone lived values and maybe give them cash but I think it's something else for someone to be recognized by a peer. That actually has so much more emotional value," he told me. As part of Traeger's Value Our Values program, once a quarter each employee can submit a recognition of a peer for exceptional contribution. The employee includes a brief description of what their peer has done, and selects one of Traeger's values it represents. The peer recognized receives $100. Andrus shares one of these submissions in every Monday meeting, where he reinforces Traeger's values and community members at their best.

Why Feedback—both Positive and Negative—Leads to Performance Gains

Radical candor provides a framework within which workers can take risks and pursue change and opportunity without fear of failure or retribution. Current and former CEOs and top leaders have repeatedly told me how they relied on a culture of radical candor to improve performance and increase innovation. For example, when Christa Quarles took over as CEO of OpenTable, a restaurant reservations website, she knew she was going to have to shift the culture, in which everyone prided themselves on being "nice." It was a "command and control culture." To change that was going to be very difficult, but her goal was to make it safe to be radically candid (which would often mean *not* being nice)—and to fail. Christa had worked with executive coach Kim Scott and believed in her friend's concept. Christa had also been in ruinous empathy situations or "in situations where someone was beating you over the head with a sledgehammer—and might actually enjoy doing that," she said. Quarles explained, "And in my view at the end of the day, it's just not effective. You're not going to be able to get what you want to get done if someone's prefrontal cortex shuts down and they can't actually hear you at all because they're in fight-or-flight [mode] or they never hear you at all because you never say it."

Quarles acknowledged that this shift was not going to be easy because OpenTable was squarely in the ruinous empathy grid. People believed that since they were in hospitality, they were supposed to be nice. Quarles thought, "But nobody's getting any shit done. Nobody is actually moving the ball up the field."

Quarles explained that she didn't realize quite how much the historical environment affected people. She spoke to employees, encouraging radical candor, but realized that to get it, she needed to give it. Quarles set the tone by publicly criticizing herself. She wanted people to know that she had these challenges. Christa saw herself as "coach or developer versus spanker or being righteous." Quarles explained, "The real goal of feedback is to get people to go climb the mountain. If you're not giving feedback well, no mountains are getting climbed."

Another problem with ruinous empathy, as Quarles saw it, was that it leads to a lack of risk taking. She wanted OpenTable to be innovative and explained that she didn't think it was possible without radical candor. Ruinous empathy meant that people weren't really saying anything, or pushing the envelope. Quarles described culture as "how decisions are made when I'm not in the room." And, if employees just sat in the room, happily exchanging ideas, or going about business, thinking everything would be fine, that wasn't going to drive innovation. She had learned that it's unsafe to take risks without radical candor.

Quarles was radically candid about the state of business. At the time,

OpenTable was focused on "fine dining and white tablecloths." She told them that there was "no more growth possible with that market." She explained, "I needed people to feel safe to take risks." She encouraged them: "By the way, when we fail, we get lots of feedback." She wasn't afraid of failing—and she didn't want that to paralyze her team.

Her team was able to use radical candor to rethink their business model. At the time, OpenTable was focused on higher-end restaurants. Casual dining restaurants weren't available in OpenTable's search engine. But after investigating its search data, the team learned that restaurants like P.F. Chang's and others at the lower-priced end of the continuum were booming, so she and her team realized that their customers wanted casual dining options. Quarles and her team thought of a radical solution. What if they put lower-priced restaurants on the site, complete with reviews and descriptions, even if these restaurants weren't linked directly to their reservations system? When she and her tribe floated the idea, people thought it was heresy, she told me. Her team pulled it off, and armed with data, were able to go to many of these restaurants and enlist them to be a part of their booking system since they had data on thousands of prospects that came to their OpenTable site, and searched the restaurant, but hadn't booked. The idea led to their best and favored tool. Christa Quarles told me that they would never have been able to accomplish what they did without radical candor. She also credited radical candor with helping OpenTable rethink international business and develop a new business model (putting software into the restaurant side). They openly challenged the current state and traded critical feedback to launch these new strategies and enable growth.

Quarles used radical candor to develop talent as well. She had a supersmart woman with three Ivy League degrees who was introverted and rarely spoke her mind. Quarles knew this woman "had the goods," but she needed to get her to a space where she would be comfortable participating in the kind of community-wide debates that Christa wanted to see in meetings. Christa urged her, telling her that sometimes she may need to speak three or four times. And, when she did say something, she shouldn't nervously laugh afterward or raise her voice. Quarles was a coach, willing to point out some of the uncomfortable common pitfalls that led to a dampened voice. By telling her that she believed in her (the "caring" part of the message), and therefore wanted to know what she was thinking that she had not shared (the "challenging" part of the message), Christa helped give her space to be heard, and over time saw this woman gain enough confidence that she could speak her mind freely. Quarles scored a win—for this talented tribe member, for the tribe, and for the larger community of OpenTable.

Chris O'Neill, former CEO of Evernote, and former managing director of Google Canada, and global business operations at Google (X), explained that during his time at Google he learned that there were many good people on staff, but that there was a big difference between "good" and "great"—or, as Kim Scott says, between "rock stars" and "superstars." Scott sees people who get exceptional results but are on a more gradual growth trajectory as "rock stars" because they are like the Rock of Gibraltar (not Mick Jagger!). They love their work and are world class at it, but they don't want the boss's job. They are happy where they are. Superstars are people who are on a steeper growth trajectory—the ones who'd go crazy if they were still doing the same job in a year. O'Neill wanted to transform the rock stars into superstars, and he knew that the only way to do that would be to provide really direct feedback—some of it quite critical. What he didn't quite take into account was that he needed to be willing to receive such feedback, too.

Soon after the announcement of his appointment at Google Canada, O'Neill publicly set forth a grand vision for his group. He said that they'd be a billion-dollar business in two to three years. While his bosses loved his ambition, his team thought Chris was crazy and out of touch. And they told him so. He went from feeling emboldened to humbled. But he listened to their feedback, and, by sharing the story of how they responded with the larger community, he allowed himself to express his vulnerability. He said the result was galvanizing—that his vulnerability led to an open dialogue among the young tribe and their entire community. So good things came out of what had seemed like a defeat for him, because his openness set the tone and momentum for the radical candor dynamic, which he was able to encourage and foster among his ambitious executive team. Chris had learned the lesson that people need to be heard. One top tech executive shared with me that the highest rated leaders had something in common. They spiked on the item "my manager regularly solicits feedback"—something all-too-few managers do.

The outcome for Chris: Their operations were rated the best at Google worldwide. It wasn't long before his executive team players got gobbled up by Google's corporate headquarters. O'Neill credits his tribe's top-notch performance to the radical candor that allowed him to fire up the young team.

O'Neill brought a similar dynamic to Evernote as CEO, and reports that it served him and his team very well there, too. The turnaround he led required a particular emphasis on the "challenge directly" piece of the dynamic, he said.

O'Neill believes that the most successful executives are adaptable. "They stay curious, and while they might have a ton of amazing applicable experience, they don't come into a situation trying to apply a playbook," he said. Staying curious, open, and adaptable requires candid feedback. That drives success, O'Neill said.

Aman Bhutani, CEO of GoDaddy, whom you met in chapter 2 and 3, is famous for encouraging radical candor throughout his career. "Feedback is oxygen. It's that tool that connects people," he told me. He shared a recent story where a direct report was really upset with a more junior leader. They stood at opposite sides of an issue. It was late in the evening, and Bhutani was super candid. He told her pointedly, "Here's the reason you're emotional," at which point she burst into tears. He respected that moment, and then strongly encouraged her to go talk to that leader further down the chain, with whom she had the issue. Bhutani pointed out that this (more junior) leader needed her help, and didn't really understand her side of the issue. "You don't really know him," Bhutani said, and although she could take all his power away, that wasn't the culture they wanted. Bhutani reminded her of the radically candid culture he was growing at GoDaddy, and that you want to support people, and to give people another chance. His report rallied and reached out to this other leader. Afterward, she followed up with Bhutani, and reported that although it was a hard conversation, it worked really well. Bhutani told me, "It was so amazing, in three days they know each other much better. They've almost become friends, talking to one another about each other's children. And, together, GoDaddy is better."

Like Quarles and O'Neill, Bhutani set the tone by role modeling vulnerability, stepping up in front of large groups to solicit feedback—the good, the bad, and the ugly. He's also not afraid to dole it out. Jen O'Twomney, whom you met in chapter 2, shared how helpful this has been for her development, and relayed a recent example. Jen was preparing an important presentation on GoDaddy's north star project. Immensely talented, O'Twomney admitted that she doesn't like presenting (at all!), so she was setting up two people to deliver the presentation. Bhutani saw a draft and told her that her words and opinions weren't coming through. Jen told me Bhutani "called me out on the fact that my voice wasn't in it. Now I'm on the path—that's love— what he asked me to do was to be more authentic." Because she knew that he genuinely cared about her and valued her opinion, Jen embraced the feedback and revised the presentation so that her voice shone through—even if she didn't deliver the talk.

Aman Bhutani told me that "one person at a time, one heart or mind at a time," change is made "because there's a multiplicative effect" in any community.

Research has shown that challenging directly serves financial advisors well. A study by Capital Preferences, T. Rowe Price, and the Financial Planning Association found that financial advisors who took the time to get to know their clients and actively challenged them, while also showing they cared, had significantly higher growth opportunities and better client relationships. In short, these successful advisors were practicing radical candor— caring personally while challenging directly. While this study focused on financial advisors, the findings seem applicable to anyone who interacts with another person in an advisor or mentor role—teachers, lawyers, and coaches.

But this is not to suggest that the ability to find the appropriate way to give negative feedback is the only key to making progress. The need for positive recognition is fundamental to optimal human performance. As Jeff Weiner, former chief executive officer of LinkedIn, has said, "Recognition can be an invaluable source of motivation and subsequently inspire people to do their best work."

In *Nine Lies About Work* Marcus Buckingham and Ashley Goodall point out that "positive attention is thirty times more powerful than negative attention in creating high performance on a team." If all our efforts are directed at giving and receiving negative feedback more often and more efficiently, then we're leaving enormous potential on the table. People need attention, especially to what they do the best.[7] High performers offer more positive feedback to peers; in fact, high-performing teams share nearly six times more positive feedback than average teams. Meanwhile, low-performing teams share nearly twice as much negative feedback than average teams.

Flex the praise muscle often, because the more you flex it, the stronger it becomes and the more natural it will be to use it. Once you begin actively looking for moments to recognize people, you'll see them throughout the day and find yourself celebrating small wins that might have gone unnoticed.

Research reveals that the most basic kinds of recognition can have a surprisingly potent effect. For instance, when teachers greet middle school students personally and with positivity as they enter the classroom, it increased students' academic engagement by 20 percent and decreased disruptive classroom behavior by 9 percent.[8]

Such a simple action, but so often neglected. Not being acknowledged or greeted by colleagues is a complaint I hear all the time. One of my most talented former honor students left his organization because his boss would blow by him in the hallway as though he were invisible. A superstar medical resident also bemoaned how much such coldness affected him and his fellow residents. He told me that the day after he'd completed a two-month rotation with a talented surgeon, the man didn't even acknowledge him in the hallway. He explained, "Even if he doesn't call me by name or anything, I mean, c'mon, I'm human!"

This kind of recognition matters more than we might think. And it costs us nothing. Why are we so stingy with it? Instead of using these simple gestures to make those around us feel a part of the tribe, we fracture any potential feeling of connection through our neglect.

Touch—and virtual or nonverbal signs of affirmation—are ways of forging connection. A fist bump or a high five might do more than just make you feel appreciated—it can help you and your team win. Michael Kraus, Cassey Huang, and Dacher Keltner studied every team in the NBA in the 2008–2009 season and found that the teams that touch the most win the most.[9] Touch predicted improved performance even after accounting for player status, preseason expectations, and early season performance.[10] "Touch predicts performance through fostering cooperation between teammates," says Keltner. "You can communicate really important emotions like gratitude, compassion, love, and anger just through brief touches."[11] "Touch instills trust," Keltner said. "It contagiously spreads good will; it makes players play better on behalf of each other."[12] The researchers found that teams who tend to have more contact are also the teams who are helping more on defense, setting more and better screens, and playing with more cooperation.[13] Some coaches are experimenting with their own teams and seeing a positive effect.

Touch releases oxytocin in the brain, a chemical that induces feelings of trust and connection. So almost every time you're giving a pat on the back to a teammate or colleague, you're creating a feeling of trust that bonds him to you. Research has shown that waitstaff who touch customers get better tips, doctors who touch patients receive more favorable reviews, and petition gatherers who touch passersby get more signatures.[14]

Touch can also provide a real psychological boost to someone who has slipped up in some way. I remember how much it helped me when I was on my college basketball team and missed a free throw. Having a coach or a team member offer a quick "five," touch, or fist bump after such a miss conveyed, "Don't worry about it, you've got the next one," which provided a huge pick-me-up. "That kind of encouragement, when things aren't going well, is really even more powerful than the high-five after you did something well," said Dr. Jarrod Spencer, a sports psychologist. "It interrupts the negative self-talk in our head."[15]

It also creates a heightened sense of belonging. Humans have a such a strong need to feel a sense of belonging and inclusion, or what scientists call "affiliation."[16] It is one of our three most fundamental needs, along with autonomy and competence, and arguably is the most important.[17] There are plenty of nonverbals and virtual signs of affiliation that provide a boost. Send a clap or high five, smile, give people a nod of approval or acknowledgment.

How Leaders Can Establish Open Discourse and Use It to Build and Strengthen Their Communities

Offer radical candor—and learn how to avoid the pitfalls.

Because radical candor can be hard to put into practice, Kim Scott developed a simple guidance and feedback framework we can use to shape our communication with tribe members, helping us to achieve the right balance between being overly nice and overly harsh, between saying nothing and saying too much.

Obnoxious aggression is when you challenge someone directly but don't show you care about them personally. Scott adds that can also take the form of praise that doesn't feel sincere, or criticism and feedback that aren't delivered kindly. Christa Quarles, the former CEO of OpenTable, now CEO of Corel Corporation, a portfolio software company, notes that people sometimes confuse obnoxious aggression with radical candor, prefacing a piece of negative feedback with "In a moment of radical candor, let me say to you..." But just because you call it radical candor doesn't mean it is. If caring personally isn't part of the message, then it's not radical candor.

Ruinous empathy is the opposite of obnoxious aggression. You care personally but fail to challenge directly. It's praise that isn't specific enough to help the person understand what was good, or criticism that is sugarcoated and unclear. Ruinous empathy may make you feel like a kind person, but it tends to be unhelpful and may even prove damaging. Scott notes that 85 percent of the mistakes—in both professional and personal relationships/communities—are in the form of ruinous empathy. The reason it's so common is that people feel that honesty would be hurtful, and they lack the courage to deliver an honest message.

Kelly Leonard explained that he himself was ruinously empathetic for much of his career. He kicks himself now for it, because he realizes he wasn't doing people any favors by failing to give them honest feedback. He feels so bad about it that in 2015, after stepping down from running Second City Theatricals, he took a former colleague to lunch to apologize to her for this, and was in tears over the meal.

Christa Quarles agrees that ruinous empathy is the most common mistake she's seen in business. When she got to OpenTable, she knew she was going to have to dismantle the "we're nice" culture because it meant that people weren't being challenged enough and this was affecting performance. She believed that radical candor could help them lift their game, and she not only offered it, she explicitly gave people license to direct it at her.

Manipulative insincerity is passive-aggressive behavior; it's when you neither care personally nor challenge directly. It's praise that is insincere, offering flattery to a person's face and harsh criticism behind their back. Kim Scott stresses that this is the worst kind of feedback fail.

Only radical candor offers the right mix of "caring personally" and "challenging directly." In fact, as Scott sees it, challenging people is often the best way to show you care. And this mix is the surest path to success.

Test whether your feedback is hitting the mark.

Sometimes there's a disconnect between how feedback is intended and how it's received. The Motley Fool, the stock advisor company, has a program called Point of View that helps discover such discrepancies when they exist. After giving feedback to an employee, a manager takes a quiz that asks about the intended message of the feedback. The employee takes a complimentary quiz, asking what came through from the manager's feedback. The manager and employee answers are compared to see if they basically match up. If there is a mismatch, the manager must return to the employee to try to communicate the feedback more clearly. The process is very useful at nipping misperceptions in the bud before they can result in the employee's trying to make adjustments because of not understanding what the manager was suggesting. The healthy dialogue also minimizes the potential for bruised feelings.

Improve feedback delivery.

Most of us don't have the luxury of the Point of View program to help us identify gaps in communication that need to be closed. But here are some tips on how to give feedback in a constructive way.

- Use the SBI (Situation-Behavior-Impact model) to guide you. Describe the specific situation in which the behavior occurred. Try to keep this description short and succinct. Give observable descriptions of the behavior in question. Avoid inflammatory or provoking language. Describe the result of the behavior and how it affected others.

- Don't give the feedback sandwich. Though many of us like to open with a compliment and end on a high (positive) note, putting the negative meat in the middle may mean that it gets lost in the feedback sandwich.[18] Why? One potential problem is that, as research shows, we often remember the first and last things we hear in a conversation. The criticism in the middle may get buried. Another problem is that many of us are anticipating a negative—we're accustomed to receiving negative, especially in a conversation about our performance. When people hear praise, they often begin to brace themselves (waiting for the other shoe to drop) such that they fail to appreciate the initial positive. They may think that compliment is meant to soften the blow.[19]

- Explain why you're giving this feedback. Starting with your intention can lower defenses. Researchers made feedback 40 percent more effective by prefacing it with just nineteen words: "I'm giving you these comments because I have very high expectations and I know that you can reach them."[20] Psychiatrist Edward Hallowell offers something similar to use with children: "I'm asking more from you because I know you have it in you." He explains that you want to challenge, but not in a punishing way.[21]

- Level the playing field. People naturally feel threatened by negative feedback. To minimize this reaction, make yourself vulnerable and human. You might say something like, "I've grown a lot from managers' and friends' feedback, and I'm trying to pay that forward." Or "I've learned that great leaders provide candid feedback and I'm working on developing that skill." Or "Now that we've worked together, it would be great if we could help each other improve by providing feedback."[22]

- Ask if they want feedback. "I noticed a couple of things about your work recently. Are you interested in some feedback?"[23] If people take ownership of receiving feedback, they will be more open to it and less defensive. In general people do want feedback and are disappointed that they don't get more of it.
- If you see a problem, offer feedback immediately, or shortly thereafter, depending on the situation. The sooner the better, because people may not remember the situations you're describing. Also, if you wait for the annual performance review, not only may they not remember what you're talking about, but they're more likely to be anxious and defensive.
- If at all possible, deliver any negative feedback in private rather than in public. Positive feedback delivered in public is typically welcome, and it's a good way to reinforce behaviors you want. However, some people are embarrassed and uncomfortable with public feedback, so it pays to know your tribe members and their preferences. If you're unsure, ask them.

Create mechanisms to give ongoing, in-the-moment, detailed feedback.

Find creative ways to make feedback a regular part of the work environment. Zingerman's, which started out four decades ago as a local delicatessen in Ann Arbor, Michigan, has grown into a large collection of local food-related businesses as well as a major mail-order shop, shipping food and gifts throughout the US. With over seven hundred employees, Zingerman's is dedicated both to maintaining its reputation for excellence and finding ever new ways to improve.

The Zingerman's "huddle," a weekly meeting convened by each of the businesses for all employees who wish to attend, is a tool that allows for almost immediate sharing of information about the performance of both individual staff members and the business as a whole. Teams track results, keep score, and forecast the next week's numbers. By documenting and discussing "code reds," which record customer complaints, and "code greens," which record compliments, these huddles offer all the employees a chance to learn and grow from tangible feedback. By sharing detailed statistics about weekly sales and whether they had matched, exceeded, or fallen behind projections, Zingerman's makes its successes and failures as an organization transparent.[24] Employees are expected to "own" these numbers and, if they fall short of expectations, to come up with ideas for getting back on track. The meetings are a magnet both for community engagement and for bonding through competition. Explaining why they created a business with this kind of openness, one of the owners said, "We wanted to invite everyone to help run the business and convey that each one of us was personally responsible for its success."

Some Zingerman's sites began instituting "minigames," or short-term incentive plans—involving goals, scorecards, and rewards—to fix a problem or capitalize on an opportunity. The Zingerman's Roadhouse restaurant staff used the Greeter Game to track how long it took for customers to be greeted. The Greeter Game challenged the host team to greet every customer within five minutes of being seated, with a modest financial reward for fifty straight days of "success." The game inspired hosts to quickly uncover and fix holes in the service process. Service scores improved considerably over the course of a month. Other Zingerman's businesses started similar games as part of their day, with incentives for faster delivery, reduced knife injuries in the bakery (which would lower insurance costs), and neater kitchens.

Become aware of who's getting your attention, and what kind.

Research shows that there are gender and other demographic gaps with feedback. One way in which women are shortchanged is in the kind of attention they receive. They are 1.5 times more likely to receive recognition for teamwork while being far less likely to receive recognition for leadership.[25]

You should also notice where you direct the majority of your attention and feedback. Alan Friedman, founder and president of J3P Healthcare Solutions, a consultancy that works with many leading hospitals and medical schools, found that leaders spend a disproportionate amount of time giving feedback to and investing in the top 10 percent and the bottom 10 percent. The middle 80 percent, who make up most of your tribe, get neglected, yet those tribe members may provide the key to performance improvements. Though they're ripe for development, it's rare for them to be a focus, he told me. The research director and top surgeon at one of the leading hospitals in the world, which is one of our clients, agreed. He told us that they spend the bulk of time and energy on the bottom 10 percent, and leadership development programs target the top 10 percent.

Who might be getting the squeeze in your tribe? What are the consequences?

Create formats for truth to be spoken to power.

Develop processes that speak truth to power. Create skip-level meetings. If you're a manager of managers, once a year try to meet with all of the people who work for each of your direct reports. If Kate is on my team and so is Ryan, meet with Kate's team without her in the room and say, "What could Kate do or stop doing that would make her a better boss or improve her leadership?" The goal is for the person to be able to speak to Kate directly and not through her boss, but it's hard to speak truth to power. Research highlights that. That's why skip-level meetings and other formats to speak truth to power are so valuable. "We're overcoming that fact of hierarchy," says Kim Scott. She says these skip meetings are one of the most helpful suggestions she ever received as a manager.[26]

Recognize and thank those who help support your community members.

A few years ago the Motley Fool sent flowers to every employee's designated significant other as a way of acknowledging the importance of their beyond-the-workplace support. Two years ago it sent beautiful, one-of-a-kind thank-you cards to the significant others.

The support that team members offer each other needs to be recognized, too. No one knows this better than Anson Dorrance, head women's soccer coach at the University of North Carolina at Chapel Hill, and former US women's national soccer team coach. And no one has used this recognition to greater effect.

Dorrance has won a stunning twenty-two NCAA national championships while at UNC, and notched a World Cup championship for the US national team. Dorrance's UNC teams have an incredible record in national championship games, winning twenty-two out of twenty-four.[27] That's an even better winning percentage than in their regular season games (which is darn good!). He attributes much of his success to getting his team to play for something greater than themselves, and then offering them recognition for the specific ways in which they've done that.

His go-to exercise is something he saves for when the pressure is on and they need it most—when his team gets to a national championship game, which it often does. Dorrance writes a letter to every senior on his roster thanking her for the incredible contribution she's made to the team and specifically to her teammates. Dorrance stays up late the night before the game, sometime into the wee hours of the morning, writing these letters. He believes that the letters are even more important than getting enough sleep to stay awake during the game. He pours himself into each one, recalling all the moments that illustrate why these women are not just great players but extraordinary human beings, and stitches them together into an incredibly meaningful letter packed with details. On game day he hands each senior her letter so that she can read what he thinks of her. And then, reading from the photocopies he's made of each of these letters, he shares them with the team, to remind them of the remarkable women they'll be playing for in the championship.

One of his former players, Caroline Boneparth, was not a superstar. Because her team was loaded with so much talent, she didn't see a lot of action. Dorrance believes she could have gone anywhere and played the moment she got there as a starter. Dorrance recognizes this sacrifice in sticking with the team, and being so supportive of her teammates despite a lack of playing time, and expresses his appreciation for it, along with what she brought to UNC's team. Dorrance notes that Caroline was an amazing leader, an incredibly strong but unbelievably soft and caring person whom the team had nicknamed "Care" because she nurtured everyone on the roster. At the end of his letter to her, Dorrance paraphrases Carl Sandburg's words about Abraham Lincoln:

Not often in the story of mankind does a person arrive on earth who is both steel and velvet, who is hard as rock and soft as drifting fog, who holds in (her) heart and mind the paradox of terrible storm and peace unspeakable and perfect.

Then he goes on to say:

This is you. You are strong and sweet and I cherish you for it. Thank you for taking "care" of everyone for four wonderful years. I am going to miss you.

—Anson

When Dorrance reads from the letters he has written to the seniors before he rallies the team to hit the field, you can imagine the effect on them—on the women who receive the letters, of course, but also on every player in the lineup, who will be fired up to do everything in their power to make sure that all the seniors graduate as national champions. This is the fuel he uses for the national championship, and he has had remarkable success with it.

One year when his UNC team got to the Final Four, it was such a tough bracket that Dorrance thought he needed to use the senior letter for the semifinal game. They were slotted to play the University of Portland, and they would be up against Christine Sinclair, the Canadian national team star, who is the world's all-time leader for international goals scored for men or women, and one of only two players to score in five World Cups. So Dorrance read the senior letters before the semifinal game that year, and they worked again! UNC did beat Portland but lost in the final. As Dorrance notes, the letters have worked twenty-three out of twenty-four times in the national championship weekends.[28]

Make your feedback clear, detailed, and as specific to the individual as you can.

"If you can say it to a dog, it doesn't count as praise." This is Kelly Leonard's favorite quote from *The Feedback Loop*, the five-episode workplace comedy series commissioned by Radical Candor to bring to life their principles about effective communication. In other words, your feedback shouldn't be generic or rote.

To offer this kind of feedback requires getting to know your colleagues, noticing what their special qualities are, observing what unique gifts they bring to the table, understanding how they can be encouraged to do better. Maybe you can't aspire to Anson Dorrance's level of eloquence, but if you are genuinely interested in your colleagues, you will learn surprising things about them.

In my early days as an assistant professor at the University of Southern California's Marshall School of Business, our department held retreats twice a year. These provided a bit more opportunity for interacting with each other than the brown-bag presentations and guest speakers at most of our other gatherings. At one particular retreat, Tom Cummings, our department chair, gave us a simple assignment: Write down one fun fact that people might not know about you. People scribbled their fun fact on small pieces of paper, which were then thrown into a baseball cap. In true academic form we waited for the results with skepticism—ready to pounce and cast judgment on exactly how ridiculous this exercise was.

Cummings, who presided over the proceedings, read from the first randomly drawn scrap of paper: "I have never pumped gasoline." What? The professors scanned the room with dumbfounded looks on their faces. "How is that possible?" someone shouted. "No way!" a senior faculty member screamed, slamming his fist on his desk. California didn't have many full-service gas stations—none that I had ever seen. After a few minutes of these expressions of disbelief, an associate professor of strategy piped up. "I haven't. My husband always fills the gas tank for me." Wow. This professor's husband, seemed like a very kind and giving soul, but still...hard to believe. A forty-plus mother of two kids who lived in California and had never held a gas nozzle, had never had to stop for gas while shuttling her kids to their various activities, picking up groceries, caring for her mother-in-law, and commuting from the picturesque mountaintop area where her family lived into the downtown campus, which was quite a distance away.

Next up, Tom began shaking, chuckling hard as he read, "I can bench-press our department chair, Tom Cummings." Seriously? This would be no small feat, and none of us were ripped bodybuilders or Ironman competitors. A quick scan of the room found no likely candidates, and no one had left the room. So who was it? People guessed the biggest guys, one by one. No, no, no, no. We were running out of options at this point. Looking back, it's embarrassing, but the person who actually wrote the note remained unnamed. Finally a thin, young, blond woman, built like a model, confidently and loudly declared, "I can bench-press three hundred and twenty-five pounds!" What?! Clearly, not a soul expected this from our new assistant professor. "Cool," I remember thinking. "Very, very cool!"

Highly entertained, Tom moved on. With a big grin, he read, "I played in March Madness." For the bewildered few, it was explained that this referred to the National Collegiate Athletic Association's (NCAA) basketball tournament, a single-elimination tournament played each spring in the United States, in which sixty-four women's college basketball and sixty-eight men's college basketball teams compete to determine their respective national championship.

Again, there were no obvious suspects, and people seemed dubious. Eyes darted around the room in search of possible candidates. They began rattling off the names of the tallest men, one by one. No, no, no. Then they started in on other men who were less likely, finally naming men who had clearly never touched a ball or graced an athletic court. I sat there, looking at my lap, doing my best to hide my smirk. "C'mon," I thought. I had put this on my CV when I interviewed, which hadn't been that long ago, and I remembered how surprised people had been at the idea of this unassuming pint-sized woman playing on a college basketball team. Over lunch after my interview they had quizzed me about my basketball experience. Now, with no one guessing that I might be the March Madness player, I wondered if they thought I had lied on my résumé. When people finally ran out of guesses, never getting around to me, I spoke up. "Yes," I said, with a huge smile, "I played in March Madness—and it was awesome." Fun times.

The afternoon could have been an excellent lesson in unconscious bias training, since so many assumptions and stereotypes were being upended, but we were ahead of our time. What it did do was provide a bonding experience. It gave us a deeper appreciation for each of our tribe members, some insight into their background and their quirks of personality, their interests, talents, and passions. The experience forever changed the way we thought about and related to one another. Suddenly we had become much more of a community. The chances of our high-fiving each other had increased exponentially, too.

_____

Feedback and recognition raise people's game. They connect community members in meaningful ways, leading to more effective collaboration, performance, and creativity. They can also create healthier, more fulfilling relationships. Yet too often community members complain that they don't receive it. This is such a waste of human potential.

So get comfortable being uncomfortable providing constructive feedback. Flex your radical candor muscles. Lean into exercises and techniques that build those muscles in both you and your tribe.

As Kelly Leonard aptly pointed out, "Meaning can be made in moments; it can also be broken in moments. . . . People can change overnight by simply learning to treat people with respect—like humans."[29] What's more, there's a multiplier effect to this dynamic. These things—both kindness and cruelty—have a way of going viral (as discussed in chapter 3).

CHAPTER **5**

Provide Meaning

There is always light,
if only we're brave enough to see it.
If only we were brave enough to be it.

—Amanda Gorman

Five days into a family vacation on a small, beautiful, quiet island in her husband's family's native Ischia, Italy, Amy D'Ambra, a partner in an insurance agency, had logged most of her time at the shoebox-sized sidewalk internet café on multiple electronic devices, juggling work demands. Even when she wasn't scurrying to the café to plug into her thriving insurance business, her mind wandered to work tasks, whether she was at meals with her family, at the beach, in churches, even on runs she took to the stunning medieval stone Aragonese Castle. Her husband, Anthony, looked her in the eyes one day and pleaded, "This has to stop. Your family is right here and you are not present to us." He offered to take her phone and computer, and contact her office in Los Angeles to inform them that they were checking out for the remainder of the vacation. She agreed to unplug.

Feeling more peaceful, Amy entered St. Anthony's church with her family. She knelt before the catacomb of San Giovan Giuseppe and prayed. She started with a simple thank-you and then asked God, "What can I do for you?" Amy, a tall, driven, naturally radiant, athletic mother of three children, felt as if there must be a better, more meaningful path for her. "I was racing through life, and was seen by others as successful. But something inside of me was breaking. Crumbling. And I was either going to break down or break free," she said. "In my heart I heard, 'Share our stories...make the saints heroes for the youth.'" Amy ran outside and told her husband what she had just heard in her prayer. He looked at her and said, "Go back in and ask him how!" Amy raced back into the church, knelt again before San Giovan Giuseppe, and asked how. She heard in her heart, "Make a necklace and bracelets, put a cool image of the saint on the jewelry, and hang a virtue tag with it. Just one virtue that pertains to the saint. Young people will understand one word. They will connect through the word or the saint, and we will do the rest!"

My Saint My Hero (MSMH) was born in 2009. The company's mission: "to create wearable blessings that empower global community through meaningful work and remind us we are loved, blessed, and protected," as the website puts it. D'Ambra started the business out of her home. Her oldest child, Ellie, who now serves as director of sales and marketing, remembers her mother huddled over their coffee table dutifully logging countless hours designing and then painstakingly stringing together bracelets and necklaces. In October of 2010, during a pilgrimage to Medjugorje, a small community in Bosnia and Herzegovina that has been attracting pilgrims for decades because of a history of visions and apparitions of the Virgin Mary, D'Ambra met a woman weaving rosaries. She hired the woman to weave one hundred bracelets. Soon she was ordering one hundred every week, then one thousand per month. Three and a half very successful years later, her company was ordering thirty thousand bracelets per month from a team of women in the village. They now employ teams of women not just in Medjugorje, but in several of the nearby villages. MSMH is focused on empowering women.

Many of those women have risen above poverty through this work. One woman, who lived in an abandoned railroad car with her family, now has a home. Another woman, from one of the neighboring villages, explained that thanks to work from My Saint My Hero, "Things changed for the better, little by little; this means financial security. From week to week we're certain that there will be an income." But money isn't the only blessing of this work. "Every week when we come get the material to weave the bracelets," she said, "there is often laughter and good atmosphere among us. In all of this hardship we manage to find time to laugh, have coffee together, share things, especially about the blessings these bracelets have brought us, the things that we are now able to afford for our children." In Medjugorje, the women typically sit at a table weaving together, providing one another with the camaraderie and support that's missing from all-too-many of our lives. "The bracelets bonded all of us," one woman noted. "At first we were only acquaintances, but this brought us much closer together." Weaving bracelets has helped the women create a real sense of community and mutual support. As the sixteen-year-old daughter of one of the weavers explained, "It's not just the shoes, food, education it provides, it's actually that when a neighbor needs work, my mom can offer this work to a family. She can help this family and this community."

Amy's company and her vision have continued to grow. At the beginning, when sales increased from one hundred the first month to three hundred monthly, "It was a big deal," she told me. But since those early days, sales have increased exponentially. From 2017 to 2020 sales have averaged between twenty thousand and twenty-five thousand pieces of jewelry *per month*. And with this growth has come the ability to lift and empower women in communities in several other places around the world. My Saint My Hero now employs about twenty women in Italy who make the hand-cast medals that are a part of the company's bracelets and other jewelry. MSMH employs ten women in Mexico. It also expanded into Cambodia, where it collaborates with Senhoa Foundation, which has established projects that address the rehabilitation, education, reintegration, and employment of human trafficking survivors. Senhoa Foundation has trained many women to make jewelry for the very extensive collections that are for sale on its website. A priest working with Senhoa Foundation said that the women there find making jewelry "incredibly meaningful—and not just financially." Again, the point is that the rewards of the work go beyond money. Since the alternative employment for many of the women would be as massage therapists or in tourist resorts, working from the private safe haven of Senhoa is a way for these former victims of human trafficking to avoid the kind of contact with clients and customers that would be painful and even risky for many of them. Instead they can come together to enjoy the rhythm and routine of beading, in community. "It's safe," the priest said, "meditative, and therapeutic." Among the women Senhoa has rescued is a sixteen-year-old who sold herself at age fourteen for money needed to pay for her mother's life-saving surgery. When she described her My Saint My Hero work, she said, quite emotionally, "I am so honored to hold Swarovski crystals...to be trusted with that. It's given me a new sense of worth."

More recently, My Saint My Hero expanded its footprint to Africa, where the company partnered with an orphanage in Nigeria and with women teachers at a school in Uganda to weave bracelets. Proceeds from their work allowed the Ugandan woman weavers to buy desks for the whole school, and to provide uniforms and other supplies for their students. Much of the weaving done in Uganda and Nigeria supports My Saint My Hero's ambitious kindness campaign. The goal of this campaign: "to change the world through love one act of kindness at a time." In 2019, My Saint My Hero came up with a design for bracelets with beads that spell "kind" in Morse code, to give people a tangible reminder, a tool of affirmation to remind them to show kindness to others—something we need more of in today's disconnected world. The company has provided a free kindness bracelet with orders during various kindness campaigns. The company hopes people wear one or share it with others who could use an act of kindness. The bracelet is packaged so you can slip it into the back of your phone or purse, perhaps to gift it to someone when you feel "a tug on your heart." People write in to My Saint My Hero to tell how these bracelets have changed the trajectory of their days—and even sometimes their lives—for the better. A bullied teenager felt cared for by a schoolmate who saw her struggling and gave her a bracelet. The bracelet is a visual reminder that someone in her community cares—she is not alone. In 2019 the company gave away 70,000 bracelets. The goal for 2020 is to reach 140,000. One day, it hopes to hit a million.

True to the unleashing concepts discussed in chapter 2, My Saint My Hero is willing to collaborate with people in ways that are adapted to the particular culture of their villages, boutiques, schools, and organizations, so long as their collaborators remain true to the core mission of the company— empowering community through meaningful work. D'Ambra understands that the women in Medjugorje will operate differently from those in Uganda, Nigeria, and Italy. Operations and logistics are bound to differ from country to country, and that's okay. In fact the differences are part of the company's strength, as she has discovered. For example, Anita, a leader in My Saint My Hero's work in Medjugorje, donates any jewelry that doesn't pass their high quality control standards to a friar who sells them at his monastery's gift shop. He's used the proceeds to fund an orphanage in Albania (home of Mother Teresa), including buying sheets and bedding for all the kids there. This is the kind of "ripple effect" that D'Ambra evokes when she talks about the "intrinsic value" of the work her company does, "which has a ripple effect on others."

D'Ambra describes My Saint My Hero as "more than a company, but *a community*." She is delighted that members of the My Saint My Hero community—which she considers to include not just employees and sales-people but also customers, suppliers, and followers, as well as the various celebrities who have been attracted to its mission—feel a connection to each other, one that creates "strength, joy, and hope...the exact opposite of isolation." That sense of being bound together in a mission is "really the crux of it." As she says, "humans crave something meaningful."

Like many business leaders, D'Ambra faced challenges that tested her purpose and the company's mission. With success came the opportunity to scale. In the business's early stages, a huge potential buyer pressed D'Ambra hard, promising access to a manufacturing plant in China that would enable them to make one hundred thousand pieces quickly. But she stayed true to the company's mission, part of which involved employing and empowering women. A TV show that offered major exposure and sales said My Saint My Hero was "too Catholic" and required that it not mention the spiritual aspect of its mission if the company wanted an opportunity on their net-work, so she said no to that, too. A mammoth department store unveiled a tantalizing offer, with the plan to prominently display pieces—but without the inspirational card that accompanies each wearable blessing, describing its meaning and the community that wove the bracelet. In each case, D'Ambra circled back to the company's why. "If I give myself space to breathe—to think about what's in line with the company's values—I can figure out what's best." Offered these as well as some other potentially lucrative propositions, she decided that she had to decline the deals. "These are hard nos—we're taught to say yes and make yes work. But it's about staying authentic to our mission, about authenticity...we say that every single bracelet is hand woven by a woman in our community." She knew that if she wavered, it could be the end of the community she'd created. "I won't forsake community members in order to turn a profit. And I'm willing to risk everything on it."

Amy D'Ambra is clear on her why. How clear are you on yours? It's worth thinking about, especially if you're a leader. Consider how your why provides meaning for your various community members. Like D'Ambra, what might you do to use that to elevate your community or attract potential community members who might further your meaningful mission?

Creating a Community Gathering Place

Kim Malek, the co-founder of Salt & Straw, an ice cream company, is another woman dedicated to using her business as a way of forging a sense of meaning and connectedness among its employees, its customers, and beyond that to the larger communities in which her shops are located. The desire for community has been her motivator, the driver of her vision, ever since childhood.

Kim was raised by parents who both grew up in families that had six kids, and when they married they brought their families into their life together. Being part of such a large close-knit extended family taught Kim the value of community. "I think you move through the world differently when you have that. You feel connected. And you propel that desire for connection from your family into the larger world around you." She happily recalled an occasion when the whole family walked into high school with her—her grandmother, grandfather, five aunts and uncles, their spouses, and her fourteen cousins— and she just felt that she had a tribe behind her. She always felt the benefits of being part of a tribe. She told me, "We generally rolled with about twelve-plus people when we showed up. All sleeping on couches and blow-up beds that night at one person's home base—because everyone traveled for hours to be there. Swedish pancakes in the morning. You show up for one another because it matters. You knew you belong. It's everything."

Having spent her formative years in a town where she was likely to run into someone she knew wherever she went also left its imprint on her: "I grew up just kind of a free range kid running around the big city of Billings, Montana, and I think what really kind of stuck with me more than anything was that feeling of community that I had…you just knew everyone. And I can remember thinking about that—that exact feeling and what that meant to me…It's had a huge impact on my life."[1] That's why from early on, when asked what she wanted to be when she grew up, she knew it would have something to do with community.

She recounted having a fantasy about opening a coffee shop within a bookstore when she was only about ten years old—"this was before the days that Starbucks was on every corner"—and describing her vision to a counselor at her summer camp. "I envisioned the shop as a means of talking, engaging, and sharing ideas," she told me.

Her work ethic kicked in early, by necessity. She was a freshman in college when she learned that her father had lost his small business and would not be able to pay her college expenses. Malek decided to stay in school, and immediately got two jobs, one of which, as fate would have it, was as a barista at Starbucks Coffee, in the early years of its espresso bar business. This turned into a position in the marketing department after she graduated. Although her parents felt sorry for Kim because they didn't think that a job at what was then a thirty-store coffee shop chain that few people had ever heard of was a promising start for someone with a college degree, she was confident in her choice. She kept saying, "It's going to be a big thing someday—I really believe in this guy Howard Schultz."[2] And it was from Schultz that she learned "that you can develop a business model based on people first," because she herself was treated with such respect even when she was only in an entry-level position.[3] She also saw that you could make community the focus of a thriving business. "During my entire career at Starbucks, we were thinking of community. We were thinking of consumers, where coffee comes from, and how are we investing?" Kim told me.

In 1996, when Starbucks sent her on a job rotation from Seattle to Portland, she fell in love with the city because of the sense of community and collaboration she felt there, and she came up with the idea of moving to Portland and opening an ice cream shop as a way of capturing her childhood dream. After all, everyone likes ice cream, so it would bring people together over something that is always a source of pleasure. But when she drew up a business plan, all the potential funders she approached were negative. One guy sent it back to Kim covered in red ink. At the top of the front page he wrote, "You can't do this. Who do you think you are, Starbucks?"

Discouraged, Kim shelved the idea and moved on with her marketing career, which over the years took her to Yahoo!, Adidas, and (RED), Bono's nonprofit to fight AIDS. In 2010, Kim was in the process of moving to New York City for her job at (RED). But before she moved she went to Portland for a birthday party for a friend, and ended up meeting and falling in love with Mike, her now husband, and with whom she has adopted three children. She quit her job, moved to Portland, and then one morning read a magazine article about artisanal ice cream as the happening thing. "This was my idea!" she said to Mike. Rather than being realistic about the obstacles to starting an ice cream company in the midst of a recession and in a city that was cool and rainy much of the time, he encouraged her to go for it. Since no one would fund the business, she cashed in her 401(k) to fund it herself, and Mike put up his home for collateral, for a company to be run by a woman he had known only a few months.[4]

In yet another propitious bit of timing, her cousin Tyler had recently returned from China and was thinking he wanted to go to culinary school rather than becoming an international businessman, as he had expected to do. Once he heard about Kim's idea, he dropped everything, moved into Kim's "not fancy" basement, and despite the fact that they were complete rookies as both entrepreneurs *and* as ice cream makers, started testing recipes on four ice cream makers he got at Goodwill for sixteen dollars. In Kim's basement, he experimented for countless hours, testing various flavors and concoctions. They sold their first ice cream out of a cart on Alberta Street in the spring of 2011, and opened their first shop that summer.

From the beginning, as is recounted on their website, the two of them "turned to their community asking friends—chefs, chocolatiers, brewers, and farmers—for advice, finding inspiration everywhere they looked."[5] Kim and Tyler worked with the Food Innovation Center, a partnership between Oregon State University and the Oregon Department of Agriculture to help companies that are going to support the local food industry and farmers. As part of this, the two of them had access to state-of-the-art facilities and food scientists who collaborated with them on recipes. On an everyday basis, they were focused on community, looking for ways Salt & Straw could partner with people to figure out recipes. "Pretty quickly, community started to be reflected through our recipe development," she told me. Every single ice cream flavor on their menu, many of them so unusual that nobody had ever tasted anything like them—smoked cherry and bone marrow, pear with blue cheese, strawberry honey balsamic with black pepper, honey lavender, goat cheese marionberry habanero—"had a person behind it that we worked with and whose story we could tell. So that feeling of community came through in the actual ice cream you were eating." Kim says people have come out of the woodwork to help them, each bringing their own expertise. They had a sea salt ice cream on their menu, and early one morning before they had even opened the shop, someone knocked on the door—"and it's Mark Bitterman, who is a James Beard Award–winning author who wrote the book *Salted*" and was the owner and "selmelier" of an internationally renowned salt shop in Portland. He had come to talk to them because he didn't think they were doing it right. "And he opens up this briefcase and it was full of salt"— which he offered them on the spot for a tasting. Out of what he taught them, they created what has become their most popular flavor, sea salt with caramel ribbons.

Salt & Straw was successful from the start. The *Wall Street Journal* gave it a rave review, and *O* magazine featured Salt & Straw ice cream as one of Oprah's favorite things. As Salt & Straw expanded from Portland—to Seattle, Los Angeles, San Francisco and other locales in the Bay Area, San Diego, Anaheim, and Miami—it never strayed from Kim's vision, making it a point in each city to work with local dairy and fruit farmers, artisans, cheese makers, brewers, tea makers, and honey collectors to incorporate their products into unique ice cream flavors that reflect their own community. Kim explains it this way: "We will sometimes talk about this idea of terroir— in the wine industry, your product has a taste of place"—and that's what they want for their ice cream, too.

Kim's idea of community, similar to Amy D'Ambra's, embraces not just the places where her products are made, but, true to the "people first" philosophy she learned at Starbucks, everyone who is involved at either the consumer or the production end of her product. "I know it sounds trite, but putting employees and your community of suppliers, vendors, and partners first is a smarter business model that is more sustainable in the end." She is sure that this is how her own company has thrived. "These are the people who are creating your success. Take good care of them. Believe in your people and your industry as a force for good."[6]

One of Malek's proudest moments was when, not quite a year after opening, the company was able to offer its employees health insurance and to expand a paid-time-off program. A couple of years later, she reported that each employee had received forty hours of training the previous year and that the benefits package was about twice the size of comparable companies. Since its inception, Salt & Straw had added at least one new benefit every year, including health benefits for all (even part-time employees), disability insurance, three months paid parental leave, employee assistance programs, and more.[7]

For customers, Salt & Straw wants to provide a true gathering place where people can run into their neighbors or meet new people while standing on line—and there have been lines out the door practically from day one—maybe even make a connection that leads to a business deal or a romance. What gives Kim the greatest satisfaction is knowing that sometimes it's more than just a momentary pleasure her customers get from the experience of being at one of her shops.

Kim told me about a customer she thinks about often. This woman told Kim, "I get home Friday night and just feel like putting on my comfiest clothes and crashing. Just melting in bed." But she knows she shouldn't do this. So instead she goes to Salt & Straw, stands in line talking to people, and reports that she always feels better after the visit. "The opportunity for people to be seen and to connect," which is what Kim has always wanted her stores to offer, may mean the difference between a good and a bad day.

A story that appears on their company website recounts the experience of Monique, one of Salt & Straw's shop managers, who saw a little boy come in wearing a superhero costume. When Monique informed him that they had a special ice cream made just for superheroes, his face lit up and he exclaimed that he was a superhero! Afterward, his mother thanked Monique, explaining that he'd been crying all the way home because he had been bullied at school, and the only time she'd seen him crack a smile all afternoon was during his interaction with Monique.[8]

"More than anything else we do," Malek commented, "that's the kind of story that makes me think we are on track with our business and feeding our culture to keep it healthy. That's how I gauge our success. Yea, we gave that little guy some cinnamon ice cream that day, but we actually give him something else...we gave him a little kindness, an opportunity to feel good about himself that day. And in a world where people are more and more isolated, that matters!"[9]

She told me another story about a child—this one a boy who had won one of the annual student inventor contests in which the children are invited to invent a new flavor of ice cream. (This contest, which is conducted in cooperation with local schools, is yet another way the shops embed themselves in their communities and try to benefit them.) The boy's school was to honor him at an assembly where he had to read the poem he'd written about his flavor. Everyone was cheering him on, high-fiving him on his way to the stage. Meanwhile his mother was very nervous because her son had a serious stutter. But to her surprise, he got through the entire reading without stuttering even once, and as she told Kim and Tyler afterward, it was the first time this had ever happened, and she was sure the whole experience must have given him a huge confidence boost. "That's what this is about," Kim said. "Changing one person at a time."

But Kim's aspirations go further than that. She remembered that in her early years she had worked for Maggie Weissman, the owner of a bakery in Seattle. Weissman was hiring a man who had just been released from prison, and she took him to a store to buy him some deodorant. Malek realized that what Weissman was doing was helping him figure out what was involved in showing up for work and succeeding, which opened her eyes to the idea that "through business you can do a lot of good." She said, "That's what you do when you own a business. You just really show up for every single person and help in any way that you can." Another of her formative experiences came when she watched a movie about the Niger Delta, which told the story of a community's struggle against a multinational oil company that had plundered their land and destroyed both the environment and their livelihoods. This made her think further about how business could play a positive rather than a destructive role in the communities where it operates. "And not just because it's the right thing to do but because it's good for business, too. Business needs to show up with government and other players to promote community." So another of the hallmarks of Salt & Straw has been Malek's commitment to social justice.

Part of this is personal, for both her partner and their three children are African American, which has made her sensitive to all the ways, subtle and not, in which racism permeates our society. Shortly after the murder of George Floyd, she posted a blog on the company website entitled "A Message from Our Co-founder: Black Lives Matter," in which she recounted her own family's experiences with racism. To her, being a force for good means using her company's platform as an agent of change—supporting Black Lives Matter, creating a job training program for women just released from prison, raising awareness of issues like childhood hunger, offering training to at-risk youth, and making sure their own workplace reflects her values. She is proud of the fact that 50 percent of Salt & Straw's team identifies as BIPOC, and 70 percent of its managers are women.

While Salt & Straw has become incredibly popular because of its one-of-a-kind flavors and the high quality of its hand-churned ice cream, it may be its commitment to community, to providing a meaningful experience to its customers as well as its staff, that is the ultimate driver of its success.

Creating Meaning for Your Community and Its Members

The desire for meaningful work, for a sense of purpose and mission, is the number one priority in a job for American employees. In 2017, a Workhuman survey of over 2,700 employees in the US found that nearly one-third (32 percent) cited the fact that they find their work meaningful as their primary reason for staying at a job.[10] As both of the entrepreneurs profiled above demonstrate, meaningful work is good business, too. It inspires employees and, as the example of Monique and the little boy in the superhero outfit shows, makes them go the extra yard in doing their job. The sense that what we do matters and serves something larger than our immediate self-interest is a uniquely powerful source of motivation.

There are reams of research documenting the value—to both employees and the bottom line of their companies—of creating a work culture in which employees feel a sense of meaning about their jobs. For example, one survey of 1,726 people, including university students about to enter the workplace and college graduates currently employed who spanned three generations, millennial, Gen X, and baby boomer, reported that workers who believe they can have a social or environmental impact through their work were twice as happy with their jobs as people who didn't feel that way.[11] The *Harvard Business Review* study that Tony Schwartz and I did of the work and life quality of over 20,000 employees across industries and organizations found that meaning was the number one driver of thriving at work. It had a stronger effect than opportunities for learning and growth, than doing what you do best, or even than doing what you enjoy most! It was also the strongest predictor of staying with the organization, as those who derive meaning from their work were more than three times as likely to stay with their organizations. These employees also reported 1.7 times higher job satisfaction and were 1.4 times more engaged at work. In another study I did across six organizations, those who reported their work as more meaningful performed 19 percent better as rated by their managers, were 47 percent more committed to their organization, and 71 percent less burned out.

Organizational psychologist and bestselling author Adam Grant demonstrated that by helping people find meaning in work, you as a manager or leader can improve productivity by more than 20 percent.[12] It can benefit you, too. Blue Zones research shows that having a clear sense of meaning or purpose helps people live seven years longer![13]

Feeling engaged in a higher purpose is something that workers crave. A fascinating Bloomberg survey of "happiest professions" revealed that the most desirable jobs were not necessarily the most financially lucrative, but rather those built around trust and human connection, along with a focus on human potential and purpose. And what was the happiest occupation? Firefighters scored at the very top of the job satisfaction scale despite the dangers of their job and their modest salaries. Their job connected them not just to a sense of purpose larger than themselves but to each other, which is another source of job satisfaction.[14] Firemen often work in twenty-four-hour shifts, living, working, and even cooking together. If you've ever seen a group of firemen shopping for food in your local stores, you get a firsthand look at their sense of camaraderie.

Yet despite all the evidence, a sense of meaning is still an underutilized tool in corporate life. Sixty-five percent of the 20,000 people in our study did not feel a sense of meaning or significance at work. Similarly, in what was described as *"good news in the American workplace* [italics mine]," Gallup, the global polling company, reported that "in 2019, the percentage of 'engaged' workers in the U.S.—those who are highly involved in, enthusiastic about and committed to their work and workplace—reached 35 percent [based on a random sample of 4,700 employees]. This is a new high since Gallup began tracking the metric in 2000." That left 13 percent "actively disengaged"— that is, miserable and likely to spread their unhappiness throughout the workplace, and 52 percent "not engaged," who will "put time, but not energy or passion, into their work," and "contribute the minimum required."[15]

Now that may be good news by comparison with previous years, but it's certainly not optimal. Such findings indicate an enormous waste of individual talent and potential—and potential earnings, too. Engagement has been positively correlated with profitability. In a meta-analysis of 263 research studies across 192 companies, employers with the most engaged employees were 22 percent more profitable than those with the least engaged employees.[16]

What's interesting to note about finding meaning is that the ability to do so is not necessarily about the job or the industry or even the organization. Some people just seem to have a gift for it. My colleagues Amy Wrzesniewski, a pioneer in the study of meaning at work, and Jane Dutton conducted a study of hospital cleaners. Though you might think it would be hard to find a sense of meaning in doing such work, in fact some of the cleaners did, particularly those who went beyond what was expected of them in their jobs. For example, some of them described how they took note of which patients didn't have visitors and then doubled back later in their shift to see if those patients would like a bit of company. One cleaner who worked on a floor with patients in comas talked about how she switched out the pictures hanging on the walls and circulated them among the rooms because she believed that changing the environment might in some way help the patients—perhaps even sparking recovery. Intrigued, the researchers asked her whether that was part of her role. She replied, "That's not part of my job, but that's part of me."[17]

The ability to see their work as a calling and not just a job, as Wrzesniewski puts it, may sometimes derive from the way certain individuals approach their day-to-day duties. But there's a lot management can do to facilitate it. Some companies actively encourage their employees to engage in what's known as job crafting in order to find ways to create a greater sense of meaning.

Jane Dutton and Justin Berg did a case study that focused on four employees at one such company—Burt's Bees, the leading manufacturer of environmentally friendly personal care products. Though these four employees worked in very different jobs, each managed to find their way to meaning, and all of them were supported by management in their efforts to do so. For example, there was Andy, a maintenance technician, who was so passionate about how to make manufacturing processes more efficient that, with management's support, he collected data and conducted experiments on how to improve these processes. This was well outside the scope of his job, but it created greater meaning for him—and resulted in greater efficiency for the company. Mindy is another Burt's Bees example. She was a customer care representative, whose work consists of taking orders and handling customer concerns. There were times when she got bored by the repetitive nature of her job. But since she loved learning new skills and taking part in events, her manager sometimes allowed her to travel to trade shows as part of the Burt's Bees team. There she could use her strong people skills to build positive relationships with clients, which helped her to see her job as something more than just answering questions and entering data. By empowering its employees to move beyond the boundaries of their jobs, Burt's Bees yields benefits for both the employees and the organization.[18]

Following are some ideas about strategies you can use to encourage a culture that makes meaning and purpose a foundational aspect of your company. It begins with hiring, making sure the people who will have the responsibility of manifesting these values share them.[ii]

Hire people who have a sense of purpose and meaning.

Kim Malek joked that Salt & Straw does more developing of its people than making ice cream. "People are central to our business and our success, and it starts with hiring," Kim told me. They hire "the unapologetically positive," a quality that is not captured on résumés but important for building community, she said. Salt & Straw asks a lot of questions, like who inspired you growing up, who is one person you look up to, and who is the best leader you ever worked for. An interviewer might also ask you to share an example of a high-pressure situation at your work and explain how you dealt with it and what you learned. Or to tell them how you like to receive feedback, how you incorporate feedback into the everyday work experience, and about a time in a previous job you had the chance to go above and beyond to make a customer happy. They also look for people who are good storytellers because Malek wants her employees "constantly telling stories about connection." Stories about their community members—their customers, suppliers, the artisans they work with—are what she's after. That's what is modeled, rewarded, and celebrated at Salt & Straw.

Leigha May, senior manager of recruitment at the Honest Company, a wellness-oriented baby and beauty supply store that has tripled its staff in the past two years to almost six hundred people, sees her recruitment teams as the gatekeepers of their corporate culture: "Our team can singlehandedly change the culture of our company if we're not hiring in the right way. With every hire, we really dive in to understand their drivers, their motivators, and whether they align with our brand."

John Phillips, SVP of global talent acquisition at Starbucks, says something similar: "The role of the recruiter is serious. You have to think beyond just filling roles, and act on behalf of what the world needs from you."[19]

---

ii   Research shows workers who believe they're having a social impact are twice as satisfied with their jobs as those who don't hold such beliefs.

Tell stories—from inside.

Malek alludes to the important of storytelling, something she feels so strongly about that her company hires for that skill. KPMG, the audit, tax, and advisory firm, doesn't at first glance seem like a company that screams the kind of purpose and meaning that would make for a good story. But it turns out that both it and its employees have a lot of stories to tell about their work, something that emerged, quite unexpectedly, when its leadership was examining the reasons for its employees' high rate of satisfaction. Tallies of employee morale conducted over several years had shown that approximately 80 percent of its 29,000 professionals reported that KPMG was a great place to work, and it had long made consistent appearances on *Fortune* magazine's annual 100 Best Companies to Work For list. But KPMG wanted to understand the factors driving these findings, and how it might use that information to do even better.[20] KPMG scoured the results of its annual employee survey and found that one item in particular was a very strong driver of employee engagement, retention, and pride: "I feel like my job has special meaning and is not just a job."[iii]

Since this sense of a higher purpose was so important to their employees, the leadership thought that one way of giving them even more pride in their company was to recount the largely forgotten stories about KPMG's history of meaningful work.[21] Like Malek, they understood the potential impact of a powerful story. So in 2014, KPMG's leadership unveiled the Higher Purpose initiative. They launched it with video titled "We Shape History" that highlighted KPMG's role in historic events, such as how it managed the Lend-Lease Act to help defeat Nazi Germany, resolved conflicting financial claims to lay the groundwork for the release of the US hostages in Iran in 1981, and certified the election of Nelson Mandela in South Africa in 1994.

Then KPMG's leaders went further. To get people to talk about what *they* do to make a difference, they invited all employees—from interns to

---

iii   This sentiment would seem to support Amy Wrzesniewski's work, which identified how people who view their work as callings (versus jobs, or even careers) may do their work in ways that allow them to experience it as a source of joy and meaning.

the chairman—to share their own stories of purpose-driven work. One employee shared about advancing science, as KPMG provides to the National Science Foundation help make important climate research in the Antarctic possible. Another employee restored neighborhoods, noting how KPMG audits development programs that contribute to the revitalization of low-income communities in Boston, opening new possibilities for every resident. A KPMG employee helps farms grow. When family farms and ranches need loans, KPMG works with the credit system to help secure them, furthering America's proud tradition of family farming.[22] They were hoping to get ten thousand stories, but to their surprise ended up with forty-two thousand from their twenty-nine thousand employees! KPMG packaged these in print, digital, and live communications.[23] The percentage of people who thought the company was a great place to work then shot up even higher—to 89 percent. The scores on the engagement survey soared to a record level, the company's turnover rate plummeted, and KPMG surged ahead on *Fortune* magazine's annual 100 Best Companies to Work For list, making it the number one–ranked of the Big Four accounting firms for the first time in their history. It also enjoyed one of its best financial years in recent memory.[24]

Seeing how powerful the effect was, to further assess its impact KPMG compared survey scores of employees whose managers did discuss purpose with those whose managers didn't. Among employees who reported that their leaders discussed the positive societal value of their teams' work, 94 percent said KPMG was a great place to work and also said they were proud to work there. For those whose leaders didn't discuss purpose, only 66 percent agreed KPMG was a great place to work and only 68 percent were proud to work there. Those whose leaders did not talk about purpose were also three times more likely to report that they were thinking about looking for another job.

To encourage managers to discuss purpose and also to teach them how to do it, KPMG has now incorporated purpose-oriented storytelling training into its leadership development programs, with the goal of helping managers to develop compelling narratives about purpose and to get comfortable with self-disclosure, too.[25] The company knows that personal experiences make for good storytelling, the kind that speaks to people's hearts as well as their minds.

Amy D'Ambra of My Saint My Hero also loves a good story and knows how important they are to her company's mission. On one occasion, as an event for its salespeople was about to begin, Amy noticed a gentleman sitting in the corner, dressed in a neat business suit, with a laptop sitting idly on the table. She approached him and, apologizing for any disruption or inconvenience, explained that this room full of ladies was getting ready to launch an event. The sullen businessman asked what kind of event it was. Amy smiled, and excitedly—and quickly—pointed to her wrist, with one of her My Saint My Hero bracelets, explaining the meaning behind these blessings. She peeled a blessings bracelet from her wrist and handed it to him. "Please take this," she said, noticing that tears immediately began to well up in his eyes and he choked up. "You don't know what this means to me," he told her. He went on to explain, "My son passed away five years ago, today. Every year, on this day, my wife and I go to church together and pray that he's okay. It's such a tough day for us, and for the first time since then, I'm not able to be home. I was expected to attend this important meeting, and I've felt terrible all day....All day I've been thinking of my son, wondering if he's okay....Thank you. Thank you so much. I feel that he's okay now." Hearing this, Amy invited him to stay for the event, and he shared his story with the audience, thanking them for the work they do. When Amy returned to the company's headquarters, she announced the story to the rest of her employees in a meeting.

Tell stories—from outside.

Amy knew that that was a story her employees would find meaningful, so she spread it company-wide, which is why I put it under the "Tell stories—from inside" heading. But it's also an example of finding someone from outside whose story would let the members of the My Saint My Hero community know that their work mattered, that it made a difference to someone who was in pain. Turns out that sometimes those stories are the ones people most need to hear.

Although the leaders of an organization can send an important signal to their employees about the importance of purpose, as those at KPMG certainly did, research by Adam Grant shows that those who benefit from an organization's products and services can be an even more potent source of inspiration than leaders. Grant began to look into this subject when he was a doctoral student at the University of Michigan and stumbled upon a sign in a campus call center that did fundraising for the university: "Doing a good job here is like wetting your pants in a dark suit. You get a warm feeling, but no one else notices."

Clearly the callers were demoralized, feeling that their work was meaningless. Grant believed that he could raise morale by helping the callers see how much of a difference the money they raised made to the beneficiaries. He arranged for a team leader to explain to the callers that the money that came in as a result of their calls contributed to the new buildings on campus, to faculty and staff salaries, and to the Michigan football and basketball teams. But, when the researchers tracked the results, they found that this didn't have an impact. Callers didn't work harder or more productively after the speech from their leader.

Grant wondered if the message came from the wrong source. The leader obviously had an incentive—even an ulterior motive—for getting his employees to work harder. What would happen if the message were delivered by another source? To find out, his team ran a study, randomly dividing the call center people into three groups. One group met a scholarship student, Will, face-to-face. Will spent five minutes with the callers, describing how their work had helped fund his scholarship and changed his life. He thanked them for their work. Other callers were given a letter with a similar message from Will but had no direct contact from him. The third group had no exposure to Will (or his message).

Over the next month, the performance, on average, of those who met with Will spiked 142 percent in weekly minutes logged on calls, and 171 percent in weekly revenues. They developed a stronger sense that their work made a difference, felt more valued, and recognized their potential effect on other scholarship students. What they learned was also something that they could share with the potential donors they called. Neither of the other groups—those who had read Will's letter, and those who had had no contact with him—displayed any changes in either effort or results.

Grant's team replicated this study five times, using different scholarship students and different callers. In one case, a short interaction with a scholarship student led to a jump in weekly revenue by more than 400 percent. The team didn't find any significant effects when leaders delivered the same message, or when a former caller addressed the personal benefits of the job (on learning and career advancement). It was only when employees heard firsthand how their work benefited a member of their community that their motivation and performance skyrocketed.[26]

Research has revealed similar effects among nurses who worked longer hours when they met the healthcare practitioners who used the surgical kits they assembled, among radiologists whose accuracy reading scans increased when the patient's photo was included in the file, and among lifeguards who read stories about rescues performed by other lifeguards and then worked longer hours and were seen as 21 percent more helpful by their supervisors.[27] Having a sense of the person at the other end of one's actions is highly motivational.

That's why The Mighty encourages its group leaders to circulate and post stories from members of their groups. Messages from members expressing gratitude to the company and its contributors for providing the support they need to face their health challenges means so much to those who work for The Mighty. At The Mighty's second annual retreat in Los Angeles, Mike shared one such story with employees. Jean Sharon Abbott had lived for thirty-three years with the belief that she had the cerebral palsy she'd been diagnosed with when she was a small child—until she saw a new doctor who said, "I don't think that's what you have." She gave Jean a pill. The following day Abbott stood up unassisted for the first time in decades. The Mighty staff, comprising just three employees at the time, read her remarkable story and were so impressed that they stopped their other work to disseminate it. Because at that time they didn't have a large cerebral palsy community, they focused on their media contacts. Within two weeks, the *Today* show featured Jean, and her story went viral. A few months later, Jean informed Mike of something even better. Twenty people had contacted her since The Mighty had championed her story, and had since discovered that, just like her, they actually didn't have cerebral palsy, either. They secured the right pills and were up and walking, too! "Think about how that one story changed all those people's lives," said Mike. "And it was just about finding a way of getting it out for more people." Mike wanted to inspire his tribe to continue working hard by letting them know that their efforts in publicizing Jean's story had transformed lives. This is one of many examples of the way The Mighty has helped people, even people who weren't in its immediate community. Sometimes its employees were aware of this, often times they weren't. He wanted to make sure they knew.

Share the metrics about the impact of your organization.

Tell your employees and other community members about what they've done to change lives. TOMS is a company that was built from day one with the explicit commitment to a "one for one" policy of giving away a pair of shoes to a person in need for every pair of shoes that is purchased. As of late 2019, according to a report it released, TOMS had donated more than ninety-five million pairs of shoes to people across thirty-eight states and eighty-two countries and was hoping to reach one hundred million pairs in 2020. Its line of eyewear, founded in 2011, had funded 780,000 sight restorations; and TOMS Roasting Co., which sells coffee beans, had provided over one hundred million liters of safe, clean water to communities in need since its founding in 2014. Founder Blake Mycoskie explains, "The 'why' of TOMS—using business to improve lives—is bigger than myself, the shoes we sell, or any future products we might launch."[28] And he makes sure his employees know that.[29]

Empower employees and community members to do their own thing.

A couple of years ago, Cisco switched the way it supports employee philanthropy from a centralized approach in which the company matched employee donations to a limited number of organizations of their own choosing, to empowering employees to make their own choices. Employees can now choose the organizations that *they* want to support, and, as a result, there are thousands of organizations for which Cisco matches donations in its Be the Bridge campaign. Employee giving has skyrocketed.[30]

Putting your employees in direct touch with the beneficiaries of their actions is another way of empowering them. At TOMS, every full-time employee gets to go on a giving trip after their first year, again after their third year, and then every three years after that. They assist nonprofit partners that are conducting eye exams or distributing shoes in Nepal, Honduras, and other countries.[31]

Cultivate meaning among your employees to help them thrive. Having a sense of purpose and connectedness helps put a dent in the isolation and loneliness that too many face. Find ways to share your purpose. Get community members as well as your employees into the game so that they are actively communicating meaning through storytelling. Meaning is a powerful motivator, as so much research shows, and it ripples throughout your community, lifting people, boosting performance, increasing employee retention, and adding to the bottom line. In the next chapter, we'll explore how contributing to the well-being of your community pays off.

Boost Well-Being

Treat those around you with respect and dignity and they will thrive. Treat them with unkindness and they will fall apart.

—Richard Branson

On September 23, 2016, Marriott International acquired Starwood Hotels & Resorts Worldwide, becoming the world's largest hotel chain in the process. Marriott spent over $13 billion in this acquisition. Despite beginning with high hopes, mergers and acquisitions (M&A) like this one often fall apart, in large part because when the cultures are very different, as was the case with these two companies, it can be hard to integrate them. There were particular concerns about the merger between Marriott, given its reputation for discipline and consistency, and Starwood, known for its unbridled experimentation and "coolness." The title of a *New York Times* article captured this dilemma: "Can Marriott Keep Starwood's Culture of Cool, and Its Customers?"

Marriott and Starwood are examples of what a group of researchers who have studied the challenges of such mergers describe as tight and loose cultures, respectively. A tight culture, according to these researchers, is known for its emphasis on rules and discipline, consistency and routine, and hierarchical structure; a loose culture values flexibility and autonomy in decision-making among its employees, openness and creativity, and favors a more egalitarian approach. In their study of over 4,500 international mergers between 1989 and 2013, the researchers found that the acquiring organizations in mergers with tight-loose differences saw their return on assets decrease by an average of 0.6 percentage points three years after the merger, or $200 million in net income per year. Those with especially large tight-loose differences saw their net income drop by over $600 million per year.[1]

Among the reasons for these disappointing results is that trying to merge two different cultures can tank employee engagement, the attention and absorption that people bring to the job, and undermine performance. This is what happened, the researchers saw, when they studied Amazon's acquisition of Whole Foods in 2017. Amazon was renowned for its structure and discipline and for its centralized decision-making, while Whole Foods was known for empowering each store's employees to make decisions that reflected their customers' tastes, and for its openness to experimentation. One year after the merger, which was when the researchers' article was published, there was unrest and unhappiness among some employees and customers at Whole Foods. Amazon's rigid, data-driven, centralized inventory procedures, which did not take into account local preferences, had resulted in frequent food shortages, and some employees who were used to much more autonomy than they were allowed under Amazon were angry and unhappy. In 2018, a group within the company sent out an email blast to all the employees urging them to support the effort to join a union. The unionization effort wasn't successful.[2] To this day, efforts to unionize have continued to alarm Amazon so much that they have developed elaborate strategies to defeat such efforts, including an algorithm that predicts which stores are most likely to try to unionize. In 2018, Whole Foods dropped from *Fortune*'s 100 Best Companies to Work For list for the first time in two decades.[3]

Yet despite the doubts, the Marriott-Starwood merger had a markedly different outcome. Two years into the massive M&A, which brought together over 750,000 employees in total (approximately 350,000 from Starwood), these two rivals defied the odds to become a global family.

Thirty hotel brands now fall under the Marriott umbrella with more than 7,000 properties in more than 130 countries.[4] Post-merger, total shareholder returns at Marriott increased while the organization's customer loyalty program has grown significantly. Moreover, surveys of employee engagement have revealed a steady pattern of two cultures becoming one. At the time of the merger, the Starwood hotels had strong employee engagement scores. But Marriott's hotels had even better scores, about five points higher. By early 2020, within three years of the merger, they had closed the gap, and the scores of the two groups were equal.

David Rodriguez, Marriott's global chief human resources officer, feels they succeeded because they were able to identify and emphasize the commonalities between the two cultures—with both cultures having a commitment to the well-being of their employees. He told me that he credits much of the success of their merger to Marriott's unwavering focus on taking care of its people, something that was part of Marriott's DNA, going back to the culture created by founder J. Willard Marriott, who is often quoted as saying, "Take good care of your employees, and they will take good care of the customers, and the customers will come back." As far back as the 1930s, Marriott's founders placed such a priority on their employees' health that they hired a company doctor as the business expanded. That legacy was continued in the TakeCare program Marriott launched in 2010. When it began, the focus of TakeCare was on promoting physical well-being through strategies that included stress management, exercising and fitness, nutrition and weight management, and smoking cessation; financial fitness was a focus, too. As you'll read below, TakeCare has since expanded into many other areas of well-being, not just personal and community-wide but societal. And it has become an integral part of the Marriott culture and identity. As David Rodriguez says, "We spend a huge portion of our lives with our employer. That's why this notion of promoting employee wellbeing is so important— you're literally partners with your employees' life partners."[5]

Employees at Starwood's headquarters got a taste of Marriott's culture and what to expect during their very first introduction to its senior leaders. "[Chairman] Bill Marriott and [the late CEO] Arne Sorenson went to the offices and spent hours shaking hands with every single employee," Rodriguez recounted. "Someone asked, 'Don't they know there's about to be a huge press conference about the merger?' But to them, that was the most important event."[6]

As one Starwood hotel general manager proclaimed at an internal global recognition event, "I was worried at first, but when I went online and found the TakeCare site, I knew it was going to be okay. They believe what we believe. You have to take care of people." It's what enables even a cool and edgy millennial brand like Moxy Hotels to fit comfortably into a broad portfolio that includes established iconic brands such as Ritz-Carlton and St. Regis. While the personalities of the brand cultures could not appear to be more different, they share the same mission of hospitality and the same core values, which put the fundamental human needs of their employees first.[7]

Marriott's core values have lent themselves to remarkable stability. Recently, the Great Place to Work Institute found unprecedented volatility in its culture audits of organizations, with some companies dropping precipitously. That was not the case with Marriott, however, which was one of only six organizations to remain on the list every year since it began in 1998.[8]

Marriott's commitment to its employees takes many different forms.

Opportunity

Because Marriott recognizes that every human being wants the opportunity to grow, it provides paths to build new skills. An Emerging Leader Program singles out high-performing employees and puts them into "a year-long development and mentoring program. More than 1,500 [associates] have gone through or are in ELP; more than half of the participants are women, and more than a third minorities."[9] Marriott International's Voyage Global Leadership Development Program is another of their initiatives aimed at skill building. Designed to arm recent university graduates with practical hands-on leadership experience in the hospitality industry, it is a twelve-to-eighteen-month program, offered in more than fifty countries, to employees in accounting and finance, culinary, engineering, event operations, food and beverage operations, room operations, and other disciplines. Participants across the world collaborate and compete in online simulations that teach them about what it takes to run a hotel. This provides fuel for a community of hungry learners eager to get a jump start into junior management roles. Marriott Development Academy, another training program, also helps prepare aspiring managers for leadership roles. It's customizable so that each person can choose the training most relevant to their personal and professional interests—a big menu based on the specifics of their appetite for learning.[10]

One typical beneficiary of Marriott's various training programs is Chi Nguyen, who is now the rooms division manager at the Renaissance Riverside Hotel Saigon in Vietnam. Associates at this hotel completed an average of fifty-three hours of training in 2019. Training included a weeklong program called "To the Journey," during which associates spent a day learning about the knowledge and skills required for a job different from their own, chatting with senior managers in different departments and hotels, and gleaning insights on career development from conversations with general managers.

Chi Nguyen began her own career at this hotel in 1999, working as a waitress. Thanks to the various trainings she received, she was eventually able to transfer to front office, where she served as a guest service agent for five years, then was promoted to club floor shift supervisor, and to club floor manager a year later. She continued to advance—to assistant front office manager, and then in 2010, to front office manager. In her new job as rooms division manager, she leads the front office, housekeeping, and health club team, with seventy-seven people reporting to her. She's come a very long way in her two-decade-plus career with the hotel. Director of human resources at the Renaissance Saigon, Minh Tam Quang Thi, raved about how skillfully Nguyen was able to leverage the experiences and development she received in Marriott's core training programs. Even now she continues to update her knowledge and skills through Marriott's various online management trainings. And as Minh Tam Quang Thi noted, she's also passing on what she's learned by training many of the managers at legacy Starwood hotels that are opening in Vietnam.

Like Chi Nguyen, those who are already managers at Marriott help train those who are aspiring to fill similar positions. They are also encouraged to recognize their fellow employees' potential and smooth the way for them to fulfill it. Abelino Martinez started working as a lobby greeter for Courtyard Marina Del Rey (a Marriott property when he was still in high school. At one point, his manager sat him down and said, "You really show that you have a passion for this company. How can I help you?" Martinez explained that his priority was completing his schooling so that he could advance. His manager made sure that his schedule allowed him to do that, which enabled him to continue with the company while he studied for a degree in business management. "It was something that I was thankful for," Martinez says, "and really something that I remembered. I do the same now with all my hosts." Armed with his degree, Martinez was promoted to manager of housekeeping at the Renaissance Los Angeles Airport, and then at the Irvine Spectrum.[11]

Another example of the way the company's employees encourage their co-workers in their ambitions came to me via DeeAnn Hobbs, executive chef at the Renaissance World Golf Village Resort in Florida. Hobbs told me about a woman who started working in housekeeping at this resort fifteen years ago. She had immigrated from Albania, and this was her first job in the US. When she said she wanted to work more hours and expressed an interest in the kitchen area, where Hobbs worked, Hobbs took her under her wing and taught her basic kitchen skills, while also giving her an overview of how the culinary industry worked. The woman did really well and enjoyed her work, but since her English wasn't very good, her prospects were limited. Knowing that the woman had real potential, Hobbs arranged for her to get English lessons. Once her English had improved, she became a supervisor in Hobbs's kitchen, before eventually leaving to become the sous-chef at a retirement community restaurant—"right down the road." But the bond she developed with the woman who was her boss continued even after she left. In fact, the very day we spoke, Hobbs had received a text from this woman telling her about her promotion to management.

Regardless of how enormous (or global) a company is, community is possible. If community is a priority and consistently developed, you can achieve it. As these examples illustrate, it often begins at the tribe, or local, level, with team leaders, or Marriott champions spearheading efforts.

Diversity and Inclusiveness (D&I)

Marriott wants everyone to feel that they belong—that there is a place for them in the Marriott family, and that there is opportunity for them to move up in the organization. One of the first things David Rodriguez looks at in the company's annual global census, in which roughly 345,000 people participate, is whether there are significant differences in employee well-being based on race, gender, or other demographics "Do I have any constituencies who are feeling disenfranchised?" he always asks himself.

Rodriguez explained that he relies not just on metrics but a gut feeling to assess how well Marriott is doing on the D&I front. He likes to check out the company cafeteria, for example, and see whether people from different ethnic and racial groups are mingling, which he views as a sign of health. "It's easy for me to spot a place where inclusion's probably on the low end because you see people of the same ilk flocking together. I don't have a direct measurement of that, but I can almost guarantee that's a bad problem for a company."[12] He has a strong commitment to inclusion because he knows from his own childhood what it's like to feel that you're not fitting in. Growing up in the South Bronx, he remembers, "I was a fair-skinned, Puerto Rican with reddish-brown hair." The Latino kids ignored him because he didn't look like them and didn't speak Spanish very well. So when he went to elementary school in Harlem, he thought of himself as African American, like his friends.[13] "A lot of my philosophy about diversity and inclusion is from personal experience—being a person who did not fit into any constituency, but still having the very human need to want to fit in."[14]

Marriott also has a strong commitment to diversity, including being an equal opportunity place for women. Stephanie Linnartz, president at Marriott, believes that the fact that there are so many women in senior positions at Marriott was one of the elements of Marriott's corporate culture that Starwood employees embraced right away. Currently, four out of Marriott's eleven board members and, prior to a recent retirement, 50 percent of the CEO's direct reports were women—unheard of for a Fortune 200 company. Forty percent of the top 850 people in the company—vice presidents and above—are women. Overall, 65 percent of Marriott's employees are minorities, and 31 percent of the company's mid-level managers are minorities in the US.[15] Marriott is well ahead of industry peers when it comes to the diversity of its executive ranks, and was recognized as the number one company for diversity across industries on the 2020 DiversityInc Top 50 Companies for Diversity list.[16] Additional diversity recognition in 2020 includes Best Places to Work for Disability Inclusion, Best Places to Work for LGBT Equality, Top 50 Best Companies for Latinas to Work for in the US, and many others.

The Three Pillars of Caring

Marriott's TakeCare program, which originated with an emphasis on physical health, has over the years become a much more comprehensive approach to well-being that now rests on three pillars—me, my co-workers, and my company's role in society. "Me" involves traditional wellness and lifestyle programs (physical fitness, weight loss, emotional well-being, meditation etc.). Since the wellness part of the TakeCare program is meant to become a way of life, not an occasional thing, in 2019 Marriott introduced TakeCare Level30, a gamified app, available to its employees and its guests as well as the general public, which offers well-being challenges to help build positive behaviors into a daily routine. Its name alludes to the notion that it takes thirty days to build a habit.

"My co-workers" consists of programs designed to connect employees with each other, including the Happiness Hero Card, in which a co-worker recognizes a co-worker for anything from her skills to her helpfulness to her style; Buddy Up, one of its many team-building exercises; On the Mend, which offers ideas for those feeling down or under the weather; and High Five Fridays, in which employees take ninety seconds to share their "highs" for the week with their team.

The "my company" part of Take Care involves contributing to society, which many company programs have done by tackling local projects in their communities. In Thailand, for instance, the JW Marriott Phuket Resort and Spa spearheaded the cause of marine conservation by creating the Mai Khao Marine Turtle Foundation, which raises funds for the protection of the endangered giant leatherback turtles that nest nearby. It promotes clean beaches and seas and educates the public on how to sustain the delicate ecosystems that the turtles live in.

The JW Marriott hotel also partnered with another Marriott hotel in the area—Le Méridien Phuket Beach Resort—to support sea turtle conservation, with a program for rescuing eggs from surrounding beaches, providing a safe home for the eggs to hatch, and releasing young turtles into the sea.[17]

Le Méridien Phuket Beach Resort has made other kinds of contributions to the local community, too. On Earth Day the hotel hosts a 2K ocean swim for the community, with registration fees donated to Trash Hero, which supports beach cleanups. The hotel has supported ten schools with its in-house engineering team. In one local school the team repaired the library, the students' canteen, and the teachers' meeting room; painted walls, tables, and chairs; and provided basic equipment the school needed. The hotel helped another school with a large renovation so that it could reopen after being closed for three years due to budgetary constraints.

Purpose

Marriott recognizes that one way of fulfilling its employees' emotional (and even spiritual) needs is by providing them with a sense of purpose. Serve 360, a social impact platform, is addressing some of the world's most pressing social, environmental, and economic issues. Local hotels customize their approach. For example, Rodriguez told me about a harrowing visit he made to Bali, where he was "a nervous wreck in car on roads because people would be driving right next to a woman and child on a bike or scooter without helmets." Out of experiences like that, Marriott developed an initiative for the Ritz-Carlton in Bali to donate helmets to local children and invite them to the hotel to decorate the helmets.

Another example of Marriott's focus on empowering its employees to deal with important societal issues is the training it offers them through its human trafficking awareness program. Because hotels are often used by human traffickers, Marriott has trained its staff in what to watch for and has broken that instruction down by role, since what a front desk clerk sees may differ from the signs that a housekeeper or bartender might observe. Jozsef Ladanyi, director of loss prevention at the St. Pancras Renaissance Hotel London, is one of these trainers.

Born in Debrecen, Hungary, Ladanyi got a job and moved to Budapest in 1996, working as a doorman at Budapest Marriott Hotel by night, learning English during the day. After cycling through various training programs, Ladanyi was asked by a former manager to come to London in 2005, where Ladanyi eventually became a customer service manager at one of Marriott's London hotels. Ladanyi decided, in the wake of the London bombings in July 2005, that he wanted to focus on hotel security, specifically on how hotels could deter terrorism. So the training that he received for his current job, which involves security matters of all kinds, including organizing the security details for high-profile visits, carrying out investigations into possible crimes, and planning effective emergency responses, has made him a very careful observer, someone who knows just what to look for to evaluate possible threats. His past experience as a doorman proved useful, too. "As a doorman you work closely with security. You're the first point of contact, reading people, and understanding the situation," Ladanyi told me. "Everyone on the floor—not just security—needs to be switched on." He added, "Associates need to feel comfortable with you so that they have confidence to come to you if they notice something is not right."

In 2016 Ladanyi received information about a pedophile who was using the very impressive St. Pancras Renaissance hotel lobby to meet with the underage girls he was grooming. He and his team monitored what was going on and reported it to the police, who wanted footage of the potential trafficker, which Ladanyi was able to supply. Thanks in part to that evidence, the police arrested the trafficker, and he was sentenced to four years in prison.

In 2018, just two and a half years after he had been arrested (he was released early for good behavior) he came back to their hotel. "One of the supervisors in the lounge area noticed the guy and remembered the circulation [internal security awareness notice warning colleagues of a certain criminal or crime targeting hotels] from years ago. She came rushing to tell us!" Ladanyi told me.

Ladanyi's team observed him that day, and although they didn't see him doing anything wrong, Ladanyi advised the police, who re-sent the circulation on this suspect. Less than a month later, the offender reserved a table at the St. Pancras Renaissance, and the lounge supervisor notified Ladanyi. His team watched closely as two young Muslim girls sat down with the trafficker. Ladanyi knew that one of the conditions of this trafficker's release from prison was that he was not permitted to be in the company of underage girls, so Ladanyi contacted the police, who apprehended the trafficker. "We intervened and he went straight back to prison."

Tony Foran, the detective who arrested the trafficker, came to see Ladanyi a week after the incident. He said that as a former police officer himself, the trafficker "knew the ins and outs, and how to cover his tracks." So Foran "was amazed that a civilian got those results," and emailed the then Marriott CEO, the late Arne Sorenson, to express his gratitude.

In January 2017, Marriott made human trafficking awareness training mandatory for on-property staff for both managed and franchised properties. Within two years they had trained five hundred thousand employees how to spot the signs of human trafficking and how to respond if they do. "Hotel workers wouldn't necessarily see a human trafficker visibly restraining a victim; they would typically see a scenario that is much more nuanced and harder to detect if you don't know what to look for," said Rodriguez. "That's why helping hotel workers identify the signs of sexual exploitation and forced labor is so important. This knowledge gives them confidence that they can do something to help." Because Marriott believe so strongly in its importance, the company has made the program, which has directly resulted in the removal of many young people from dangerous situations all over the world, available to other hotels, including Marriott's competitors, who are using it to train tens of thousands of people.

There have been times when Marriott's commitment to employee well-being was tested, but the company remained true to its values. After 9/11, when the global travel industry plummeted, Marriott went from a 75 percent to a 5 percent occupancy rate, and employee hours had to be cut. To make sure that employees didn't lose out on their insurance and other benefits, Arne Sorenson, backed by Bill Marriott, waived the thirty-hours-per-week minimum requirement for health and benefits coverage.

Something similar happened when the recession hit in 2008 and many Marriott employees began to lose their health insurance because they didn't meet the minimum hours to qualify for benefits. David Rodriguez remembers the morning he brought the problem up at a staff meeting. "I was just 30 seconds into my plea when [Bill Marriott] cut it off and said, 'Well, this is obvious what we need to do. Suspend that rule.'"[18]

Unfortunately, the challenge of navigating the devastation wrought by

COVID-19 has been far more difficult than anything Marriott has ever faced—worse than the effects of 9/11 and the 2008 recession combined. With governments around the world restricting travel, Marriott was forced to furlough some employees in March of 2020, which allowed employees to retain their insurance and other benefits. With a loss of $234 million in the second quarter, or 72 percent of revenue, the hotel planned to lay off 17 percent of its corporate staff, and in December 2020, informed over eight hundred non-union employees that they would lose their jobs in March.[19] In a video address to employees, shareholders, and customers, their late CEO Arne Sorenson explained the actions the company was having to take and also noted that neither he nor Bill Marriott would be drawing a salary in 2020 and that the salaries of the rest of the executives were being cut by 50 percent.[20] Though the pandemic led to employee losses, many more people would have been laid off had Sorenson and Marriott not given up their salaries and cut other executives' pay.

Rooted in its founders' beliefs, Marriott and its leadership team prioritize employee well-being, which drives engagement and loyalty, which, in turn, drives retention and better service, which drives customer experience, which drives revenue. Marriott's data reveal that properties that score higher in employee engagement have better financial results.[21] "In the service industry, you're only as good as the wellbeing of your people," Rodriguez puts it.[22]

As you'll see from the next example, you don't need to be a mammoth within your industry, loaded with resources, to create a culture of caring in your company. The small but mighty Motley Fool, a company dedicated to helping the world invest better, boasts an award-winning culture that focuses on employee well-being. Though Marriott and the Motley Fool may seem very different, because they share essential values about what matters, they feel oddly similar.

Motley Fool

I first met Tom Gardner, the co-founder and CEO of the Motley Fool, at the same Google re:Work event where I met Astro Teller. Tom presented on the importance of culture—and the role it plays in the company's investment strategies. The Motley Fool has been studying investments for over twenty-five years, consistently crushing the market over that period. (Its Stock Advisor program Motley Fool generated a 505 percent return since 2002 versus S&P's 101 percent return.) Gardner told us that its core advantage is that unlike Wall Street, which thinks short term, Motley Fool advisors look very, very closely at an organization's ongoing culture. Referring to the notion of leadership guru Peter Drucker that culture eats strategy for breakfast, Gardner joked, "Or maybe culture just gets a seat at the breakfast table with strategy. If they're even close, then you and we and all of us in every organization we're involved in—the company we work at, the nonprofits that we volunteer with, the schools that we interact with—we have to be trying to innovate our culture as rapidly as anything else that's happening in that organization."

Later that evening on a bus ride back to our hotel after dinner, I had the opportunity to sit with Gardner and my friend Amy Wrzesniewski, the three of us sharing stories and laughing together. Amy quietly nudged me. "You really need to study them and their culture, Chris," she whispered. "They're living it. Go visit their office and see for yourself."

Soon after, I followed her advice. And she was so right! Founded in 1993 by brothers Tom and David Gardner, the Motley Fool, with 575 employees,[23] helps millions of people attain financial freedom through its website, podcasts, books, newspaper column, radio show, mutual funds, and premium investing services. From its early years, Tom and David believed that employee engagement would drive motivation and, ultimately, performance. Because they want their employees to be Fools for life, they have gone to great lengths to ensure Fools' happiness and well-being through their mission and their work culture.

The result? The Motley Fool's turnover rate is less than 2 percent, which is remarkable by industry standards.[iv] The company has also racked up a

---

iv   The company's growth—from 375 to 575 employees this year—continues to provide opportunities for employees. It may also help that the Motley Fool enables meaning through job crafting (see chapter 5). Gardner has asked employees, "Think about what you would (and wouldn't) do if you could take a 15 percent pay cut, but design your own role." The Motley Fool doesn't cut people's pay but does want them to design and engage in meaningful work.

trophy case of culture awards, including landing on *Inc.*'s Best Workplaces 2020 list. But its achievement is about much more than awards—it's a feeling you sense immediately if you've ever spent time in the Motley Fool's office. One Fool wrote in an engagement survey, "If crisis reveals character—and I believe it does—then the connections and care I've witnessed and been a part of are a testament to the quality of the people at our company. I believe we are unmatched as a collective group of truly good hearted humans."[24] This could explain why Motley Fool's co-founders, David and Tom Gardner, were among the twenty-eight people at twenty-three companies named "Heroes of Conscious Capitalism" by the Conscious Capitalism organization, whose credo states: "Conscious businesses have trusting, authentic, innovative and caring cultures that make working there a source of both personal growth and professional fulfillment. They endeavor to create financial, intellectual, social, cultural, emotional, spiritual, physical and ecological wealth for all their stakeholders."[25]

The founders' values are reflected in the company's name, the Motley Fool, which, as Tom Gardner explains on its website, "is in homage to the one character in Shakespearean literature—the court jester—who could speak the truth to the king and queen without having his or her head lopped off. The Fools of yore entertained the court with humor that instructed as it amused. More importantly, the Fool was never afraid to question conventional wisdom." Clearly, Fools are expected to be as original and fearless—and honest—as any of Shakespeare's Fools, who play critical roles in both his tragedies and his comedies. This helps to explain why "trust" in its employees is one of the hallmarks of its culture.

Trust

The trust Motley Fool extends to its employees is expressed in a number of ways, including their work schedules. Employees have extraordinary flexibility and discretion about where and when they do their work. As Tom Gardner

---

(re:Work with Google. [2014, November 10]. *Motley Fool's Tom Gardner on Investing in Culture* [Video]. YouTube. https://youtu.be/DGqzRUfH52o.)

explains, "To unleash the talent that will expand your company's potential, you have to institute work schedules that are as flexible as possible."[26] This trust is also reflected in the Motley Fool's unlimited vacation policy, which began in 1993 (the year the company launched). Most Fools take between three and four weeks, but as former communications manager Laurie Street put it, "No one in HR is counting our vacation time as long as we get our job done." And if someone "needs an extra day to get over jet lag, or to travel on off-peak days," that is also up to the employee. It's assumed that employees will use good judgment and not violate the company's trust.

A similar approach applies to sick days. Gardner doesn't believe in having a set number of days for sick leave. To him, it's simple: "If you're sick, please stay home." He believes "this is common sense. We're all adults here."[27] Staying home is not just for the well-being of the employee but for the rest of the staff, too, since coming in sick puts everyone else at risk. And if a manager feels that someone is taking advantage of this policy, the time to address it is in a performance review. But Gardner doesn't worry about this problem coming up very often, because he feels confident that if you've established your organization's meaning or purpose, tribe members will want to come to work—it may even be hard to get them to stay away. Tom told me about one employee who complained about the Motley Fool trying to get people to stay at home for several days during a bad snowstorm. "C'mon," the employee urged, "I really want to come to the office and see other Fools!"

For Tom, sick-day policies are "classic examples of managing to the lowest performers. That's never a good idea. It makes *everyone* feel low. Distrust is far more dangerous to a company than days off for the common cold."[28] The Motley Fool is also generous with maternity and paternity leave, offering new parents up to four months of leave time during a child's first year.

The Motley Fool's workplace has a playful appearance, with all kinds of toys and fitness gear and board games scattered throughout the space. Chief people officer Lee Burbage once described it this way: "From my desk right now I can see 1) large inflatable pool toys (swan, orca, shark, walrus, turtle) 2) a Nerf gun battle 3) several art pieces created by Fools at a happy hour 4) Five board games 5) wizard's chess, wands and broomsticks (Firebolt and Nimbus) 6) a dozen jester hats."[29] But this playfulness does not come at the expense of effectiveness. Quite the opposite. As Tom Gardner explains, "At the heart of our craziness we are building a culture of trust," because this is the kind of culture that "makes our Fools happy, improves recruiting, and leads to great employee retention and a healthy office environment."

The purpose of trust, Gardner says, is as much about doing well in business as it is about doing good: "The part that many people don't understand is that trust equals speed. Professional trust is very closely related to productivity and output. Trust in the workplace leads to faster decisions, higher collaboration, and greater autonomy. In a high trust relationship, you focus on the future, and everything moves faster. You can say the wrong thing and still be understood. You can make a mistake and recover quickly—and your team will help you. In a low trust relationship, the focus is on the past, mistakes are hashed and rehashed, time is wasted choosing the right words, and then reversing them. Your ability to cover yourself overshadows the need to move forward and focus on the future, and your team will blame you."[30] After decades of work with leaders, Stephen M. R. Covey, author of *The Speed of Trust*, has found this, too. He says trust is "the most overlooked, misunderstood, underutilized asset to enable performance."

Gardner's advice to other employers: "If you are looking at your own corporate culture—reinforcing, rebuilding, reframing—don't start with fun. Start with trust." Neuroeconomist Paul Zak would agree. Quantifying trust by measuring the brain's production of oxytocin, a chemical that switches on the cooperation networks in the brain, he has found that compared with people at low-trust companies, people in high-trust companies report 74 percent less stress, 50 percent higher productivity, and 76 percent more engagement.[31]

Gardner also understands the importance of having employees who are healthy, which explains why in 2013 the Motley Fool hired someone whose title is chief wellness officer.

Wellness

Over the years it gradually dawned on Tom Gardner that, due to the sedentary nature of their work, his employees were gaining weight. According to Samantha Whiteside, the person who currently has the chief wellness officer title, it was called the Foolish 15, because that's how many pounds on average the Fools were gaining after being hired.[32] So over time Gardner began investing in wellness efforts. One of the first steps he took was to remove all the soda and candy vending machines. He also convinced one of his employees, who had been planning to leave and become a fitness trainer, to stay on the job and dedicate part of his day to personal training and group fitness classes for the other Fools.

When Whiteside was hired to become the company's full-time chief wellness officer, she created what is now known as the FoolFocus program, which encompasses four categories: exercise, nutrition, health promotion and disease prevention, and brain health.[33] FoolFocus offers all employees Foolish Fitness classes (boot camp–style classes), yoga classes, Zumba classes, and twice-weekly open gym where Fools enjoy basketball, floor hockey, soccer, and volleyball together. Fools also have access to personal training sessions and highly subsidized twice-a-week massage sessions. Eighty-nine percent of the employees participated in the classes offered through FoolFocus in the first two years, and that percentage has grown since then. Whiteside also devises one-month challenges like the Fool-wide Push-Up Wellness Challenge the company held one year, which had a collective goal of one hundred thousand push-ups for the month, and, dipping into one of the other "buckets" of its wellness program, a philanthropy challenge where Fools tracked hours of volunteer work and charitable donations.

To encourage Fools to utilize stress management resources, which Whiteside considers to be crucial to brain health, she brings in employee assistance program counselors at least twice a year to answer questions, and each Fool gets six free counseling sessions a year to address a specific issue. Other programs, like an active book club and speaker series with world-renowned entrepreneurs and businesspeople such as John Mackey, and the Bookie Monster, which gives employees free books, are part of the company's emphasis on keeping its employees mentally active, engaged, and healthy.

Because the Motley Fool recognizes the dangers of employee burnout, it offers four-to-eight-week sabbaticals for employees serving ten years or more. Workers who have been there at least a year also get a shot at a leave through the Fool's Errand—a program that David Gardner came up with. Each month there is a Fool's Errand drawing whose winner will receive $1,000 to spend on anything they want—on the condition that they leave the office and disconnect completely from work for two consecutive weeks out of the following four. This not only gives the employee an unexpected break but also encourages employees to make sure that if they need to be out for a much less pleasant but equally unexpected reason—illness or a family emergency—their team members will know how to fill the gap in their absence so that the workflow will not be interrupted.

To encourage healthy behaviors on a daily basis, Motley Fool keeps its refrigerators filled with organic snacks that anyone can take without charge. Healthy items in the cafeteria are also either free or highly subsidized, by as much as 90 percent. WW (formerly Weight Watchers) is subsidized by 50 percent. The company has brought in a nutritionist to speak to employees interested in healthy eating. And, multiple times a year, a food cart gets brought out to deliver tasty treats to employees at their desks—often it's to celebrate an achievement. Each year Fools are given a certain amount to spend on anything wellness related—from bikes to hiking shoes, swimming lessons to nutrition or meditation classes, whatever form fitness takes for them.[34]

Though health is the primary goal, employees describe how their fitness programs build greater collaboration and camaraderie. Stepping up to—and often struggling through—tough challenges unites them and brings them closer together. Gardner wishes the company had hired its wellness coordinator fifteen years ago. As he summed it up: "The net result is a convenient solution for our employees that yields higher productivity, lower health insurance costs, and greater levels of satisfaction."[35]

A Fool's Welcome: Foolientation

From the start, Motley Fool went to great lengths to integrate new employees into the community through Foolientation. Before new Fools even start working, their managers will call to congratulate them and answer any questions they may have.[36] New Fools also get a welcome email before their first day on the job, but it's different from what you might expect. It includes something fun for them, a gift card for dinner out with their spouse, family, or friends, or maybe for funds they could use toward decorating their office desk. The Motley Fool wants new employees to feel good about their job from their very first day. "Taken care of" would be another way to describe it.[37]

Before showing up at the job, the new Fool must fill out a questionnaire asking about the Fool's favorite things—foods, sports, movies, vacation spots, hobbies, and more. Upon arrival, the Fool will then find a desk decked out with items that reflect these preferences. For example, a new Fool who loves traveling may get a scratch-off map or a book about the best places to visit in the world. The greeting will also often include a huge stock of the Fool's favorite snacks. So one employee was greeted at his desk with "Steve!!" spelled out in colorful Starburst candies, along with a huge bag of them, a couple of books on zoos, and plenty of Motley Fool swag. Another Fool was welcomed with a stack of hard hats with the Dodgers logo on them, lots of playful fortune-telling games, a rubber palm of a hand (to read), and the biggest bag of gummy bears I've ever seen. These personal touches are fun for the new Fool, and they also provide colleagues with a snapshot of the new hire's personality and help to identify mutual interests.

On their first day, which is always a Friday, Fools receive a First Day Survival Kit and are taken on an office tour led by a Leadership Fool to highlight the company's high-performance culture. Lunch with Fools outside of their department helps them to make company-wide connections, and the day ends with a team party and a send-off with a "Treat Yo Self"—one hundred dollars to spend on dinner. The second day of Foolientation includes an interactive office operations tour to learn how the office functions. The Fool also meets their Fool Buddy—a tenured Fool who will regularly check in to answer questions. The new Fool also completes a Foolish Scavenger Hunt, which involves riddles and a search for clues about the Motley Fool community.

Community and Collaboration

Tom and David Gardner and their team do a lot to cultivate community among employees so that they'll feel the same way as the Fool who was dying to come to work and see the other Fools. They offer a multitude of resources for connecting with each other: social and sporting events ranging from playing on a local softball team to hitting up concerts on the weekends. Todd Etter, one of the Motley Fool's founders and the man with the title chief collaboration officer—the first person in corporate America to have such a title—uses a variety of other techniques to bring Fools together, some of them learned from his decades as an improv teacher. He's introduced team-building exercises, company-wide puzzle hunts, and board games that take place at least three times a week in the cafeteria. Fools from all over the company come together, get to know each other, learn to collaborate, and build relationships as they play these games.[38]

As an incentive to get to know each other in an enjoyable way, the Motley Fool offers its employees ten-dollar Starbucks cards. The catch: Fools must use the cards to treat a fellow co-worker—ideally one they don't know well—to a drink. Tom Gardner encourages using the cards as a chance to learn about others' projects; identify best practices their fellow Fools use; and collaborate on challenges or ideas. Company-wide challenges can bring awesome employee abilities to light, from impressive handwriting skills to puzzle-solving mastery and cooking talents. On one occasion, a chef-turned-Fool hosted a butchery course to much applause.

One of their most memorable contests was when Gardner, who felt strongly that bonds between employees were crucial to creating a better culture, challenged all of the company's employees to learn the names of all the other employees in order to unlock the 20 percent annual bonus—the catch was that everyone had to participate for the bonus to kick in. The Fools rose to that challenge and the bonus was delivered.

Motley Fool has also implemented a peer-to-peer employee-recognition program through the rewards platform created by Kazoo. To celebrate each other's accomplishment, Fools can reward their co-workers with "Gold" (which can later be converted to cash or gift certificates) for any action they feel worthy—for example helping with projects, hitting a major deadline, or mentoring. Kazoo's live feed allows employees to read all posted compliments. It's a way to provide feedback, spur recognition, and boost employee engagement.

To cultivate and sustain community, the Motley Fool hosts many different kinds of social outings and events. Each employee's work anniversary is marked with a gift and a balloon. Special anniversaries (five-, ten-, fifteen-, and twenty-year anniversaries) are denoted with a bouquet of balloons. The Motley Fool also holds monthly birthday celebrations. Each month, a small group of Fools who were recognized for performance are selected to attend an exclusive off-site event. It could be a soccer match, a concert, or an arts event, but whatever it is, it is meant to create a strong sense of collaboration among the Fools who are brought together. The company's annual retreat, Foolapalooza, offers another opportunity to spark new friendships. The full day of business meetings culminates with a celebration at a local restaurant.

Inclusiveness and Equality

Tom told me that early on, leadership felt the company was doing well—80 percent of employees reported being engaged, which was well above the average. But when he thought about it, he realized that that was like having eight out of ten rowers rowing hard, pushing toward the goal, while the other two, who are disengaged and potentially causing all sorts of problems, are basically just whacking their paddles around, sometimes against the actions of the rest of the paddlers in the boat. Since then Tom has had the company put more effort into asking how people are feeling—whether they feel included, whether they feel like their voices are heard. The Motley Fool now does quick, very short pulse surveys (which can be done on a phone or computer), which it reports have been incredibly helpful in tracking employee mindset and engagement. Analyzing this pulse survey data by demographics has been particularly illuminating. The company learned that while statistics on feeling psychologically safe to speak up were remarkably high, they were significantly lower for women. Being aware of the differences in how certain swaths of its community feel has allowed the Motley Fool to make adjustments quickly.

For example, after seeing data like this, along with research illuminating how salary negotiations have played a role in the gender pay gap, the Motley Fool introduced Ask for a Raise Day. Historically, men ask for raises more frequently than women do, and men's requests are met more often. Women risk all sorts of backlash for merely asking.[39] The Motley Fool wanted everyone—extraverts and introverts, all genders, races, and cultures—to feel comfortable asking for a raise. Gardner explains, "We want to try to reduce the bias that can create an obstacle to the success for any member of our team or any of our stakeholders." So he proposed to other executives: "What if we flip it open and have *everyone* ask for a raise?"[40]

Kara Chambers, vice president of people insights, and Lee Burbage, chief people officer, spoke about the program on a Motley Fool podcast, sharing ideas for how to participate. Burbage thought one internal Fool had a great way of figuring out the value you're adding. He encouraged people to think about what would happen if you weren't here, if you weren't doing the things you're doing. Employees who chose to participate could get coaching from Chambers and her team, for an evaluation of their position and an estimate of what would be a reasonable salary range, before they met with their manager to make the big ask. Gardner sweetened things, too. Even those who didn't succeed in getting their desired raise or promotion would be awarded $200 just for asking. About half of the Motley Fool's employees went for it, with the gender breakdown of askers mirroring the company as a whole. Most of those who participated received raises of between 3 and 10 percent. Only about one-third walked away with just the $200. After Ask for a Raise Day, a regularly conducted survey of the Motley Fool employees showed that positive responses to "I feel like I'm paid fairly" increased by 13 percent. The program didn't break the bank for the Motley Fool and actually saved at least one employee from leaving.[41]

Lee Burbage told me, "We don't believe perks drive our employee engagement, but feeling like your leadership team cares about you and what you want or need to be happy does drive engagement." As shown by so many examples cited thus far, including Marriott and the Motley Fool, community increases engagement, which drives performance—and profits. The literature on this is vast and persuasive. But there are other ways of quantifying the results, not all of which can be captured in dollars and cents.

The Benefits of Creating a Caring Culture

They say you can feel it when you step into a place. It's palpable. It's what researchers Sigal Barsade and Olivia O'Neill saw in their study of cultures based on what they call "companionate love." They define companionate love as consisting of "feelings of affection, compassion, caring, and tenderness for others," which they say can be manifested in a number of easily observable ways—workers "expressing caring and affection toward one another, safe-guarding each other's feelings, showing tenderness and compassion when things don't go well." They include a quote from an employee at a medical center who said, "We are a family. Everyone cares for each other regardless of whatever level you are in." Another employee, a woman who had been diagnosed with multiple sclerosis, described how her co-workers responded: They "showed me more love and compassion than I would ever have imag-ined. Do I wish that I didn't have MS? Of course. But would I give up the opportunity to witness and receive so much love? No way."[42]

What Barsade and O'Neill wanted to know was whether companionate love would have a measurable effect on the workplace. To answer the question, they surveyed 185 employees, 108 patients, and 42 family members of patients at a large nonprofit long-term healthcare facility and hospital. The researchers believed that if managers and leaders encouraged and reinforced these close workplace relationships, they would see benefits. And did they ever! Look-ing at measurable variables within attitudinal, emotional, behavioral, and health domains, and assessing them at two time points, separated by sixteen months, Barsade and O'Neill found that employees who feel connection and caring from colleagues perform better and are more engaged. They have less emotional exhaustion, less absenteeism, better teamwork, and higher levels of satisfaction. The benefits of the culture flowed to clients, too. Patients reported more positive moods, better quality of life, better health outcomes, and fewer trips to the emergency room. This culture of connection, or love, led in turn to their families' satisfaction with the long-term care facility, because they felt their family members were being treated well, and therefore a greater willing-ness to recommend it to others.[43] The researchers wondered if these results would hold across settings. They surveyed 3,201 employees in seven different industries from financial services to real estate and found similar results. Employees who felt free to express care, affection, and compassion for one another were more satisfied with and committed to the organization.[44]

The reason that creating a sense of community and caring among employees has such a widespread effect is that actions and feelings ramify and multiply through social networks. In their book, *Connected: The Surprising Power of*

Our Social Networks and How They Shape Our Lives, Nicholas Christakis and James Fowler reveal how each of us has a much bigger impact than we can see, because our happiness and well-being (or the reverse) manifests not just from us to our friends, but even to our friends' friends, and their friends. This is an effect that happens in communities of all kinds, and it can be quantified. A person is about 15 percent more likely to be happy if someone they are directly connected to is happy. The happiness effect for a friend of a friend of a friend is 6 percent. Christakis and Fowler documented that the spread of happiness did not depend on deep, personal connections. In a study of thirty-three professional male cricket players with pocket computers that recorded their moods four times a day during a match (which can last five days), there was a strong association between a player's own happiness and the happiness of his teammates, independent of the state of the game. Further, when a player's teammates were happier, the team's performance improved.[45] It's obvious how this kind of effect would operate in an office or other work environment.

How to Create a Caring Culture

Marriott and the Motley Fool are terrific examples of caring cultures. But there are many other ways to create such a culture that are not dependent on either the vast resources of Marriott or the quirkiness, playfulness, and originality of the founders of the Motley Fool. Following are a few low-tech, no-cost, common sense approaches to catalyzing connection and community in the workplace. They may seem quite diverse, but what they have in common is that they are all ways of showing respect for people.

Talk to your employees and your colleagues in person when possible.

So much of office life gets conducted via email that we forget the value of in-person interactions. But creating a genuine sense of psychological contact with others depends on social and gestural cues—eye contact, direction of gaze, facial expression, etc.—that the human brain can only pick up on when people are in each other's physical presence, explains Dr. Patricia Kuhl, a co-director of the University of Washington's Institute for Learning and Brain Sciences. Kuhl and her colleagues found that nine-month-old babies who were spoken to in person, in a second language (Mandarin or Spanish), focused intently on the person talking and then recognized those speech sounds later. However, babies who [merely] heard the same speech sounds on audio or video recordings couldn't do the same.[46] Kuhl explained, "There was phenomenal learning in the live group and no learning at all via a disembodied source."[47] Although you are probably not trying to teach anyone in your workplace Mandarin, Dr. Kuhl's studies of language acquisition relate directly to the profound human need for connection.

If you're not actually in the same room as the person you're talking to, Dr. Kuhl advises, find ways to replicate as many of these cues as possible—make eye contact, nod your head, interject and change your gaze, as you'd do in a meaningful back-and-forth conversation—in order to send signals that you're paying attention and actively listening. This can be done, as millions of people are now newly aware, with tools that allow for people not just to hear you but to see your expressions and nonverbals. During the pandemic, when she was unable to meet in person with her lab staff but connected with them via video calls, Kuhl realized that she was getting to know her people in a different way now that she saw them bouncing babies on their laps or zooming from their children's bedrooms. "It's not face-to-face, but we'll come back with a new understanding of each other."[48]

The need for social connection is primal, as present in nonhuman animals as it is in us, and as basic a craving as our desire for food. In fact, when neuroscientist Dr. Rebecca Saxe and her colleague Dr. Livia Tomova looked at fMRI images of adults' brains scanned before and after a day of social isolation, they saw patterns of neural activity that were almost the same as those of people who had fasted all day. People who are isolated crave social interaction the way a hungry person craves food.[49]

People who do have chances to interact with their colleagues in the workplace report feeling a much greater sense of belonging—and therefore of motivation and engagement. Even the simplest kinds of interactions matter. For example, one study of one thousand employees found that 39 percent of respondents felt the greatest sense of belonging when their colleagues checked in with them (personally and professionally).[50]

Small daily exchanges like "How are you doing?" or "How can I support you?" go a long way. So do expressions of interest in another person's point of view when it differs from your own. In instances where you know you disagree, instead of debating, you might ask them to tell you more about their thoughts, or note that you've never looked at it from that perspective. You might also look for opportunities to let your colleagues know about challenges you are facing. Expressing vulnerability is a way of humanizing your relationship with others.

Such actions are likely to lead to more positive connections and even friendships in the workplace. Research by Tom Rath and Gallup shows that people who have a best friend are seven times more likely to be positively engaged.[51] This is yet another indicator of how human connection is a major predictor of performance.

Create shared experiences.

Develop ways for your people to connect through shared experiences. Sanjay Amin, head of music subscription partnerships at YouTube, will share personal stories, suggest his team listen to the same album, or try one recipe together. It varies and is voluntary. He's tried to set the tone by being "an open book" and showing his human side through vulnerability. Amin's also started his team's meetings with a deep question card, which he sent to participants the day before. It is completely optional, but allows people to speak up and share their thoughts, experiences, and feelings in response to a deep question. People recognized a shared humanity, he told me, and bonding.

Reduce time spent on email.

Many people are inundated with email. Over two hundred billion email messages are sent and received every day.[52] Most of this email is work related—and most of it is internal. The average employee spends 23 percent of his or her workday on email, checking their inboxes thirty-six times (or more!) per hour. Research has shown that regardless of actual time spent on email, it increases emotional exhaustion and negatively impacts well-being and job performance. In other words, even when we aren't using our technology, the fact that we might need to at any moment creates stress.[53] And of course any time spent on email is time not spent on connecting in person—or at least on the phone. Sometimes a quick phone call or a five-minute sit-down with a colleague can clarify things much faster than the endless back and forth of email. In fact, because emails are so hastily composed and often so sloppily expressed, they can end up creating more confusion than in-person communications, and therefore consume even more time.

Thierry Breton, CEO of French IT services company Atos, compared the barrage of electronic notes to pollution. Calling for a massive cleanup of email pollution, Breton said, "We are producing data on a massive scale that is fast polluting our working environments and also encroaching into our personal lives. We are taking action now to reverse this trend, just as organizations took measures to reduce environmental pollution after the industrial revolution." At his behest, Atos began a series of projects designed to streamline and improve internal communication. Breton wanted to reduce the number of internal emails sent to zero within three years. As so often happens with lofty goals, Atos failed—and yet it made huge strides toward this goal.[54] Atos reduced its overall email by 60 percent.

Over that same time period, Atos's operating margin increased from 6.5 percent to 7.5 percent in 2013, earnings per share rose by more than 50 percent, and administrative costs declined from 13 percent to 10 percent. While the reduction in email can't be credited with all of these improvements, the correlation is certainly very strong.[55]

A growing body of research suggests that email is overloading our mental capacity. Reductions in email are linked strongly to reductions in stress, and increased job satisfaction and productivity. With some leaders acknowledging the mental burdens associated with internal email some organizations only allow employees to use email at certain hours of the day.

Reduce time spent in meetings.

Meetings are another drain on time, and despite the fact that they are done in person, there seems to be nothing to indicate that they increase social connection—or productiveness. Rather they just seem to make people unhappy and exhausted. In his book *The Surprising Science of Meetings*, professor Steven Rogelberg finds that nonmanagers routinely attend eight meetings per week, while managers attend twelve, and most of these are an hour long. The higher you climb in the organization, the worse the problem gets, with some 60 percent of CEOs' working hours dedicated to meetings!

Most people *loathe* meetings, especially the regular meetings that often occur more out of habit than necessity. A 2014 survey by Harris Poll found that 50 percent of respondents said they'd rather do "any unpleasant task" than attend a regular meeting (based on status updates). A leader with a telecommunications company reduced the number of meetings by half by using prerecorded five-minute videos to convey a message that previously would have required a meeting. Strive for the smallest number of meeting participants possible. Don't include spectators there to listen. Invite people for part of the meeting. Rogelberg has found that some people may worry about being excluded. He suggests not inviting them, but sharing meeting notes with them soon afterward (so they don't feel like an afterthought).[56]

Evidence shows that shorter meetings boost satisfaction without reducing the quality of decision-making. So be thoughtful about whether you need a meeting, and if you do, consider whether that meeting needs to be as long as it usually is. Shoot for twenty-, thirty-, or forty-minute meetings that have clear agendas and goals rather than the more common sixty-minute default. Or switch to shorter, more frequent "huddles"—ten-to-fifteen-minute meetups.[57] Consider what your employees' time is worth, and keep in mind that meetings cost time not just while they are going on but before they even begin. Studies reveal that when people had a meeting coming up, they got 22 percent less done in the hour beforehand. Researchers found that free time seems shorter to people when it comes before a task or appointment on their calendar. Looming tasks on our calendar make us less productive.[58]

Periodically evaluate meetings. People who lead meetings are biased and think they're more effective than their community members do. Ask how you can improve them—listen, and make changes. You might train people in what a good meeting looks like, as former CEO of Intel Andy Grove did. One study found 75 percent of those surveyed received no training in how to conduct or participate in meetings.[59]

What can you do to improve the culture of your workplace? When work creates opportunities for people to connect in deeper, richer ways that foster community, the employees benefit, but the organizations and their shareholders do as well. As the Motley Fool and Marriott have found, it pays to take care of your people and to invest in your community's culture. Creating a culture of well-being and caring for people doesn't require rich resources. Small actions that signal care matter. And these effects ripple throughout communities.

PART **2**

The Challenge: It Starts with You

Everyone thinks of changing the world, but no one thinks of changing himself.

—Leo Tolstoy

Most of us aspire to be part of a community filled with positive, uplifting people who will be supportive and caring, helpful and generous, encouraging us to live up to our own most aspirational expectations. Yet most of us feel a void. We lack the community we long for.

So what should we do? The solution is to be the change we desire. Part 2 examines what is required to put ourselves in a position to thrive. We'll take a deeper look at how physical and mental well-being, rest and recovery, and a positive mindset help us become our best selves. And because of what Tony Schwartz and I have identified as the multiplier effect, which occurs when leaders both model *and* encourage thriving, becoming our best selves will also lift our organizations and our communities. In part 2 you'll meet some of these multipliers and see the exponential effect they have on their communities.

One such multiplier is Nina Vaca. The third of five children, Nina was born in Quito, Ecuador, and grew up in Los Angeles, where her parents operated a successful travel agency. At age fifteen, Vaca began working at the family business, and after her father passed away when she was only seventeen, she became responsible for running it. Later she went to college, and after graduating—the first in her family to do so—Nina moved to New York to start her career in technology.

In 1996, at age twenty-five, she founded the Pinnacle Group from her living room in a tiny apartment in Dallas.[1] What started as a one-woman IT staffing firm has grown into a global workforce solutions powerhouse that provides talent and staffing services as well as payroll and other IT resources to companies as diverse as telecommunications, financial services, transportation, and technology. Pinnacle has appeared on the Inc. 500/5000 list of fastest-growing companies thirteen times.

Vaca is dedicated to bringing more Latinas into positions of power, and as a very active philanthropist, she is also dedicated to contributing to her community. In fact, Pinnacle's motto is "The community IS our business." She credits her mother for this, reporting that her mother taught her, "Do not strive to be a person of success, strive to be a person of value." Her charitable work encompasses organizations that improve the lives of disabled veterans, people experiencing homelessness, families of children battling cancer, women and children in domestic violence shelters, as well as students, parents, and teachers in Title I schools. She is particularly focused on expanding opportunities for women and girls in STEM fields, and women and Hispanics in business.

But how does she manage to do all this—on top of being the mother to four kids? Vaca radiates energy, which I caught firsthand when we had dinner before a panel we did together at the Texas Conference for Women. The key to her energy, I learned, is caring for herself as a Corporate Athlete— something she's prioritized ever since reading "The Making of a Corporate Athlete," by Jim Loehr and Tony Schwartz, in *Harvard Business Review*. The article explains how incorporating physical, mental, emotional, and spiritual practices and concepts builds the kind of resilience and energy that leaders require. Vaca got the message. "Keeping my energy levels up, my physical health in check, and my mental state steady is vital to my work. That's why these things are important, and that's why I place so much emphasis on taking care of myself in the same way a professional athlete does."[2]

Before she decided to focus on building a healthy way of life, Nina had found it easy to get stuck in a cycle of constant activity and stress, and admits that there were times in her career when she worked so much that she slept on a couch in her office. But she now prioritizes regular exercise, mindful eating (low sugar, regular, smaller meals, and avoiding processed foods), and sleep. Her passion for exercise (and giving back to her community) has led her to participate in triathlons, including one that provided funds to rebuild homes in Ecuador after a disastrous earthquake, half Ironman competitions, and other athletic events such as the 170-mile BP ride for multiple sclerosis. She's done this bike ride and other events with clients and potential business partners. "Trust me," she says. "You will feel very bonded with someone after you drag yourself through mud, over walls, and up hills with them!"[3]

But for her, sleep is the single most important element of her personal regimen. When she "got serious about sleep," she "became a better businesswoman and person because of it."[4] The mental and emotional and spiritual focus has helped, too, especially the goal of aiming for something that takes her beyond the immediate targets of corporate success. "In the same way that an athlete typically plays better if he or she is playing to help the team or family, or for something more important than money and fame, connecting with something more important can help us avoid burnout, feel more energized, and perform better," she said.

Her commitment to her personal well-being is something she consciously seeks to model for her employees. "As the CEO, when Pinnacle associates see me prioritizing my own health and wellness, it can encourage them to make it a priority in their own lives." Not only does she model and evangelize for fitness and a healthy lifestyle, but she has made it one of the cornerstones of the culture at Pinnacle, from the types of snacks offered at the workplace, the activities teams enjoy together, and various fitness challenges.

However, her own journey to health hasn't been without obstacles. Life threw her a curveball in 2014 with a case of appendicitis so severe that she was laid low by the aftereffects of it for months. "This was such a shocking blow for me, as I have always focused on having an active and healthy lifestyle." But the same discipline she had brought to maintaining her health for all those years paid off when she applied it to getting well again. "I began my recovery as soon as possible, by walking slowly to the mailbox, then to the end of the street, then around the block, then twice around, and so on day by day, step by step, until I had regained my health and my strength." It took Vaca a full year of committed rehabilitation before she felt like herself. But this was again something she shared with her employees in order to model the capacity for recovery. "Proving that I could regain my health and my lifestyle was a way to show myself and others that we are stronger than we think and if we put in the work, we can do more than we believed possible," Vaca said.

Captain

Even if you're not a leader at the very head of your organization, like Nina Vaca, your actions can have a potent effect on your tribe. This is something Sam Walker found in studying the world's greatest sports teams. In his book *The Captain Class*, Walker identified sixteen top sports teams through history and noticed something "that stopped [him] cold." It wasn't just one team whose performance, for better or worse, corresponded to the arrival and departure of one particular player. They all did. "And with an eerie regularity that person was, or would eventually become, the captain," Walker said. Captains lead in a way that is not about directing people but connecting with them, inspiring and motivating them. Because they don't have any actual power, whatever authority they do have is derived only from the respect they earn from their fellow teammates.

In my work with organizations, I've noticed that, too. You don't have to be the top leader in an organization in order to have a big influence on your team—as a manager or even as a peer. Someone who exemplifies this is Carla Piñeyro Sublett, whom I met at the same Texas Conference for Women where I met Nina Vaca. Originally from Uruguay, she has a very Latin American warmth and vivacity, which she brings to everything she does.

Although she is now a senior vice president and chief marketing officer at IBM and has more than twenty years of experience leading global sales, operations, and marketing teams in the technology industry, it was early in her career, long before she occupied such an important position, that Sublett discovered the impact one person could have on corporate culture. At the time she was working in the sales division at Dell, overseeing a call center. She realized very quickly that the people who worked there weren't healthy. A study of the employees conducted by Dell's wellness team revealed that based on health statistics, people were ten years older than their biological age. She also learned that people would put on an average of fifteen pounds in their first thirty days at the call center! In her first month she herself gained more than ten pounds, and she noticed other new hires struggling with the same experience due to the "sedentary butts-in-seats culture." "It was inhumane," Sublett said.

The problem was exacerbated by the vendors who serviced the call center, providing cupcakes, chips and queso, and all sorts of other fattening, empty-calorie treats. When another vendor brought in cake balls, Carla hit a breaking point. She yelled, "No more cake balls!" She decided that she'd bring in food at her own expense, only it would consist of juices, smoothies, and locally sourced fresh fruits and vegetables. In a radical move, she also announced a new policy: Anyone who wanted to work out could take an hour off in addition to lunch. She'd even supply a trainer who would run fitness sessions three times a day. Carla called it "on my dime and my time." She participated, too, though at the start she was "sucking wind in a parking lot after running a mere mile."

The reactions from outside the call center were not so positive in the beginning. Some of the higher-ups in the organization thought the idea of giving people time off to work out, which was part of the program she named Thrive, "was sacrilege!" At that time, things like this just didn't happen in their organization, anywhere. Yet Carla found it was working. Although staff spent less time at their desks and more time exercising, the call center's productivity jumped by 25 percent. Two employees lost over one hundred pounds. More than seventy-five people lost fifteen pounds or more. People who had never worked out before began running long distances. One gentleman found his passion, logging six-minute miles and running marathons. When Carla met his eighty-year-old mother, she thanked Carla personally for helping her son. Thrive was such a hit, and word of it spread so quickly, that it wasn't long before some Dell employees strolled across campus and asked to join it.

An unintended but entirely welcome side benefit of the program was that Thrive "broke down hierarchies. Communication between leaders and employees opened up. It seemed to erase barriers of power and status," Sublett recounted. People ran next to each other, learned from each other, and became friends along the way. And the company benefited, too, as this sales division's productivity increased—and profitability increased by 48 percent, she said. And though Sublett left Dell in 2015, the Thrive program she created was such a success that it not only lives on to this day but has gone global.

In the pages that follow, you'll meet several more of these multipliers—leaders (and in one case a "captain" rather than a leader) whose philosophy about self-care has made an impact not just on their own well-being but also on their colleagues'. You'll also meet some inspiring tribes and communities that are moving from surviving to thriving, together.

CHAPTER 7

Self-Awareness

Do the best you can until you know better. Then when you know better, do better.

—Maya Angelou

Aman Bhutani, whom you met in previous chapters, is obviously a very effective leader. But at one stage of his work at Expedia, he realized that something was throwing him off his game. He had a habit of responding even to relatively routine requests for information with a sense of great urgency, especially if the requests came from an important person at work, like the CEO. As soon as he got such a request, he would fly off and fire an email to as many as 150 people in a frantic attempt to provide an answer in twenty-four to forty-eight hours. Sometimes it took several days to hear from all the people he emailed. But meanwhile Aman might already have responded to the original email request, so all of the time and energy he sucked from others often ended up being for nothing.

Aman knew that this way of doing things was counterproductive, and that he was much more effective at his job when he was calm. His mother has been an avid reader of science and spirituality for the last forty years, so he was well aware, through her, of the benefits of mindfulness and meditation. "I knew I had to change my emotional response—excited or negative. I had to be calmer so I could create." He made a decision that he would make a conscious effort to get out of this reactive mode. Being calmer and more deliberate in his responses would prevent him from wasting so much of his own energy, and because his actions had a cascading effect on others in the workplace, it would benefit them, too. The challenge he now faced was how best to make this change. What was required, he thought, was to bring his attention to all the moments in the day when he was making those wasteful energy expenditures. Only when he was conscious of them could he do anything about them.

True to his data-driven approach, Bhutani created an Excel spreadsheet to track this problem in his work life. "When I tracked it in Excel," he told me, "I found that I was excited/happy or excited/sad four to five times per week. Within five to six months, I realized that it took me twenty-four to forty-eight hours each time this happened to get calm." Once he had the data in front of him, he began to make changes. Rather than shooting off emails to dozens on his team to get the answers he needed, he would slow down, and often he found that if he "could come at it calmly," he could find the answer himself. If he couldn't, he could think more carefully about who might be able to help him, and usually it would be only one or two people whom he would have to reach out to for help. Ever since he started tracking, he's been mindful of trying to limit the time and energy he used to expend in those email frenzies, and to avoid exposing his team members to this energy suck.

Although Bhutani says he's still a work in progress, his efforts seem to be paying off, based on both his own and others' assessments. He is one of a number of examples you will read about in this chapter of how to achieve self-awareness. Bhutani's route, which I would call "using data to track," involved being "methodical about self-awareness," as he puts it. First he used the data he'd collected on his Excel spreadsheet to make the problem "transparent." That drove awareness. Once aware, he tracked the outcomes of the awareness, in what became a constant circle of feedback, which resulted in an ever-deepening sense of self-awareness. It's all part of his deep belief in the scientific method. It's hard work, Bhutani says, but worth it.

Needless to say, Excel spreadsheets won't be everyone's chosen route to self-awareness. There are probably as many ways of achieving it as there are definitions of what it is. But however defined, and however achieved, self-awareness is one of the foundational skills for success in the twenty-first century. Bill George, former CEO of Medtronic, considers self-awareness to be the very starting point of leadership. Self-awareness helps us lead ourselves with authenticity and integrity—and, in turn, better lead others and our communities.[1] Self-awareness also allows us to know when we are thriving and when we are not, which is particularly important for those in leadership positions, because a leader who is not thriving is likely to infect his company with his own malaise.

There is considerable consensus about the importance of self-awareness—but not about what it is. How it's defined will depend on whom you are talking to. For some it's the culmination of deep inner exploration; for others it's a sense of purpose and path; for still others it's being conscious of how one interacts with and affects one's family, friends, colleagues, community; and for many it's about learning to see themselves—their shortcomings as well as their strengths—accurately enough to achieve excellence in their field. From the people you'll meet in this chapter, you'll hear many different, often overlapping iterations of what self-awareness can mean, how they have achieved it, and the impact it has had not just on the person who possesses it but also on their community.

The Self-Awareness Unicorns

How would you know if you have self-awareness? Ask yourself: Do I think I have an understanding of myself (internal self-awareness) and of how others see me (external self-awareness)? Based on data Tasha Eurich culled from thousands of people all around the world, a whopping 95 percent of people believe they're self-aware. What percentage do you think actually are self-aware? Again, based on Eurich's criteria—10–15 percent.

You might brush this off, thinking you're among the 10 percent or 15 percent who have mastered the skill to understand yourself and how others see you. But it was by comparing people's own assessments of their self-awareness with the assessments that others made of them that Dr. Eurich, author of *Insight*, arrived at her conclusion that 80–85 percent of people have an inaccurate perception of themselves. Knowing this, perhaps you will wonder whether your own concept of yourself is realistic, or whether it might also be contradicted by the view of someone close to you. The study that Eurich and her team did to test self-awareness consisted of an in-depth seventy-item quiz for people to fill out with their assessment of how self-aware they are. Typical items on the quiz are "I have clearly defined values that outline what is most important to me" and "I know what I want out of life"—internal self-awareness—and "I am aware of the impact I have on those around me"— external self-awareness. The test-taker had to rate each of these seventy statements on a sliding scale of very true to very untrue. A similar quiz went out to someone who knew the person well, who was asked their own assessment of how the person ranked on each of those criteria. Then the researchers looked at the degree to which those assessments matched up—or didn't—to arrive at a determination about the person's self-awareness. As part of her studies, Eurich wanted to understand how the self-aware got to be that way, so after finding that small minority they identified as self-aware, Eurich and her research team interviewed a number of them. But what they discovered was that almost all of them just seemed to have a natural sense of self-awareness, something they had had all along—it was just the way they were wired. They weren't able to articulate any processes they had gone through to develop that quality. This was somewhat discouraging because Eurich was hoping to understand how those who aren't simply born with it can cultivate it.

Frustrated by this apparent dead end to their inquiries, the researchers then went in search of people who didn't start out as self-aware, who entered adulthood with only low or moderate self-awareness, but who had been able over time to learn to see themselves more clearly. After exhaustive research, they were able to find fifty such people, whom they dubbed unicorns because there were so very few of them. But what they learned, and what a substantial body of research confirms, is that despite the rarity of self-awareness unicorns, self-awareness is a surprisingly developable skill.[2] You don't have to be born with it. But you do have to really want it and go after it.

So what do these unicorns do to become such paragons of self-awareness?

Unicorns build self-awareness in slow, steady steps.

The team discovered two things that surprised them about these fifty people. First, they came to their self-knowledge only incrementally. Eurich explained to me that most of us think of self-awareness as an almost magical process—something happens that causes us to wake up one day and have the realization that this is why we were put on earth. But such epiphanies are not actually the way most self-aware people gain self-knowledge. Instead, they actively work, every day, on making the small changes that eventually result in greater self-awareness. There's nothing magical about it. As she noted, it's something like going to the gym on a regular basis, slowly but surely building the qualities that are part of self-awareness and not allowing them to fall into disuse.

Unicorns have to work to build self-awareness.

The second thing the team discovered was that the unicorns actually worked much harder on their self-awareness than most people do. There were no shortcuts. "Unicorns made a conscious decision that they wanted to know the truth, and they committed to a regular practice of searching. They had a sense of curiosity about themselves, and the sense that, like exploring space, there is always more to know," said Eurich.

Another key takeaway from these unicorns was that while they're highly self-aware, they are simultaneously very self-accepting. Eurich told me, "What those two qualities do together is they allow you to keep learning, and to self-correct. You don't take your mistakes as an indictment of you as a person, but you say, 'Wow, I learned something from that that I can now act on.'"

Unicorns seek quality feedback.

Like many people, including those who are not very self-aware, unicorns actively sought feedback about themselves from others. But unlike people without much self-awareness, the unicorns were very picky about whom they asked for feedback; they tended to seek it from an average of only three to five people. These unicorns understood that (1) not all feedback is helpful, and (2) not all feedback is well intentioned. Unicorns focused on gathering feedback from people who (1) had their best interest at heart and (2) would deliver radically candid feedback. Their sources of feedback were "loving critics," as Eurich's team called them.[3]

If unicorns received unsolicited feedback from some random person, for example, someone who approached them at the end of a meeting and said, "Can I give you some feedback?" they recognized that this kind of drive-by feedback wasn't necessarily useful, especially if it was something they hadn't heard before that didn't ring true. But if they wanted another opinion, they would activate their loving critics and ask for their thoughts. "Somebody told me that I interrupt people in meetings and talk over them," they might say. "You have always told me the truth when I needed you to and I know you always will. So is that something you've seen me do?"

Unicorns are emotionally agile.

Another thing that researchers, including myself, found is that unicorns have emotional agility, or what Dr. Susan David describes in her book of the same name as the ability to "unhook." That is, they are able to tolerate high levels of stress and to endure setbacks, all the while remaining open, engaged, and receptive. As David writes in *Emotional Agility*, "They understand that life isn't always easy, but they continue to act according to their most cherished values and pursue their big, long-term goals."[4] That doesn't mean that they don't experience anger, sadness, disappointment, and frustration if they fall short of their goals or receive very critical feedback. The difference, David told me, is that they can step back from such difficulties in order to approach them with curiosity, self-compassion, and acceptance, instead of being overwhelmed by negative emotions or allowing themselves to be derailed from their ambitions.

Emotional agility is crucial to navigating the journey of self-awareness, according to David. She writes, "Recognizing, accepting, and then distancing ourselves from the scary, or painful, or disruptive emotional stuff gives us the ability to engage more of the 'take the long view' part of us, which integrates thinking and feeling with long-term values and aspirations, and can help us find new and better ways of getting there."[5] The emotionally agile are able to remain not just accepting but excited, enthusiastic, and invigorated in the face of challenge.[6] As Tasha Eurich so aptly put it, we choose to become braver but wiser. "I'm going to buy a ticket to the self-awareness journey.

And I'm going to stay on that train forever because the scenery is great and I'm enjoying the ride."

Unicorns ask what, not why.

Tasha Eurich believes that the kind of introspection that involves asking "why" questions is one of the biggest traps the un-self-aware fall into. The more they introspect, the greater the negative results! Since it will always be impossible to access many of the unconscious thoughts, feelings, and motives we think may be key to self-understanding, we are destined to be disappointed in our search. This can cause us to get lost in an unproductive spiral of thought that, as research shows, often results in depression, anxiety, and a sense of hopelessness. So, for example, if I have a fight with my significant other, and I say, "Gosh, why is this happening? Why can't we have a better relationship? Why have I gone so wrong?" or if I don't get a promotion, and I say, "Why didn't I get this?" I may simply end up tormenting myself rather than asking the kinds of questions that would enable me to move forward.

Unicorns asked different questions of themselves. Poring through hundreds of pages of interview transcripts, Eurich and her team discovered the word *why* appeared less than 150 times, but the word *what* appeared more than 1,000 times. Applying the "what" questions to that disagreement with your significant other, you might ask: "What do I want out of this relationship?" or "What do I need to do in the future to make sure this doesn't happen?" or "What am I going to do the next time the same issue presents itself?" *What* helps us stay objective, future focused, and empowered to act on our new insights.

How Self-Awareness Benefits People and Communities

Those who are self-aware are happier, more confident, and better communicators. The more self-aware have stronger and deeper relationships at work and at home. People who are self-aware are happier in their marriages. They even raise less narcissistic and more mature children.[7]

Their communities win, too. People who are self-aware tend to perform better at work, are more successful in their careers, more innovative, and better leaders.[8] Companies with a high percentage of self-aware employees are more profitable, whereas companies comprising large numbers of un-self-aware employees were 79 percent more likely to show poor financial returns. Another study revealed that leaders who are self-aware tend to lead more profitable companies.[9] To hire self-aware people, you might ask an interviewee to tell you about a time when she was convinced she was right about something but then came to change her mind. Or ask her to think of someone she wasn't close with—or didn't get along well with at work. How would that person describe her? Those with (greater) self-awareness can think of someone, and describe how they work with others, noting areas of awareness (sometimes because they've sought such feedback).

In a study of several hundred leaders and their direct reports, Tasha Eurich and I found that tribes benefited from leaders who were more self-aware in a number of ways. Those with greater self-awareness, as measured by Eurich's criteria, received higher ratings of their effectiveness and had better relationships with their employees. Employees whose leaders had self-awareness were happier both with their supervisors and with their jobs; they reported a stronger commitment to their organization, a stronger sense of belonging, and a stronger attachment to it, too.

Yet, as Tasha Eurich told me, "Self-awareness is a skill that almost nobody prioritizes because they think they're already there. But what we found in our research is that when we can make even incremental improvements in how clearly we see ourselves, the benefits touch every part of our lives." Since her three-year study was published in 2017, we've learned just how much they touch others' lives, too.

Self-awareness about the extent to which one is thriving—defined as feeling energized by an ever-evolving sense of progress—is particularly important given its potent and contagious effect on a tribe or community. Thriving individuals feel that they are growing and developing over time, the opposite of feeing stagnant and depleted. We've found that an individual's thriving affects team thriving and team performance. Yet so few people realize how they're energizing—or more importantly, de-energizing—their tribe. Often this is through small actions (as discussed in chapter 3).

Laura, a technology executive, is an example of someone who could have spread her own feelings of depletion and stagnation to her team. But she was self-aware enough to recognize that, after years of loving her job, she was no longer thriving in it. She was exhausted, demoralized by conflict with a toxic board member, and dreading the task before her, which involved laying off a number of employees, including colleagues she cared about but couldn't tell about the imminent downsizing. Given that the organization was undergoing massive change, and was dependent on her to carry much of it out, she decided to leave. What she didn't want to be was what author Jon Gordon has referred to as an energy vampire. It wouldn't have been intentional, but she recognized that, for her own good, as well as for the good of the people she cared about, she should resign. She told me that the move turned out to be great for her, and beneficial to the community, too. Her replacement successfully guided the organization through this transition and has had a great career in this industry since then. The replacement came in thriving, with boundless energy, immune from the toxic history of this firm.

As Alexandra Gerbasi, Andrew Parker and I have found, sometimes it takes only one person who's de-energized to reduce a team's ability to function well together, especially if it's a person who is in a leadership position. The team members' engagement, collaboration, performance, and job satisfaction can all sink.[10] And it doesn't take long. In our social network studies, we've found that when long-term high performers are no longer thriving, the negative effects ripple throughout the larger community very quickly (as evidenced in chapter 3 too).

How to Foster Self-Awareness and Thriving

Whether you're seeking to improve your own self-awareness, or you're a leader looking for ways to strengthen your or your tribe's self-awareness, following are some proven strategies you can employ:

ASK FOR—AND GIVE—FEEDBACK.

When asking for feedback, first think about what your aspirations are. For example, if your goal is to be CEO in five years, share that with the people from whom you're soliciting feedback. Then frame questions about how to reach that goal in very specific terms: What's the next step I should take? What additional skills will I need to improve my chances of getting where I want to go? What do you see as things that might be holding me back? What changes do I need to make?

Getting good, candid feedback is especially important if you're a leader, because research reveals that there is often an inverse relationship between our self-awareness and how powerful we are. The higher we climb on the corporate ladder, the less self-aware we tend to be, even if we don't start out as less self-aware. One study found that more experienced managers were less accurate in assessing their leadership effectiveness than less experienced managers. A study of more than 3,600 leaders across a variety of roles and industries found that relative to lower-level leaders, higher-level leaders valued their skills much more highly than their observers did. In fact, this pattern existed for nineteen out of the twenty competencies the researchers measured, including emotional self-awareness, accurate self-assessment, empathy, trustworthiness, and leadership performance.[11]

What explains this? First, senior leaders simply have fewer people above them who can provide them with candid feedback. Second, the more power a leader wields, the less comfortable people will be to offer constructive feedback for fear it will hurt their careers. One VP of human resources told me that she felt sorry for people as they rose through the ranks because they got less and less realistic (and less helpful) feedback. Third, as leadership guru Jim O'Toole noted, as people's power grows, their willingness to listen shrinks, either because they think they know more than their employees or because they believe seeking feedback will come at too steep a cost.

Leaders need to cultivate their own self-awareness, but also that of their tribe, as Anson Dorrance, head women's soccer coach at the University of North Carolina, has done. As recounted in chapter 4, Dorrance has won a record twenty-two NCAA national championships. His UNC team has defined eleven core values, such as tough ("We will not whine"), caring ("We care about each other as teammates and as human beings") and classy ("We treat everyone with respect"). Twice a year, players evaluate one another on each of these core values on a scale of 1 to 5, and then see how their teammates rated them. The system allows players to raise their teammates' self-awareness—and effectively coach one another, by giving them specific feedback to drive adjustments, as needed.[12]

Dorrance told me that this system has transformed their culture. You see, for years, he never shared the rankings with the players. It was something for his eyes only, because he feared that seeing negative feedback would be too painful. (Dorrance was guilty of ruinous empathy.) But one day Dorrance became so frustrated with one of his players that, at his wit's end, he decided to share the woeful results of her teammates' evaluations in a one-on-one meeting with her in his office. He then asked her, "Are you glad I shared this with you?" "Yes," she said in a very low, sheepish voice. He asked her why. She looked at him and said, "Because now I know I need to change."

Dorrance claims that it was the most incredible metamorphosis he's ever seen. She could have been defensive or shut down, could have crumbled before the criticism, could have exploded with anger at what she heard. Afterward she could have let her emotions eat at her, and become a fraction of herself—on and off the field. Instead, this player, in a demonstration of extraordinary emotional agility, took the feedback to heart and got to work on what she learned about herself. Dorrance said that this formerly troublesome player's end-of-the-year speech was one of the greatest he's ever heard. From this experience he realized how valuable it would be for the women to see their evaluations. He now says, "Of all the things that we've done to implement character growth in our program, this is the absolute best."

Others' feedback can propel us forward. It is a gift, though it may not always feel that way, especially in the moment. Feedback that enhances our awareness can be a difference maker that moves us from untapped potential to our best self in a relatively short amount of time, as it did for Dorrance's player within the space of one short fall soccer season. And it can have a huge effect on our team or community.

HIRE A COACH.

If you want in-depth feedback, in real time, you might consider hiring someone to provide it. Even if you're already good at what you do, you can always get better. Dr. Atul Gawande is an accomplished surgeon, a professor at Harvard Medical School, a brilliant writer for the *New Yorker*, and the author of several *New York Times* bestsellers. But ten years ago, when he was eight years into his surgical career, Dr. Gawande wondered whether he had plateaued. He felt he could improve. And everywhere he looked, he realized that other professionals—teachers, concert-caliber musicians like Renée Fleming and Itzhak Perlman, Olympic-level athletes—had coaches. If Rafael Nadal and nearly every elite tennis player in the world had a coach, why shouldn't doctors? he wondered. Why shouldn't he?[13]

So he hired one. He asked Dr. Robert Osteen, a retired general surgeon whom he had trained under during his residency, to observe him, to see if there were ways he might enhance both his surgical technique and his already admirable outcomes.

Osteen's suggestions surprised Gawande, particularly after the quick first surgery that his coach witnessed. It had gone beautifully. Yet, as they sat in the surgeons' lounge afterward, Osteen had a number of technical suggestions. Granted, they were "only small things." But, as Gawande recounted in the *New Yorker* piece in which he wrote about the experience, Osteen told him, "If I were trying to keep a problem from happening even once in my next hundred operations, it's the small things I had to worry about."[14]

Osteen asked Gawande to pay more attention to his elbows. "You cannot achieve precision with your elbow in the air," he told him. A surgeon's elbows should be loose and down by his sides, and as Osteen explained, "When you are tempted to raise your elbow, that means either you need to move your feet...or to choose a different instrument." In fact Osteen had a long list of observations like this. "His notepad was dense with small print."[15]

Other blind spots he pointed out: The way Gawande draped the patient for surgery gave him perfect vision of the procedure but blocked the view of his assistants across the table. While this was invisible to Gawande, it was obvious to his coach. Because Gawande operates with magnifying loupes, this restricts his peripheral vision so much that he had been unaware of the blood pressure problems that the anesthesiologist was monitoring. That one twenty-minute discussion with his coach, Gawande reported, "gave me more to consider and work on than I'd had in the past five years."[16]

In later sessions Osteen pointed out possible improvements not just in his surgical technique but in how he worked with the residents assigned to his team. He suggested that Gawande allow the residents to struggle for thirty seconds more when he asked them to help him with a task. "I tended to give them precise instructions as soon as progress slowed. 'No, use the DeBakey forceps,' I'd say, or 'Move the retractor first.' Osteen's advice: 'Get them to think.' It's the only way people learn."[17]

Gawande continued to have Osteen coach him for a number of months. There came a time when he made an error in judgment that resulted in some serious problems during one of the operations he did under Osteen's observation. Although he was able to salvage the situation by changing his strategy and the patient did fine, he was mortified to have his coach see him in a situation where his judgment had failed. But as mortified as he was, he kept up his arrangement with Osteen because he found that after following Osteen's suggestions, a few at a time over a number of months, his complication rates went down. Avoiding just one major complication can save a life, and on average, $14,000 in medical costs. While he found his time with his coach well worth it not just because his complication rate went down but because of the many improvements he was able to make, the experience did come at a price: exposure. You have to be willing to allow people to see you when you may not always be at your best, which can be very hard on the ego.

This is of course true in all situations where you solicit feedback of any kind. Inevitably you are going to have to learn things about yourself that will be painful. But if feedback consisted only of praise, there would be no point to it. Embracing its lessons, as Gawande did, and as Dorrance's young player did, is the key to learning from mistakes and achieving excellence.

ENLIST YOUR CO-WORKERS AS COACHES.

Peers are an underutilized source of feedback. When hired as CEO of UMass Memorial Health Care in 2013, Dr. Eric Dickson wanted to create a culture of innovation. During his first five years, however, "things were getting better, but not at the pace we needed," he said. He concluded that it hadn't yet fostered an environment in which people felt comfortable speaking up and offering their ideas for improvement. In short, it needed to create a culture that made people feel respected, but he wasn't clear about how to do that. Then Allison Lemay, chief of staff and associate vice president of strategic initiatives, came to him with an idea focusing on developing commonly agreed-upon standards of respect. She surveyed six thousand employees about what makes them feel respected, and boiled the many answers down to six Standards of Respect (SoR): Acknowledge, Listen, Communicate, Be Responsive, Be a Team Player, Be Kind.

To follow up on its SoR training program, UMass Memorial designed Stepping Up Respect: Manager Feedback, a multistep process created to help managers develop more self-awareness about how well they are adhering to the Standards of Respect. Each manager nominates several raters to provide anonymous feedback via a survey that will indicate which behaviors the rater thinks the manager demonstrates well and which need improvement—along with suggestions for how to improve. The raters rank the manager on adherence to specific behaviors within each of the six basic standards. For example, under "Listen" they rank "stops other activities to focus on the speaker; asks clarifying questions to ensure and show understanding; stops using technology when others are talking; asks if everyone was heard; pauses before responding." The raters may be peers, or they may report to the manager, or the manager may report to them.

The next part of the process for those leaders who have participated in it is to commit to specific actions they can take to improve in those areas that have been pointed out as weaknesses. For example one leader was told he needed to avoid using a rude tone. And among the actions he committed to was to walk away if he was feeling heated and return to the conversation later, to develop greater consciousness of when he sounded rude, and to avoid speaking harshly to staff in front of patients and their families.

The third part of the process is for the leaders to name a peer coach—a manager, direct report, friend, family member—who will ask them, each week, how well they are executing the specific actions they committed to as part of this process.

As the intro to the survey explains, the ultimate goal of all this "is to elevate respect across UMass Memorial Health Care by providing each leader with customized specific suggestions for how they can further apply respect 'strengths' and avoid mistakenly showing signs of disrespect." And it has made a real difference in changing the culture at UMass Memorial.

As Dr. Dickson told me, "The Standards of Respect program is the linchpin that has led to a big increase in patient satisfaction, an increase in engagement, improved execution on projects and in a way that people feel respected. There's also been a palpable increase in performance." He said, "I don't know what I'd do without the Standards of Respect." And the peer feedback process has been an integral part of these results.

GO OUT FOR A DINNER OF TRUTH.

Another form of feedback, which is a favorite of Eurich's, is the "dinner of truth." Developed by communications professor Josh Misner, it dovetails with the "be braver but wiser" theme. Find someone you're close to with whom you want to improve your relationship, and invite her to dinner. At dinner, ask her, "What do I do that is most annoying to you?" And then listen, soaking in the insights. Don't justify, defend, or explain away any of the behavior that the feedback critiques. Just try to delve into it with questions like "Can you give me an example of a time where that's been an issue?" or "Have you seen it get worse over time?"

Tasha Eurich relayed her own experience of this. She intentionally picked one of her most crotchety friends. She expected him to respond with "Oh, I am so glad you asked. Here's the litany of things." In the days leading up to the dinner, Tasha went into a tailspin as a train of negative thoughts about what Mike might say swirled through her mind. But when she plucked up her courage and asked the scary question that night, what came out wasn't nearly as bad as what she dreaded. Mike thought for a moment, then said, "Well, here's what I'll offer you. I love you in person, but I hate you on social media." Surprised by what he told her but eager to find out what he meant, Tasha responded, "Wow, tell me more please, Mike." Mike shared with Tasha that while in person she was focused on others—providing them with information when needed and being helpful in other ways—on social media, she was not getting it right. She seemed too focused on herself and her brand. It felt like she was all about "me." He said, "Not only is it not who you are, but I find it just annoying. And I wonder if any of your readers or anybody else feels this way, too."

Tasha and Mike spent some time talking about what she could do differently. She's worked to be more mindful in the moment, and is especially wary of humblebragging. Now before she posts, she always asks herself, "What is my goal in this?" "If it's showing how awesome I am, then I change the post," she said.

Tasha told me that every one of the dozen dinners of truth she has done since then has strengthened the relationship and also helped her become more self-aware. The feedback has been surprising, but affirming overall. Three years ago, when she asked her husband, Dave, whom she's been married to since 2009, for feedback, he said, "Sometimes you can be dismissive." Dave reminded her of the time that he couldn't wait to share some exciting news he received. But when he told her, he recounted, she was so busy on email that she didn't seem to share his excitement. Hearing that, Eurich told me, "broke my heart," but she understood it was something she needed to know, and in the end it was more helpful than hurtful.

Many others share a similar experience. For example, Tasha received an email from someone who did this with her five-year-old son. A brave thing to try, since who knows how a kid will reply when asked that question! Her son said something to the effect of "Mommy, it really annoys me that you don't ever take any time for yourself. You're always taking care of me, or you're taking care of Daddy and it makes me worry about you."[18] As Eurich commented, "There is no question that whatever we're going to hear will be useful, and it will almost never be a realization of our worst fears."

DISCOVER YOUR RECIPE.

Kim Scott, author of *Radical Candor* and coach extraordinaire whom you met in chapter 4, described what she had learned from Fred Kofman when she worked at Google. He drew a wheel on a whiteboard. At the center of the wheel, he told her, is you. You want the wheel to turn really fast. If the wheel is out of alignment, however, you can't do well, lead well, work well.

Scott recommends that you figure out what your recipe is—the things you need to do in order to stay centered and thrive. Everybody has a different recipe. Some people like me love exercising and being in nature—others not so much! Some people love to meditate, while others hate it. Kim shared her recipe: "I need my nine hours of sleep, an hour of exercise, and at least twenty minutes of conversation with someone I love. If I can do those three things every single day, no matter how unstable the world seems, I feel like I'm on solid ground. If I don't do those things, then even when the world around me is very stable, I feel very unstable. So it's really important to figure out what your recipe is, and follow it every day."[19]

You might even reflect on whether there's a particular order in which the ingredients to your recipe should be incorporated. In Dan Pink's *When*, he traces the timing of activities and their impact. For example, for some people like me, working out in the morning is the key to jump-starting their day. To discover your recipe, and trace the effects of different ingredients (and their timing), take the Energy Audit—designed by Gretchen Spreitzer and Traci Grant and inspired by Jim Loehr. Chart what you are doing and how you feel throughout the day, hour by hour over several days. A day or two of charting can provide insights, but several days is even better, since we've all had days that get away from us or that aren't very representative of our normal schedule.

Once you have your chart, look for patterns. When did you see energy spikes? When did you see dips? Were there certain activities that led to a boost in your performance or well-being—and when were those boosts most likely? Take notes on any ripple effects activities and energy had on others—for better or worse. One consultant noticed that when she took a break at home and walked for even as little as twenty minutes before or after dinner, she felt much better. She was calmer and more patient with her kids, too. MBAs and executives whom I've asked to complete this audit are often surprised by how enlightening it is. One executive took a break from both his phone and his online activities on Saturdays and Sundays. He and his wife made a pact: They allowed themselves a thin slice of time on email early Saturday morning, and again at the end of Sunday. Otherwise they were untethered, off-line. They noticed how they thrived as people, a couple, and a family.

DO A DAILY CHECK-IN.

Something we can all do that is enormously helpful is a regular check-in at day's end. Eurich encourages us to review how our day was without overthinking it. Ask yourself the following:

1. What went well today?
2. What didn't go well today?
3. How can I be smarter tomorrow?

The check-in can also give you detailed insights you can use to be more aware of your interactions with others. How did your sense of thriving affect how you approached a situation or person?

WRITE A USER'S MANUAL.

One interesting exercise in self-awareness asks leaders to create a user's manual they can give to their colleagues and team members to describe their own unique preferences and quirks so that people in the workplace will know how best to deal with them. I've assigned this task to MBAs and executives, asking them to write a one-page bullet-pointed memorandum listing what they see as their assets and liabilities as managers. Another possibility is to ask colleagues to write one for them, or provide feedback on their draft to remedy any blind spots. This is a powerful way to connect with members of their community and cultivate better relationships. But it's also useful to the person doing it because the process forces you to reflect on how you interact with others.

Is your office door always open? Always closed? Do you prefer to keep people at a distance and communicate only via email? Do you like to have one-on-one meetings? If there are problems, do you want to hear about them directly or have them brought to your attention by a senior executive? Do you remain in your office most of the day, or do you circulate among your employees and enjoy getting to know them in brief chats as you stop by their workstations? Are you a fast decision maker or a slow one? Short-tempered?

Impatient? Reflecting on these personal characteristics may clarify which of your leadership skills are strong and which need work. It may also help you to understand what kind of culture you set and the practices that you expect your followers to follow.

A hospital chief, Dr. Ron B. Goodspeed, wrote his manual while trying to find a vice president of performance improvement. He wrote, "Ask me to 'get to the point.' Hint: If I use analogies that are not clear, please ask me to be more concrete." The manual asked the job candidates to warn him if he "was charging down the wrong path." He suggested that they supply more rather than less information, and not try to test the waters before making recommendations.[20] Dr. Goodspeed then shared his draft with five colleagues. His chief operating officer suggested Dr. Goodspeed add, "I can sometimes refer to statistics and research data when I am uncomfortable with an idea." This manual was helpful to employees as well as prospective job candidates. Some formerly timid employees started to question him more in meetings, and even asked him to curb his verbosity and clarify points. These requests improved Dr. Goodspeed's effectiveness.[21] And as someone who has actively pursued critiques from both superiors and subordinates, he was glad to have the input. While writing a manual for candidates for a position in performance improvement, he ended up improving his own performance.

Leaders I've worked with who have shared their user's manual in one-on-one meetings, or after taking over a team, have found that it speeds up the learning process and provides a rich touch point with community members. Colleagues really appreciate this kind of show of vulnerability and openness in a leader.

Are you thriving? Or merely surviving? As a great deal of research has shown, we are inclined to see ourselves in a more positive light than is perhaps warranted. Renowned executive coach and bestselling author Marshall Goldsmith calls this the "highlight reel of our successes."[22]

But if you want to become aware of areas in need of improvement, to keep growing and developing rather than congratulating yourself on what you have already achieved, I encourage you to move beyond that reel and home in on your blind spots. Gathering feedback is critical to developing the necessary self-awareness.

While many routes to self-awareness involve various kinds of personal tracking, like Aman Bhutani's and the daily check-in, feedback from groups can be particularly effective. Anson Dorrance and his team have found that to be true, as has my brother Mike with The Mighty, Cleveland Clinic with its shared medical appointments, and many, many other people, in areas as diverse as sports, business, dieting, addictions, and physical and mental health. By coming together in an intimate, open, and emotionally safe place, small groups of like-minded people who are supporting one another in the pursuit of shared goals are a formidable source for personal growth of all kinds. When our fellow group members ask us questions and offer their observations of our behavior, that gets us thinking and provides an opportunity to contemplate and recalibrate. In the end, that's the whole purpose of self-awareness: change.

CHAPTER 8

Physical Well-Being

> I believe that the greatest gift you can give your family and the world is a healthy you.
>
> —Joyce Meyer

Mark Verstegen and his wife, Amy, started Athletes' Performance, a training facility for elite athletes, in 1999. In 2006, Verstegen and his team expanded beyond their original focus on athletics and started working with the US Navy and Special Forces to prepare soldiers for deployment, help them heal from injury, and assist their transition back to civilian life. Their team has since trained over 425,000 sailors worldwide and 5,000 command fitness leaders—those who coach military troops to maintain a successful physical fitness program and good health.

But in 2013 they shifted gears once again and changed the focus of the company to improving performance in every realm, not just sports and the military. And with that shift came a new name—EXOS. As it says on the company website, Exos comes from the word *exosphere*, which refers to the highest level of the atmosphere, and its mission is to help everyone—athletes and people in the armed forces, but also people in diverse work settings and at all ages and stages of fitness—perform better. Ultimately EXOS's goal is to put people in control of their health so that they can succeed at anything. To the extent that you are becoming a healthier, better version of yourself, everyone in your personal and professional life benefits. This chapter builds on chapter 6, detailing specifically how physical well-being upgrades your life, allowing you to bring a stronger, more focused and energetic, happier, productive self to your personal and professional tribes. The theme of part 2 of this book is that it starts with you. Be a role model for your tribes, and consider what you can do to nudge your community to be healthier. Move yourself from surviving to thriving, together.

Success—and upgrading lives—is something Mark knows a lot about. Sitting in his modest-sized EXOS office in Phoenix on a spring afternoon a couple of years ago, I could see that it was strewn with signed jerseys from the men on the World Cup–winning German soccer team, signed cleats from some of the biggest athletic stars, and all kinds of other football, basketball, baseball, and track-and-field memorabilia. Thank-you notes from athletes and team managers were scattered across corkboards and walls. Photos depicting the tough, grueling training Mark puts his athletes through, along with newspaper photos of teams lifting trophies, or receiving Olympic medals, dotted the office. Yet for someone who had spent decades devoted to lifting athletes to the pinnacles of their professions, Mark Verstegen was remarkably the same as he ever was—humble, grounded, authentic, and kind.

I met Mark and Amy Verstegen the summer after graduating from college, when I began working at International Management Group's sports academy, IMG Academy. A former college football player, and a pioneer of integrated sports science, Mark had launched IMG Academy's Performance Institute as its director after receiving his master's degree in sport sciences. He began with a 1,200-square-foot area—one room stocked with weights and a few tread-mills and other machines, along with another small room of weighted balls and kettlebells, and a small area in which to stretch. By the time I left, only a couple of years later, he had expanded to an impressive domed turf field next door where we (his staff and friends) played some epic Thanksgiving football games against the (overly) confident tennis instructors and staff. Two years after I left, he and Amy, whom I worked with at IMG Academy, left to launch Athletes' Performance. Since then, in each of his ventures, he's continued building and scaling.

Mark's genius was to use science and analytics to improve athletic perfor-mance, and he quickly became known for taking talented athletes who were looking to go professional, and molding them into their best selves. He did this by designing a system that got the maximum mileage out of every last ounce of an athlete's potential. Much of his emphasis was on movement training, which focuses on function and balance rather than sheer strength and endurance, since research shows that mobility dysfunction and imbalances are the cause of many injuries. Mark was unique in that he took a holistic approach, combining elements of proper movement, nutrition, recovery, and mindset—what he calls the four pillars—into his overall program. He wanted high-level performance, but also sustainable performance. Therefore his program took into account not only how athletes perform but also how they get injured, and how best to protect them from injuries. His goal was to "prepare and repair." As the founder and president of EXOS, Verstegen has continued to focus on player safety and welfare, having served as director of performance for the NFL Players Association for nearly two decades.

Our conversation in Verstegen's office that spring day didn't revolve around athletes or coaching, however. I wanted to know more about how he defines his mission at EXOS. He recounted how, many years before, he realized how many people there were who were not able to live their lives to the fullest because of their lack of fitness. He asked himself how he could help people become healthier and improve their well-being. This was one of the inspirations for the founding of EXOS. Through his work at EXOS, Verstegen hopes to be able to help fix what he's described as a national crisis in well-being. Evidence of this crisis is the fact that poor health and obesity cost US companies $225 billion every year, according to the Centers for Disease Control, and the number is escalating quickly.[1]

"Reactive healthcare is broken," he says. "Seventy percent of the issues clogging our healthcare system are lifestyle-related. If we can remove them, if we can get people upstream of the disease state, it's a win-win for everyone."[2] The mission for him and EXOS is to help people to become proactive about their health, rather than relying on the "reactive healthcare system," which focuses on repairing the damage done by our unhealthy lifestyle, rather than preventing it in the first place. Verstegen wants to upgrade the lives of as many people as possible so that everyone can flourish at doing whatever they want to do, on the playing field or at their desk job. Since the vast majority of us are not professional athlete prospects, however, working out on punishing treadmills and pumping heavy weights is not the solution. So he and Amy had to give a lot of thought to how to pivot the business and scale it in a way to take advantage of what he learned from working with athletes for all those years and adapt it to the needs of a general population.

EXOS has grown in several ways to fulfill this mission. In 2014 the company acquired MediFit, which had fitness gyms in corporations, hotels, resorts, and community centers, many of which are active adult or senior care facilities. This allowed them to scale into the corporate and community space more quickly. They could staff the existing gym structures with fitness trainers and programs and plug into a rich network that they could grow to reach more people in those buildings, campuses, and centers. Since EXOS's founding, Fortune 500 corporations like Adidas, Humana, Intel, Google, LinkedIn, and Walgreens have flocked to EXOS in hope of minimizing ballooning healthcare costs and maximizing the health and fitness of their employees. In pursuit of these goals, EXOS delivers "personal game plans" to individuals in these workplaces. In some cases, EXOS may send trainers and chefs into the workplace to provide additional support for the wellness goals, or they may design the food offerings in corporate cafeterias and cafes. EXOS collaborated with the Mayo Clinic on a 3D Movement Quotient tool they developed that uses video analysis and biomechanics to assess movement quality instantly for the purpose of designing individualized training plans that will enhance mobility and prevent or alleviate pain.

Much of EXOS's work now focuses on people who want to improve their health in order to make changes in their performance at work. Because Verstegen comes from a sports background, the programs EXOS designs for them use language that sounds like what he might offer his elite athletes. Participants are given a holistic customized "game plan" and a "coach" (or team of experts) to advise them; they join forces with a group of similarly motivated "teammates" who will share feedback and support; a "scoreboard" tracks and quantifies their progress so that they can see what they have achieved and where they still need to make improvements.

Verstegen and EXOS have demonstrated that no matter what their job, people can learn how to operate at the highest level, day in and day out, and enjoy a better quality of life, if they make improvements in their physical well-being. Verstegen calls it high-performance DNA. He explains that we're the sum of our behaviors, and that 90 percent of our actions are driven by habits, whether positive or negative. So a lot of their focus is on habit change—undoing bad habits, and forming new habits, such as regular physical exercise.

This chapter will offer examples and case studies that show how people and communities have been able to instill high-performance DNA in themselves and their members through movement and nutrition—and how they have benefited as a result. When communities invest in their members, it's a win-win for everyone.

If your company doesn't have any type of program that focuses on physical care, consider what you might do to jump-start one, even if the available resources are limited. You could organize a tribe of weekend warriors who hike or go on runs or bike rides together, or encourage people to spend part of their lunch hour speed walking or just taking a walk. Or you could enlist a group of employees interested in participating in a daily fitness challenge. The challenge can be something very simple, like agreeing to take a twenty-to-thirty-minute movement break at least once a day. Even something as basic as setting a timer to remind themselves to stretch, take some deep breaths, and focus on something besides the task at hand for a few minutes every couple of hours or so is beneficial. And none of these ideas require management to spend money or provide any kind of special equipment.

High-Performance DNA the EXOS Way

A few examples of how EXOS works, in environments as diverse as a finance company, a warehouse, and a hospital, illustrate how learning to take care of themselves physically lead to wins not just for the employees but for their tribes and communities—and their employers. In an industry known for burnout where employees manage intense workloads in stressful environments, Michael Forman, the chairman and CEO of FS Investments, wanted to support a culture that would "allow employees to be as present and engaged with their families at 8 p.m. as they are at work at 8 a.m."[3] He believed that if there were more resources integrated into their working environments to help employees move better, eat better, and recover better, employees would become healthier, happier, and more productive both at work and in their personal lives. Of 327 employees (55 of whom worked remotely) who participated voluntarily in FS Investments' program with EXOS, 22 percent were overweight or obese, 74 percent reported pain, 43 percent were active less than three days a week, 53 percent had poor cardiovascular fitness, and 85 percent had poor diet at the beginning.

EXOS was brought in to create a performance and movement program that included personalized plans and digital tools to track and record activity, a café that served free healthy food and snacks, and mindset training and support. The results were impressive: a healthier, more resilient workforce—and a projected savings of $2,052 per employee annually, in large part because of vast physical improvements. Employees collectively reduced their body fat by 10 percent in the program's first year.[4] Eighty percent or more of employees reported less stress, more energy, and a greater understanding of fitness. More than 70 percent of participants said the program increased their productivity and said the program made them more likely to stay with the organization. The percentage of overweight participants shrank to 16 percent. Only 17 percent reported pain (down from 74 percent!). Only 13 percent reported being physically active fewer than three days a week, and only 13 percent had poor cardiovascular fitness (down from 53 percent). Forty-two percent of the participants who had been in high or moderate health risk categories moved to low or no health risk categories.[5] All of the high-risk participants increased their physical activity levels, and the vast majority reduced their stress.[6]

One employee reported that his participation "has allowed me the opportunity to become a better version of myself, not just for FS Investments but for my family." Another participant said, "I'm more cognizant of how to relieve my body from everyday injuries—how to relieve stress with simple techniques that I can also do at home." Another highlighted the nutrition benefits: "Smaller portion sizes here in the café have helped me eat less outside of work. Also eating healthier foods outside of work."[7] Summarizing the benefits, the manager of the EXOS program at FS noted that in addition to helping the firm's employees, the opportunity to participate in it had added to their appreciation of their employer: "The program improved the building's morale as people feel appreciated, that we care, and that we are investing in them."

In 2017, EXOS worked with industrial athletes—employees who drive forklifts and selectors within a warehouse environment, often referred to as "pickers"—to decrease pain, injuries, and the number of accidents on the job; to improve productivity and reduce downtime due to injury; to improve employee attendance and retention; and to boost morale. A twelve-week program included one-on-one coaching and nutrition consultations, personalized meal plans, weekly check-ins, pre- and post-movement sessions, educational sessions based on the four pillars of human performance, and the creation of on-site areas where healthy food and drinks were available. Specific fitness goals tailored to the particular challenges faced by these employees included improving movement mechanics and lifting posture; enhancing quality of movement during repetitive tasks; and creating healthy habits. Even if you're not working with a coach, you can adopt plenty of habits that will improve your health. These habits don't need to involve lots of resources. Verstegen has found that 70 percent of employees in their studies are dehydrated. He coaches people to start their mornings well, drinking a glass of water when they wake up, spending a few minutes doing three movements or stretches, and considering their mindset for the day and for their lives. Stay hydrated throughout the day (the clearer the better), and eat clean and often (snacks every three hours).

Pre- and post-evaluations showed a 13 percent improvement in movement quality scores. One participant noted, "I've increased my productivity by 15 to 20 percent and am now one of the top selectors. I'm able to spend more time with family instead of sleeping." Another participant said, "Movement prep helped me be more prepared for my shift and reduced soreness after ten hours of work. This allowed me to sleep better, have more time in my personal life, in turn giving me a positive attitude and improving my performance at work." Overall, employees' body composition—proportion of fat to lean tissue—improved, which improved health and productivity. Turnover decreased 123 percent as compared to the previous twelve months, which equated to an estimated $1.3 million in turnover savings. Pain injury claims drastically dropped, which led to injury claim savings (annualized) of

$2.3 million. The industrial athletes reported 49 percent greater energy, 74 percent better sleep quality, 21 percent productivity improvements. Over the last thirty days of the twelve-week program, productivity among participants soared by 35 percent, there were zero injuries reported, and over 93 percent of new hires were retained (versus the 30 percent benchmark).

What about caregivers in medical settings? Might they benefit from the kinds of programs EXOS offers? We might think healthcare workers are masters of physical health, yet they're a population that's stretched physically and emotionally, day in and day out, in ways that would lead most mortals to buckle. The toll over time is enormous. So Cancer Treatment Centers of America identified caregivers who exercised less than three days per week, and EXOS designed a twelve-week program for them. The health of the 116 participants shifted dramatically. Both mental and physical energy increased an average of 23 percent, and pain plummeted. There were decreases in body fat and in workdays missed due to health issues. An independent consultancy found that the monetized value of ten outcomes that were tracked resulted in a savings of over $850,000. It's easy to see how the employees' ability to care for others improved, too. The chief of gynecologic oncology reported, "As a surgeon, physical flexibility is important, and because of a shoulder injury I was having difficulty performing surgery because of the pain." Crediting the individualized attention she received from trainers with her improvements, she said, "I've been able to increase my range of motion and decrease the pain. This has impacted my ability to take care of patients." A radiology assistant noted, "[I had] never done anything like this in my life. I'm toning up, building up, getting stronger and having less pain—as far as the normal aches and pains that you get as you get older. It seems to be helping with my joints, so I really like it!"[8]

Wegmans

Wegmans Food Markets, a leading supermarket chain across New England and the mid-Atlantic, is another company that discovered the value of investing in their employees' well-being. In 2007, Wegmans' healthcare costs were skyrocketing. Wanting to understand how its employees valued different parts of the company's overall benefits offerings, including their healthcare plan, it commissioned an employee survey. Through this Wegmans learned that employees valued health coverage benefits so highly that they were considered a reason both for joining and for staying with the company. They also found that offering even basic healthcare coverage to employees who were not currently eligible, at a cost of $107 per employee, would cost $1.5 million, but it was worth $32.5 million to those employees, a figure arrived at by examining the trade-offs they were willing to make among hypothetical "packages" of healthcare and compensation.[9] Jack DePeters, senior vice president of store operations at Wegmans, told us about these findings, and the actions Wegmans took as a result, at the Google re:Work event mentioned in previous chapters. Wegmans now offers life benefits (including paid vacation time, and employee assistance to help find childcare, eldercare, legal consultations, and financial planning) and generous health coverage options, as well as wellness services that include blood pressure testing, flu shots, tobacco cessation programs, and even a yearly on-site health screening that covers blood pressure, cholesterol, weight, and BMI—all for free! Its Eat Well Live Well program focuses on changing eating and physical activity habits, and its Know Your Numbers initiative focuses on blood pressure. The company also offer coaching and guidance from pharmacists and dietitians, on-site yoga, Weight Watchers at Work meetings, fitness discounts, and a free smoking cessation program for both employees and their spouses. In 2008 Wegmans also stopped selling tobacco products in its stores.

Data collected between 2008 and 2013 show that the share of the 44,000 Wegmans employees with high blood pressure has dropped from 24 percent to 14 percent, along with a similar drop in the share of its workers with high body mass index, a measure of body fat.[10] During that same period, the percentage of employees with healthy weights rose from 29 percent to 40 percent, and those considered obese dropped from 32 percent to 25 percent.[11]

Wegmans went one step further, deciding to invest in the well-being of the communities in which it operates. CEO Danny Wegman, whose activist philosophy has given him a reputation as an ambassador within the industry, has challenged his industry to make more progress in battling obesity, diabetes, and other related societal problems. Like Verstegen, he sees society losing the battle against these conditions, and he wants Wegmans to offer solutions to the problem. As part of Wegmans' attempt to inspire the local population to be more active, the company created a Passport to Family Wellness program. In collaboration with city-sponsored recreation and fitness programs and park conservancy groups, Wegmans customizes and distributes a pocket-sized "passport" for families looking to explore local nature trails. It contains easy-to-read maps, fitness tips, and motivation in the form of prizes for trails hiked. In New York's Genesee Valley Greenway (GVG), for example, the Wegmans passport contains a map of fourteen GVG hikes from 2 to 7.5 miles long. Each trail has a marker post somewhere along it, which participants use to make a rubbing on their passports to prove they have been there. After completing six hikes, they are eligible to receive a coupon redeemable for Wegmans products. Those who complete ten hikes are eligible for a drawing for an Empire Passport, which provides free vehicle access to all New York State parks for one year.[12] In other communities, people who bring in their passport with six hikes completed get a Wegmans Passport to Family Wellness T-shirt. Wegmans has also contributed to community-built playgrounds and sponsored youth sports along with local walks and runs.

These types of commitments to the physical well-being of its employees, as well as its communities, have helped to land Wegmans on the Fortune 100 Best Companies to Work For list for the twenty-third year in a row, ranking third on the 2020 list.[13] It is quite unusual for a regional grocery store, with primarily hourly employees, to land on the list. The company was also ranked number one for corporate reputation among the one hundred most visible companies, according to the 2019 Harris Poll Reputation Quotient study. Wegmans has also scored plenty of positive media attention and won scores of fans in the communities that are using its passport and other programs to get healthier. Wegmans is routinely ranked as one of the highest-rated grocery chains in the nation when it comes to customer satisfaction.[14] Robert Wegman, the late chairman of the board of Wegmans, was famous for the saying "We can only take care of our customers if we first take care of the needs of our people."[15] And that philosophy, which we've also seen expressed in the corporate cultures of Marriott and Southwest Airlines, has translated into satisfied, loyal employees who have made Wegmans customers feel satisfied and loyal, too.

Exercise: The All-Purpose Remedy for Mind as Well as Body

The goal of all EXOS's work is "to unlock people," as Allison Schoop, senior vice president of strategy at EXOS, told me. "You need to uncover what's holding someone back" so that they can "bring their whole self to work," their best self. And exercise, as EXOS has demonstrated time and again in its work with the dozens of organizations that have brought them in to devise programs for their employees, helps us become our best selves. This is something that has been confirmed in study after study, including the one that Tony Schwartz and I did of twenty thousand employees across diverse industries and organizations.

Exercise boosts brainpower and is a powerful way to reduce stress[16] and stress-related diseases.[17] Regular exercise can transform the default state of the nervous system so that it becomes much more balanced and less prone to fight, flight, or fright.[18] Exercise promotes alertness, concentration, and cognitive performance, so people learn more efficiently following exercise. People who exercise regularly benefit from astonishing gains in cognitive performance—memory, reasoning, attention, problem-solving, and even fluid intelligence.[19]

Exercise boosts our happiness.[20] Over time, regular exercise remodels the reward system, relieving depression and expanding our capacity for joy. Our muscles are like a pharmacy, pumping out "hope molecules" (myokines) when we contract in exercise.[21]

Psychologist Kelly McGonigal, author of *The Joy of Movement*, believes that adopting a regular exercise routine can often enable a powerful inner transformation, too. "Even deeply held beliefs about ourselves can be challenged by direct, physical experiences, as new sensations overtake old memories and stories," she says.[22]

Exercise can erase self-doubt because it allows us to tell ourselves (and others) that we've achieved goals, overcome obstacles, broken what we once thought of as barriers.

McGonigal found that through movement, we can even cultivate courage, which can translate into all sorts of wins for our communities, from being radically candid, to being willing to take the risk of speaking our minds or sharing our ideas, to setting (and tackling!) audacious goals. It's no mystery why the language of bravery is expressed through metaphors of the body. "We walk through fire," "carry burdens," and "lift one another up." We are warriors. We may be weekend warriors, or part-time warriors, but when we lace up our shoes, our words and mindsets begin shifting along with our bodies, and we are on the road to becoming the people we want to be. As McGonigal puts it, "The mind instinctively makes sense out of physical actions. Sometimes we need to climb an actual hill, pull ourselves up, or work together to shoulder a heavy load to know that these traits are a part of us."

I know this from my own experience. Whenever I've felt myself shrinking into a smaller version of myself, often because of professional or personal failure or disappointment, exercise is my refuge. I start there. It is a way to pull myself out of a hole. I know that whatever small wins I feel through exercise I will carry with me everywhere. They become a part of the fabric of who I am.

Our moment-to-moment sense of self-confidence is shaped by the qualities of our movement. If we're lifting weights, we feel stronger. Running may make us feel powerful. Yoga, joga, or Pilates might elicit a sense of balance and self-care. Working up the nerve to go to an exercise class that we were previously intimidated by—no matter what kind of class—is a way of conquering fear. All these actions translate into the words we use to label ourselves. We go from feeling weak, powerless, out of balance, and fearful to thinking of ourselves as strong, in control of ourselves, balanced, focused, and brave. "Physical accomplishments change how you think about yourself and what you are capable of, and the effect should not be underestimated," writes McGonigal. This helps explain why we show up differently at work when we become physically fit. Physical activity helps us have a sense of purpose.[23]

Sarah Robb O'Hagan, currently the CEO of EXOS, has had a career focused on fitness, having been an executive at Nike, president of Equinox, and CEO of Flywheel Sports. Her view of exercise as a key to both physical and mental fitness shares a lot with McGonigal's approach. O'Hagan's book, *Extreme You*, takes as its credo the belief that pushing yourself physically will drive a higher level of personal achievement. She has developed a six-week program combining fitness challenges, nutrition counseling, and personal development coaching to help participants leverage the connection that exists between physical fitness and mental strength. So she suggests that if you're feeling overwhelmed by a challenge, start with a physical one. Once you choose and share your small or big challenge, you're much more likely to achieve it and feel "the awesome beginnings of your Magic Drive momentum engine kicking in." As she says, "It's amazing how starting with a physical goal quickly fires up drive that can be applied to other life challenges."[24]

Movement also primes us to connect with others by increasing the pleasure we derive from being around other people. Endorphins don't just make us feel good—they help us bond, and strengthen relationships.[25] One study found that when married couples exercise together, both partners report more closeness later that day, including feeling loved and supported.[26] Another study found that on days when people exercise, they report more positive interactions with friends and family.[27]

Fuel for It: Nutrition in Community

Food fuels our bodies and brains. Healthy eating improves well-being and can lead to a healthier, more productive workforce (as discussed in chapter 6). But eating well can be complicated, involving having to make more than two hundred decisions about food every day—many of which tend to be bad decisions. Which is why about 60 percent of the food we buy is highly processed, sugary, fatty, or salty.[28] That in turn is why we now have a serious obesity crisis in this country—the obesity rate having risen dramatically in recent decades to over 42 percent in 2017–18 (a rise of more than 10 percent in less than two decades), according to the Centers for Disease Control. Obesity is not just a major factor in the $225 billion the CDC estimates it costs US companies to deal with the ill health it causes, but it is also a contributing factor to hundreds of thousands of premature deaths.

A lot of research has gone into exploring what can be done to fight these trends. In their book, *Nudge: Improving Decisions About Health, Wealth, and Happiness*, Richard Thaler and Cass Sunstein reveal how indirect suggestions and positive reinforcement can be more effective than mandates and commands. Making it easier to make good decisions is another effective "nudge" strategy. Because the costs of obesity and being overweight are such a problem for employers—resulting in more absenteeism and less-than-optimum performance on the job, as well as higher medical expenses—many corporations, among them Google, are putting into effect versions of the principles outlined in *Nudge* to make it easier for its employees, and visitors like me, to eat wisely.

To nudge Googlers and visitors to make better food choices, the Google Food Team started offering healthier snacks. And with the not-so-healthy M&M's—the company favorite—instead of offering them in bulk and stocking four-ounce cups to pour them into, which often resulted in people filling their cups, Google started putting the candies in smaller, individually wrapped packages. The average serving size fell 58 percent, from 308 calories to 130 calories. The company also found that if cookies and crackers and other snacks were placed farther from the beverage station in a break room, people were less likely to grab the snacks when they went to get their coffee. Data from an experiment involving more than one thousand employees showed that if the beverage station was located six and a half feet from the snack bar, people were 50 percent more likely to grab a snack with their drink than if it was seventeen and a half feet. For men, this translated into one pound of fat per year for each daily cup of coffee![29] Google also nudged employees by putting up colorful posters with trivia facts about the "vegetable of the day" (unpopular vegetables like cauliflower, brussels sprouts, and beets) next to the food station where the vegetable was served. The result: The number of employees trying the featured vegetable increased 74 percent, and the size of the portions rose 64 percent.

Not all workplaces can afford to offer complimentary helpings of healthy food. A mere 21 percent of the over twenty thousand employees Schwartz and I surveyed reported that their workplaces provided healthy food or snacks. But there are still things companies can do to make it easy for people to choose healthier options. For example, Dr. Mark Hyman, the renowned medical expert featured in chapter 1, advises companies to upgrade their vending machines with healthy offerings like fruit and nuts instead of candy, and flavored waters instead of soda.[30]

Eating Together, the Firefighter Way

Google and many other corporations have on-site cafeterias where employees can eat free or subsidized meals. There are many reasons for providing these communal eating spaces, among them the belief that they will promote healthier eating, and increase productivity by reducing time spent going off-site to eat. Another reason offered is that these cafeterias will encourage employees to eat together, the idea being that the togetherness over meals will translate into greater cooperation and collaboration at work. "Cook together" is actually one of Traeger's five values—and employees do it Monday through Friday.

One environment in which shared meals are a long-standing tradition is the firehouse. The firefighters' culture typically features eating—and cooking—together, since firefighters usually work in ten-, twelve-, or fourteen-hour shifts and can't leave the firehouse for their meals. They do, of course, have the option of bringing in food from home or ordering takeout, but the culture of shared meals and meal preparation is so ingrained—and celebrated—that participation is the social norm. The firehouse usually comes equipped with the facilities for cooking, such as refrigerators, stoves, and sinks, but not the food, so the firefighters pool their money to buy supplies, design the menus, do the cooking, and share cleanup duty afterward. These shared meals are famously convivial occasions. As the son of a firefighter, Kevin Kniffen, a researcher at Cornell University and the lead author of a study entitled "Eating Together at the Firehouse," wanted to investigate whether this culture of eating together had any actual effect on job performance.[31]

Part of the study involved his visiting thirteen firehouses in a large American city and interviewing the firefighters and their supervisors about their experience. None of the firefighters mentioned cost savings or time savings as the reason they cook and eat together. Instead they reported that eating together creates a family-like feeling and is crucial to keeping their teams operating effectively. Firefighters believed that sitting around a table over a shared meal resulted in their developing genuine feelings of connection and building trust among themselves. In the dangerous situations they often confront, caring about each other and knowing they can count on each other can sometimes be the difference between life and death. They felt their communal culture actually helped them save more lives. A firefighter named Bob, who came from a family of firefighters, offered one example of how this happens. One day he was chatting over lunch with his colleague, Dominic, who told him, "You would never know this about me, but as a kid, and even now sometimes, I'm afraid of heights." "Afraid of heights," Bob said. "Really?" This was the last thing he would ever have expected of a firefighter. Four hours later, the fire alarm went off, and Bob, armed with new knowledge about this member of his team, used it to make strategic decisions about how to deploy the team. Since part of the effort involved scaling considerable heights, Bob made sure to put Dominic in another role where he would be more effective, and the team successfully (and safely) conquered that fire.[32]

Follow-up surveys of 395 supervisors validated the firefighters' belief in the value of their communal meals: There really were positive correlations between eating together and team performance. The supervisors assessed cooperative behavior as being considerably greater—about twice as high—among team members who shared meals than among those who didn't.[33] The benefits of eating together were likely reinforced by the other cooperative behaviors underlying the firefighters' meal practices—collecting money, shopping, menu planning, cooking, and cleaning—and taken together all these shared activities resulted in stronger job performance.[34] "Eating together is a more intimate act than looking over an Excel spreadsheet together. That intimacy spills back over into work," said the study's author, Kevin Kniffin. It's a "kind of social glue."[35] For companies, what this study suggests is that it may be worth investing in and facilitating group eating facilities at work. Yet Tony Schwartz and I found in our study of twenty thousand employees that only 23 percent of them had leaders who encourage people to get away from their desk for lunch. Even organizations that don't have resources for a cafeteria or subsidized food—or management support for such initiatives—can find ways to bring employees together over a meal. A manager might invite the team to a lunch of takeout food in a conference room, or organize a walk to a nearby restaurant for a brainstorming session, or just a chance to socialize over soup and sandwiches. Another possibility: At an off-site meeting, team members might be asked to cook an elaborate meal together as a means of figuring out how to work collaboratively on something out of their usual range.

I still have vivid memories of one such event that I was fortunate enough to attend. It happened more than fifteen years ago, when I attended a Positive Organizational Scholarship event at the University of Michigan's Ross School of Business. During the day we heard great presentations, ate a tasty lunch catered by Zingerman's (see chapter 4), and participated in lively small group discussions to move our research forward. The evening event proved particularly memorable, however. As is so often the case at U-M, it raised the bar with the activities that night. We were divided into three groups, each of which would walk to one of three nearby professors' homes in Ann Arbor where we would be expected to design and cook a meal. Our team walked through a dark little forest to a beautiful, warm home—a restored barn. Once there we were shown to the kitchen and provided with a wealth of ingredients to choose from in devising our menu.

A colorful array of fresh vegetables, fruit, and a pile of large lettuce leaves sat on the kitchen countertop, and on a farmhouse-style dining table we found potatoes, pasta, tortillas, and cooking basics like olive oil, flour, and butter. As we planned out our meal, people volunteered for tasks specific to their abilities. One person joked that he didn't have any cooking skills and therefore he'd clean up. A couple of others chimed in with suggestions for making versions of their favorite dishes, and in short order we'd planned a menu, divvied up responsibilities for making it, and figured out the timetable for each part of the meal. One thing that emerged from our discussions, however, in which a number of us confessed to not having made a meal in months if not years, was how pressured we felt by our professional ambitions. Time was so tight that we tended to avoid anything that diverted us from what we had to do to make progress on the tenure track (specifically, publishing in top academic journals), so shopping, cooking, and, in some cases, even eating much beyond a bowl of cereal just seemed like too much trouble.

It felt like a group therapy session, similar to the shared medical appointments in chapter 1. The beauty was that people not only com-miserated but also shared strategies they'd found to cope with their career challenges. These were people I admired, peers and mentors at the top of my field, admitting to anxieties that I'd thought only I felt. Finding out that I was not alone in sometimes feeling stuck or paralyzed was a priceless gift.

Prepping dinner as a team cracked people open in unexpected ways. We started revealing our greatest professional fears and hopes. Over a candlelit dinner of pasta with sautéed vegetables and a delicious salad, we went deeper, dancing into a conversation about who we really wanted to be, what we hoped to contribute through our work. At the end of the meal, we packaged up the decadent chocolate-laden desserts we'd created, then traipsed back through the woods, where we joined the larger group and celebrated by sharing the desserts each team had made. Every part of the evening felt like a bonding experience, which deepened the relationships among us. All these years later, I can instantly recall what it was like to wander through the unknown woods together with flashlights, in the company of a group of people most of whom I had just met, wondering what lay ahead for us. One thing was clear for me: I had found my professional tribe.

A Few More Nudges

Walk and work.

Holding walking meetings is a way to introduce some much-needed activity into your employees' lives—and help combat the loneliness epidemic, too. People are sitting 9.3 hours a day.[36] As many a magazine article on the subject has noted, sitting is the new smoking. One-on-one walking meetings with colleagues get people out of the office, on their feet, and in motion. It also brings them closer together because they are sharing something that is enjoyable. But the effects go beyond health and togetherness. Research indicates that people were 60 percent more creative while walking. Creative juices continue to flow afterward, too.[37] At design firm NBBJ, employees have moved from traditional sit-down meetings with agendas to "meeting walks" with "itineraries."[38] Encourage people to venture outdoors or move about your office with walking meetings. You could also consider installing standing and treadmill desks.

Make room for fitness.

Even if your company doesn't have a dedicated gym, you can set aside space in a conference room for employees who want to stretch, run on a treadmill, lift some weights, or do some yoga or Pilates moves. If the space is there, people will use it.

Hire a personal trainer for the staff.

This is always a great perk for employees, and a very popular one. Tom Gardner, whom you met in chapter 6, explains that the net result for the Motley Fool community "is a convenient solution for our employees that yields higher productivity, lower health insurance costs, and greater levels of satisfaction."[39]

Make self-care part of the corporate culture.

Encourage people to serve as champions or ambassadors of well-being, as Marriott does. Such people can help create a culture in which their colleagues become focused on taking care of themselves, physically, mentally, and emotionally. They can organize fitness challenges, offer classes in practices like mindfulness and meditation that support mental health, and give people the opportunity to join groups where they will support each other in their self-care goals. Such groups and classes can make wellness fun—and build camaraderie.

Dedicate a day.

Have your company set aside a day to devote to physical well-being. In 2019, as part of its commitment to trying to make Earth Day a national holiday all around the globe, the North Face gave employees the day off on April 22. It closed down headquarters and all 113 of its stores, and encouraged everyone to disconnect and explore the outdoors, or do some kind of volunteer work in their communities. People shared what they did on their explore day through the North Face's internal social network, a way of promoting the company's values and its commitment to the outdoor life

REI is another company that makes it corporate policy to get its employees into the outdoors. Since 2015, REI has opted to close its doors on the busiest shopping day of the year, Black Friday, for what it calls #optoutside day, in order to encourage people to get outside into nature because it's good for their well-being. REI also offers its employees two Yay Days a year, one every six months, to encourage them to "go outside and play ... [and have] a chance to get inspired by the outdoors, by engaging in their favorite outdoor activity," according to its corporate website.

As Amanda Carlson-Phillips, senior vice president of strategic partnerships and insights, who has led many of EXOS's nutritional programs and research since 2003, told me, "If you build it, they might come, but if you build it and you use it and you put it into the culture of the organization, they definitely will come." The good news, Carlson-Phillips told me, is that "you don't have to have the Cadillac to create impact."

How can you build physical well-being into the culture of your tribes? Habits are crucial. There are many ways to start small that will still result in measurable improvements. Verstegen often says, "Simple things done savagely well." Start there. Once you get started, the momentum will build. I discuss the other two pillars of Mark Verstegen's holistic approach to wellness and high performance next. These will add jet propulsion to the momentum.

CHAPTER 9

Recovery

Sleep is an investment in the energy you need to be effective tomorrow.

—Tom Rath

Jen Fisher joined Deloitte, a tax and financial consulting services company, in 2001 as senior marketing coordinator. From there she ascended the ranks, serving as chief of staff to the chief operating officer (later CEO) and eventually working with the chief marketing officer.[1] Fisher was energized, learning and growing from her work with very senior leaders. She worked anywhere, at any time, without boundaries, often logging nineteen-hour workdays. She thought she was taking care of herself, because she always set aside time to exercise. A former college soccer player at the University of Miami, she viewed that hour a day as her "me time" and was strict with herself about sticking to it. Fisher believed she only needed three to four hours of sleep, and although she tended to eat healthy, there were days when she was so busy she would just forget to eat. "Powering through" the next deadline or event seemed to work for her for a while. Over time, however, this punishing schedule began to take a toll on her, and people who cared about her began to notice.[2]

First it was Fisher's husband. But when he drew her attention to what it was doing to her, she wasn't ready to hear—and in particular, not from him. "You know, we never like to be told these things by our spouses. So, of course, I denied it, didn't want to accept it. To me that would have meant failure, that I couldn't handle all of these things, couldn't be everything to everyone at every time. In other words, I couldn't be a super woman."[3]

But the pressure she was under was also affecting her work relationships. A dear friend who worked for Fisher left her team and sat her down to explain, with kindness and candor, that she was leaving because it was so tough to work with her. Fisher still wanted to believe that the problem had nothing to do with her. However, as more and more of her colleagues, mentors, and people she knew cared about her started to tell her she was driving herself too hard, it started to sink in. Her mentor at the time, Deloitte's former chief marketing officer Diana O'Brien, brought Fisher over to work with her. But O'Brien recognized that Fisher wasn't herself. So when Fisher asked what she would be doing in her new role, O'Brien told her, "Well, the first thing that you're going to do is, you're going to take some time off, and you're going to figure out who Jen Fisher wants to be." Fisher was reluctant at first. She thought, "I don't need time off. I'm ready to dive into my next role."[4]

However, O'Brien issued some "forced time off" and asked her to think about her own well-being—what she thought well-being meant, how she was or wasn't supporting it, why it was important. Once Fisher really disconnected, it finally hit home how exhausted she was. Fisher went to bed, and pretty much stayed there for three weeks. She began to reevaluate not just her health habits and sleep routines but the overall direction of her life.[5]

When she returned to work, she spent several months easing her way back in. During this time, as she continued to recover, to reengage in life and in her job, she continued to reflect on what mattered to her, and who she wanted to be. She now understood that she had defined well-being far too narrowly. "I had been working non-stop and believed at the time, that if I got my daily workout in, then I was ok. But in reality, I was ignoring all of the other important areas of my life, like sleep, recovery, connection, etc. That's when I realized that well-being is about more than just the physical, it's also about your mental, emotional, and social health, as well."[6] Sometimes she needed time at the gym, but sometimes, she realized, she needed time to rest, reflect, read, meditate, or just relax on the couch and do nothing. And as she continued to learn more about her needs, she found that she wanted to help other people discover their own. "Regardless of how passionate people feel about their jobs," she said, she now understood that "they're going to burn out if they don't take time for rest and recovery."[7]

In the end, burnout transformed her. She had learned that burnout is not the price you have to pay for success, that in order to create a more meaningful life you have to remove your "badge of busyness."[8] She became passionate about wanting to communicate that message to others. And once she realized how much it meant to her, she began thinking she might become an executive coach or something like that. Fisher assumed that because no role like this existed at Deloitte, she would need to leave. She met with Diana O'Brien to tell her that she was going to resign to pursue this new passion. O'Brien's response surprised her: "If you need this, don't you think others need it, too?" She went on to say, "You're not going anywhere. Just because a role doesn't exist, doesn't mean there shouldn't be one. We create roles all the time in organizations."

O'Brien urged Fisher to write out a case for why well-being mattered for the performance and bottom line of the Deloitte community and pitch it to the leadership. Fisher did just that. The result: Deloitte leaders appointed her to chief well-being officer in June 2015.

Jen's first step in her new role was to create a comprehensive well-being strategy. This was not about just throwing money at apps, tools, or programs. Rather, it was about cultural transformation. She knew that change had to become embedded in the daily life of the workplace. She engaged with Deloitte employees to understand their needs and discovered that well-being is not one-size-fits-all, and took that into account in her planning. Later that year she helped develop and launch Empowered Well-being, Deloitte's wellness program. The goal was to broaden the definition of success to encompass not just job performance and the financial bottom line, but to include—and emphasize—personal well-being. "If we don't support employee well-being, we are sub-optimizing our people's potential," Fisher says. "As a professional services organization, Deloitte is analyzing complex problems that require their people to show up as their best selves."[9]

Empowered Well-being focuses on the whole person, including mental and emotional health, personal purpose, and financial well-being. Deloitte now offers flexible work options, sabbatical choices, mindfulness meditation, yoga, energy breaks during meetings, well-being days for employees to collectively unplug electronically, and education on topics like nutrition, stress management, positivity, and the impact of technology on well-being.

Fisher is especially proud of Deloitte's emphasis on mental health, which is unlike many company well-being programs. There's also an emphasis on reframing attitudes and perceptions regarding sleep and rest to see them for what they are—the ultimate performance enhancers, Fisher says.[10] Programs like the Collective Disconnect, in which Deloitte employees disconnect together for the last week of the year, are helpful. Employees still have their paid time off (PTO) throughout the year, but the Collective Disconnect allows for all members of the community to focus on rest and recovery at the same time. Genius.

In May of 2016, just months into her new role, Fisher noticed a lump in her breast. A few days later she learned she had breast cancer. Fisher was shocked. She felt healthy and had no family history of this disease. But now she thought she was going to die—just as she had begun doing such meaningful and necessary work for the Deloitte community. She didn't think she could continue in her role. But a pivotal moment for her occurred when she told her boss, Mike Preston, former chief of talent, of her diagnosis, and said she thought she should probably step aside, because surely a chief well-being officer needed to be healthy. She remembers that after she said that, "he paused for what seemed like an hour. He's an incredibly thoughtful, caring, compassionate human being. And he said, 'Jen, you're one of the smartest people I know, and this has to be the dumbest thing I've heard you say.'" "You're going to get through this," he insisted. "You're going to come out the other side and this is going to give you a platform to talk about wellbeing in a different way. Because it's one thing to get up on a stage and tell people to take care of their health and wellbeing if you've never struggled with your wellbeing because that's easy. But if you've actually struggled with your own health—be it your physical health or your mental health—you're actually coming from a place of experience." Fisher told me, "That changed the whole trajectory. And it also changed how I went through the whole cancer process. I hung up the phone and I thought, 'I've got this.'"

Her boss had provided her with not just hope but a new sense of purpose—not only to fight, but to use cancer as a platform to connect with people and teach them, by example, to take care of themselves. Given how passionate she was about her work, which she felt would engage her and give her a feeling of normalcy while undergoing treatment, and seeing how it might be all the more meaningful to the Deloitte community because of what she was going through herself, she decided to stay on the job. But she redesigned the job to give her greater flexibility during her treatment. She prioritized recovery. She slept more and scheduled daily recovery breaks into her calendar—"I hung a virtual 'do not disturb' sign on my door" during nap time, she said—and was very open about what her needs were. She found that when she set clear boundaries, people respected them.

Fisher made it through eight months of cancer treatment, including two surgeries, chemotherapy, and radiation, successfully. And she herself benefited from a program Deloitte instituted in September 2016. Their paid family leave program offers sixteen weeks of paid leave for new parents and for family caregivers, such as those caring for aging parents or sick family members, who need time off. Since Fisher's husband is also a Deloitte employee, it meant he could take some paid leave to support her during her treatments.[11]

Thanks in part to her own experience, Fisher continues to grow in her understanding of well-being, and specifically of the recovery aspects of well-being. After bouncing back to health, Fisher noticed that she had let go of some of the healthy habits she had maintained during treatment. She wondered if it would be selfish of her to continue to prioritize recovery the way that she had, boldly publishing it on her calendar for others to see. But after reflection, Fisher asked herself, "Why is it okay to take care of myself when I'm sick but not when I'm healthy?" And that is now one of the messages she communicates to Deloitte employees. Incorporating time for rest and recovery into your daily life is not just for when you're sick.

Fisher was lucky that she had a mentor, leaders, and team members to call her attention to her burnout. "Stress is inevitable in the workplace and in life," she says. "But it doesn't have to be pervasive. Organizations can and should play a more active role in preventing burnout."[12] Fisher has found that when a company actively supports its employees, "this impacts the way they show up every day. It impacts their productivity. It impacts our clients. It impacts the way we go home at the end of our day and week."[13]

This chapter explores why companies should value the health and well-being of their employees, not just out of altruism but out of an understanding of how they can affect the bottom line. Just as Fisher learned how we hurt ourselves when we don't practice self-care, companies must learn how this hurt extends to the community as a whole, its negative effects rippling and ramifying in surprising ways.

Because recovery is so important to our overall well-being and effectiveness, there are many practical suggestions in what follows for how leaders and managers can promote recovery in the workplace. As Mark Verstegen says, recovery is balance. Because stress is a daily drag on your body and mind, recovery should be a regular part of your life. Consistent recovery routines help build resilience to stress so you can bounce back quickly when it hits.

Sleep as the Key to Health

Let's start with what may be the very foundation of good health. Can you recall the last time you woke up without an alarm clock, feeling refreshed, and not having to reach immediately for a jolt of caffeine? If you're like more than two-thirds of adults across all developed nations, chances are you are not getting the recommended seven to nine hours of sleep per night. "Sleep in some ways is the neglected stepsister in the health conversation of today," says Dr. Matthew P. Walker, professor of neuroscience and psychology at the University of California, Berkeley, director of the Center for Human Sleep Science, and author of the bestseller *Why We Sleep*. "We've spoken a lot about diet and physical activity as being essential to good health. We used to think of sleep as perhaps the third pillar of health. But I actually think sleep is the foundation on which those two other things sit,"[14] he says.

If sleep is indeed the foundation for health, we have a lot of work to do to fortify that crumbling foundation. In 1910, American adults averaged 8.25 hours sleep per night. That figure is now 6.75 hours per night. And a large-scale study indicates that 29.9 percent of Americans get even less than that, sleeping fewer than six hours per night.[15] Studies from Korea, Finland, Sweden, and England indicate that America is not alone; the sleep epidemic is global.[16] Its effects are wide-ranging and devastating.

Every major disease that is killing us in the developed world—from Alzheimer's to cancer, cardiovascular disease and stroke, diabetes and obesity—has significant links to insufficient sleep.[17] So, if we want a healthy community, sleep matters.

Sleep matters to the corporate bottom line, too. A study led by Dr. Ronald Kessler at Harvard Medical School reported that sleep deprivation costs American companies $63.2 billion a year in lost productivity.[18] A RAND report on the epidemic reports that up to $680 billion is lost each year across five countries—the US, UK, Germany, Japan, and Canada—due to insufficient sleep.[19] Low sleep quantity or quality has been associated with low job satisfaction,[20] poor motivation,[21] a reduction in executive functioning,[22] less innovative thinking,[23] and poor task performance.[24] Sleep deprivation also causes safety lapses and work injuries.[25] Lack of sleep and poor sleep leads to absenteeism,[26] difficulty with organization, impatience, cyber loafing,[27] bad behavior in the workplace, such as rudeness[28] and even unethical behavior.[29]

An individual who sleeps on average less than six hours per night has a 13 percent higher mortality risk.[30] This may in part be because insufficient sleep undermines the strength of our immune system. In an experiment, participants were restricted to four hours of sleep for a single night. This resulted in a 70 percent drop in the activity of the immune system's natural killer cells (which are like the secret service agents of our immune system, detecting and eliminating early signs of disease). Dr. Walker described this as "a concerning state of immune deficiency." It helps explain why there are so many significant links between short sleep duration and the risk for numerous forms of disease, including bowel, prostate, and breast cancer. In fact, the link between lack of sleep and cancer is so strong that the World Health Organization has classified any form of nighttime shift work as a probable carcinogen.[31] "There's a simple truth: the shorter your sleep, the shorter your life. Short sleep predicts all-cause mortality," according to Dr. Walker.[32]

And there's more bad news. Research suggests that the worsening of memory that occurs as we age may in part be because we don't sleep as well as we age. There is some evidence that poor quality, and quantity, of sleep may contribute to dementia and Alzheimer's disease.

Conversely, the good news is that getting adequate sleep helps our cognitive functioning. Sleep is all about reflection, Dr. Walker says. It helps us distinguish between what's novel and new and worth remembering, and what we can let go of and forget. It essentially clears out the storage space in our mind and makes room for what we need. This is another way in which sleep increases our chances of survival.[33]

Sleep as the Glue That Binds Us in Community

In the context of community, what I find most interesting about sleep is that it is critical to forming social connections. Dr. Walker and Eti Ben Simon did a study of more than 1,350 participants who had varying amounts of sleep and sleep deprivation. When the researchers put participants in an fMRI scanner to see what was going on in the brain, they had them watch a video of a person walking toward them. They found that in those participants who had had lots of sleep, a neural network called the "theory of mind" network lit up when the person walked toward them. The theory of mind network is what allows you to understand another person's state of mind, which is one of the foundations of our ability to bond with each other. So the fact that the cells in this region of the mind lit up was a very pro-social reaction. When people who were sleep deprived watched the video, the pro-social network was shut down by another neural network—the one that signals possible danger from an approaching human. This suggests that if we're sleep deprived, we are less able to connect with others, which has obvious implications for the capacity for cooperation and collaboration on the job (and of course in many other areas of life as well). What the researchers found is that how well a person slept could accurately predict how sociable the person would feel the following day. "Just one night of good sleep makes you feel more outgoing and socially confident, and furthermore, will attract others to you," says Dr. Walker.[34]

Lack of sleep puts serious limitations on our ability to connect with others in our community. "We humans are a social species," said Walker. "Yet sleep deprivation can turn us into social lepers."[35] Walker goes on to say that "human beings were not designed to be alone. Sleep is a glue that, biologically and psychologically, binds us together as a species. Ironically, sleep is often viewed as something that takes us away from social activity. The opposite appears to be true. Sleep reconnects us with our social circle; with our friends, colleagues, partners and even with strangers."[36]

A lack of sleep takes a toll on community, as the sleep deprived have trouble regulating moods and emotions.[37] Poor sleep is linked to frustration, impatience, hostility, and anxiety. Sleep deprivation hurts the relationship between leaders and their subordinates,[38] and how much help they provide each other.[39]

There is a silver lining in all of this. Sleep is a treatable issue. It's something that we can seek to improve—to prioritize and change. Experts like Dr. Walker say that sleep is the single most effective thing we can do to reset our brain and body health every day. Information about how to form good sleep habits is readily available in books (including his and Arianna Huffington's *The Sleep Revolution*), health columns in magazines and newspapers, online at many health-related websites, at doctors' and psychologists' offices, etc. And I provide information later in this chapter about what employers can do to promote and enable it among their employees.

Working Less, Achieving More

Multiple research studies reveal that a shorter working week would make people happier and more productive, while statistics from the Organisation for Economic Co-operation and Development (an intergovernmental economic organization) show that countries with a culture of long working hours often score poorly for productivity and GDP per hour worked.

The twenty-thousand-employee survey that Tony Schwartz and I did yielded similar results. We found that the more hours people work, the worse they feel, and the worse they perform. Conversely, employees who work forty or fewer hours a week report the highest levels of focus, engagement, satisfaction, and positive energy at work.

Our study also found that employees get a positive performance boost from each additional break they take during the day. Those who take a break approximately every ninety minutes report a nearly 30 percent higher level of focus across the day. Vacation breaks are productive, too. We found that the more vacation people are able to take, the better they're able to focus when they're working, and the more engaged they become.

A study conducted by Ernst & Young showed that for each additional ten hours of vacation employees took, their year-end performance ratings from supervisors improved by 8 percent.[40] Frequent vacationers are also significantly less likely to leave their firms. And they're likely to live longer, too, according to one of the most extended longitudinal studies in the world, the Helsinki Businessmen Study, which followed 1,222 male executives born between 1919 and 1934 for many decades.[41]

Yet this message has not gotten through to American workers, who left a record number of vacation days on the table in 2018—768 million days, according to new research from the U.S. Travel Association, Oxford Economics, and Ipsos. More than half (55 percent) of workers reported they did not use all their allotted time off. Presumably this is because they felt pressured to achieve more—but in fact they would have done better by working less.

Make Rest and Renewal a Team Effort

Tony Schwartz, the research collaborator I referred to throughout the book, is the founder and CEO of the Energy Project, a consultancy that helps individuals and organizations manage their energy more skillfully in order to avoid burnout. He told me about the work his group did with a team from Ernst & Young, the accounting firm. For accountants, tax season, which runs from January through April, is always an extremely intense, busy time, but in 2018 this team had been working on a particularly challenging project during the busy season, with the result that the team members became so exhausted and demoralized that a majority of them left the company afterward.

To try to change this destructive dynamic, the forty-person EY team worked with the Energy Project to develop a collective Resilience Boot Camp for the 2019 busy season. The Resilience Plan focused on teaching people to take more breaks and get better rest in order to manage their energy—physical, emotional, and mental—during especially intense periods, when people often worked twelve to thirteen hours a day, seven days a week. Here are the five key behaviors the Energy Project suggested:

1. Do your most important work when you first arrive at the office, for an uninterrupted sixty to ninety minutes. Then take a break.
2. Get up from your desk at lunchtime for at least thirty minutes. Do

some type of movement.

3. After every ninety minutes of work, take a break of five minutes or more. If that isn't possible, do one minute of deep breathing.
4. When you stop work for the day, do something that allows you to transition mentally and emotionally between work and home.
5. Set a pre-sleep routine and a bedtime that ensures you get seven hours of sleep or more.

At the beginning of the busy season, the Energy Project ran a daylong session for the EY team, to teach them the principles and practices of managing energy. As a follow-up, every other week for the fourteen weeks of the busy season, the EY employees attended one-hour group coaching sessions during which the team members discussed setbacks and challenges and supported one another in trying to embrace new recovery routines. Each participant was paired with another teammate to provide additional personal support and accountability.[42]

Thanks to the significant shifts in behavior that they made in their work with the Energy Project, the EY team became more efficient, completing their work in fewer hours. So they agreed to take off one weekend day each week. Many left the office significantly earlier than in previous busy seasons. "Employees were able to drop twelve to twenty hours per week based on these changes, while accomplishing the same amount of work," Schwartz told me.

By the end of the busy season, team members felt dramatically better than at the end of the previous one. The team's lead partner reported, "It showed us the extraordinary value of intentionally taking care of ourselves." And five months after the busy season, when accounting teams typically lose people to exhaustion and burnout, this EY team's retention stood at 97.5 percent. A striking contrast to the year before![43]

Tony told me that his "main takeaway" from that experience was "the power of community." Although he and his team at the Energy Project were able to drive great results at other organizations using similar principles of rest and renewal, he believes that the fact that EY made it a community effort in which the team members actively supported one another was what delivered exponentially better, more potent results.

How Companies Can Foster Rest and Renewal

Promote sleep.

Mark Bertolini, who was the CEO of the healthcare company Aetna from 2010 to 2018, and before that its president, is a big believer in the importance of sleep. "You can get things done quicker if you're present and prepared, you can't be prepared if you're half asleep.... Being present in the workplace and making better decisions has a lot to do with our business fundamentals."[44] Bertolini put his company's money (at least a little bit of it) where his mouth was. Under his leadership, Aetna paid employees a bonus of twenty-five dollars per night if they slept for more than seven hours a night, for twenty nights in a row, with a maximum bonus of $500 per year. Not a lot of money, but it sent a message, and the fact that it came from the top probably made it more powerful.

Living the message matters, too. In Rasmus Hougaard and Jaqueline Carter's study of 35,000 leaders and interviews with 250 more, they found that the more senior a person's role is, the more sleep that person gets.[45] Turns out that many of the most high-powered executives, people so famous they need no introduction, now prioritize sleep: Jeff Bezos says he gets eight hours a night, Bill Gates, seven hours, Arianna Huffington, eight hours.[46] Satya Nadella, the CEO of Microsoft, has publicly committed himself to getting eight hours of sleep, which sets an example for everyone at Microsoft.[47]

Offer nap time (and a place for it).

Organizations concerned about employees getting enough rest can also facilitate taking naps. Nike, Cisco, Google, Ben & Jerry's, and Zappos are among the many companies that have recognized the value to their employees' well-being, and also their job performance, of being able to nap on the job. Although not every company has the resources to provide their employees with $13,000 nap pods, as Google has done, most workplaces can set aside a quiet, dark room where employees can take a power nap when needed.

Encourage short breaks.

For leaders, no behavior has a larger effect on lowering employee stress than encouraging their employees to take regular breaks. Breaks don't need to be long! Five to ten minutes is restorative, particularly if you get up and move. (They also help you avoid deep vein thrombosis, or DVT, a blood clot that forms in the vein deep in the leg.)[48]

Make time off a priority.

Our data revealed the bottom line value of recovery in all its aspects, including opportunities for rest and renewal during the workday, disconnecting from work in the evenings and on weekends, getting adequate sleep, and also taking vacations. But because, as mentioned, so many employees don't take enough of their vacation, some organizations have gotten creative. FullContact, a technology company, led an effort to provide one of the best vacation policies in the country. After a year of employment, employees are offered $7,500 for vacation in addition to their paid time off. The catch—they must completely disconnect—no checking work emails, or using Slack, or working on projects. And, they have to go on vacation, or they don't get the money.[49]

Offer sabbaticals.

Another way to encourage renewal is to offer sabbaticals. Sabbatical leaves of six months or more reduce stress levels, particularly for those who fully unplug from work.[50] Many companies are experimenting with mini-sabbaticals in which employees remove themselves from their day-to-day job roles and offer their expertise to nonprofit organizations or entrepreneurs from disadvantaged communities for periods of one to three months.

One leader in technology told me that taking a couple of months' sabbatical "removed a lot of negativity" he harbored from the workplace, and helped him realize that his "internal dialogue was off." The time and space to unplug also gave him a clearer sense of his purpose, which he decided was "helping bring people together." After returning to work energized by his time off, he developed routines to connect to people in his office so that people felt less isolated, and like a tighter knit tribe. He also carried forth some routines that he'd found helpful in maintaining better energy, such as setting aside some time in the morning, and again in the evening, for meditation, and for taking walks outside.

Help your team disconnect.

Multitasking lowers people's job satisfaction, damages personal relationships, adversely affects memory, and negatively impacts health.[51] And multitasking is aided and abetted by all the many devices we are plugged into. In the workplace it's no longer considered unacceptable to look at our phone in a meeting while a colleague is speaking. However, we may pay a price for this, even if we're unaware of it. Research shows that smartphones hijack our minds. Cognitive capacity and overall brainpower are significantly reduced when smartphones are within glancing distance—even if they're turned off and facedown. According to one study, just having a smartphone on their desk reduced participants' working memory capacity by 10 percent, fluid intelligence by 5 percent.[52] The good news is that when the smartphone was placed in another room, all study participants—regardless of preexisting degree of smartphone dependence—returned to their normal levels of performance on cognitive capacity tests.[53]

Leslie Perlow, professor at Harvard Business School and author of *Sleeping with Your Smartphone*, led an in-depth study of the effects of digital disconnection at Boston Consulting Group (BCG). What started as a modest experiment with a six-person team and a skeptical manager in BCG's fast-paced, intense environment generated such powerful results for employees' work lives, the team's work process, and ultimately the client they were working with at the time, that the study triggered a global initiative. Four years later, over nine hundred BCG teams from thirty countries on five continents participated. Perlow found that the consultants who had regularly scheduled nonwork times each week when they disconnected from their mobile devices reported more open communication and greater learning and development. They also delivered a better product to the client, experienced better internal communication, increased learning, and improved delivery to their clients. Employees were also more satisfied with their work-life balance—and their work. BCG was better able to recruit and retain employees.

Just as the Energy Project's work with EY was turbocharged by being a communal effort, Perlow believes that BCG's results were enhanced by the fact that they required collaboration and mutual support. In order to make the disconnection viable, team members had to agree to each other's schedules for time off ("Predictable Time Off," or PTO) each week so that the rest of the team would be available to clients. "It's about learning to cover for each other," said Perlow. "One person will be off today, another person will be off tomorrow…and I mean off—no smartphone, no computer for business purposes. It's about not getting emails or texts that you feel compelled to respond to, and instead freeing this time to do whatever you want that is non-work-related." Team members also supported each other in taking time off, having regular discussions about how well each member was achieving the goal, and being flexible about changing schedules when necessary. These were small changes that had big results:

- 51 percent of people on PTO teams were excited to start work in the morning, versus 27 percent on other teams,
- 72 percent (versus 49 percent) were satisfied with their job,
- 54 percent (versus 38 percent) were satisfied with their work-life balance,
- and significantly more of those on PTO teams found the work process to be collaborative, efficient, and effective.[54]

In short, disconnecting improved not just employees' work lives, but the effectiveness and efficiency of the work process itself. The good news, Perlow noted, was that none of this required an organizational makeover or support from the CEO. All that was necessary was collaboration among teammates who were motivated to make the small changes.

It's helpful to be explicit about limits and expectations, both for yourself and your team. For example, Jen Fisher coaches people to be careful about sending emails on the weekend if they're not urgent. A former member of a different team, Ya-Ting Leaf, chose to go off-line from 4:00 p.m. to 6:00 p.m. every weekday when she was at Deloitte.

Set an example.

Of course, if there is an example set from the top, so much the better. The late Arne Sorenson, CEO of Marriott, used to hold hours of meetings with no phones, computers, or other devices allowed in the room.[55] As a leader, don't underestimate how much your actions may affect others. In a classic study, the anthropologist Lionel Tiger found that the average baboon looks at the alpha male once every twenty to thirty seconds for guidance. Human beings aren't much different. We look to those with the most power in any given situation for cues about what is acceptable behavior and what is not.

Prioritize work-life balance.

This is another arena in which leaders can be very effective by setting an example.

Dan Helfrich is the CEO of Deloitte Consulting. Helfrich actually has two jobs—he's CEO, and he's also the broadcast announcer (the play-by-play voice) of the Georgetown University men's soccer team. As a former college player there and lifelong fan who is so passionate about sports that he almost took a job in broadcasting after college, he's been announcing these games for the last sixteen years. Both of these roles are important to him, and while it might seem to an outsider that anytime there was the potential for a conflict in scheduling Helfrich would of course prioritize the demands of his CEO job over his broadcasting responsibilities, that is not the case. At Deloitte, having a sense of personal purpose, not just organizational purpose, is something that the company's well-being program really encourages, and Dan himself exemplifies that dual focus. His broadcasting work is important to him, so he never neglects it.

"For me to be a complete person who has the energy and the drive to be successful as a CEO, I need a fulfilling life with my four kids and my wife and I need things that give me energy outside of work because that creates oxygen for me to be great when I am at work. And for me, broadcasting is one of those things. Which is why I tell my 56,000 person team that when there's a game at 2:30 on a Wednesday afternoon in the fall that conflicts with an important business meeting that same day, I am going to choose to do the broadcast. I think that sharing that with them is a small way of giving my team permission to make their own choices about what they need to do to create a fulfilling life outside of work."[56] Helfrich feels that giving people the work-life integration message through his own actions is part of his responsibility as a leader. "I never once lied about what I was doing [soccer announcing]. I didn't say I'm sick, or I've got a family commitment. I said this is important to me. And I want others to do the same. That's why I've always empowered people to prioritize and not have to be hiding what's important to them," Helfrich told me.

And people have noticed. Jen Fisher said, "From the time he was a baby consultant to CEO he's been a role model. He's never lost this sense of purpose, it's been a consistent drumbeat."

Jen tries to make sure that she does what she can to encourage this same kind of balance for those on her own teams. At the start of new projects, she will pull them together to have a conversation not just about what is going to be involved—maybe it's going to require a lot of hard work and long hours for six to eight weeks—but about how they can maintain their well-being during the push. Like the teams that Perlow studied at BCG, Jen's teams discuss in advance the personal priorities that are most important to them. Maybe someone is going to need to go home early on Thursday nights because they play in a soccer league, or they have to take a weekend off right before the deadline to attend their child's out-of-town college graduation. Whatever the case may be, if they have this conversation at the outset, it gives everyone the opportunity to make sure their needs are met even at times when a lot is going to be demanded of them.

Ya-Ting Leaf noted that during her time at Deloitte the focus on work-life integration was critical to people's ability to set healthy boundaries. "Prioritizing balance made a big difference." The fact that they did this as a team, having those discussions about what everyone's priorities were, was also important. "The community piece is huge," she said. "We aren't an island." The idea that none of us operates in isolation—as an island—is something to take with you, whether as a member of a team, or as a leader.

A Minister of Education with a Vision and a Young Woman with a Dream

The examples of communal effort given so far have concerned work teams, some large, some small, at various companies. In Bhutan, a country probably best known to the outside world for its Gross National Happiness Index, we have an example of an entire country that made a commitment to well-being—by teaching the skills relating to mindfulness-based emotional intelligence to its teachers, and its government employees. The lessons are being shared with young students in classrooms in Bhutan by principals and teachers.[57] It all started when Norbu Wangchuk, who was then Bhutan's minister of education, heard a keynote by Chade-Meng Tan, author of *Search Inside Yourself*, in 2017. He was intrigued by the neuroscience-based approach to mindfulness, and interested in the programs at the Search Inside Yourself Leadership Institute (SIYLI) that taught these skills. After participating in a full program with SIYLI CEO Rich Fernandez and SIY-certified teacher Yizhao Zhang, where he learned useful breathing and mental habits that helped him achieve calm and clarity of mind, he decided to invite them to Bhutan to conduct a two-day training with Bhutan's teachers. Bhutan's predominantly agrarian way of life, which had endured for many centuries, was experiencing rapid change as it underwent modernization, and Wangchuk thought what he had learned could help the Bhutanese manage the stresses that accompanied such a radical change.

Bhutan is a tiny Buddhist kingdom sitting on the eastern edge of the Himalayas, between India and China. Famous for its rich, ancient traditions, and for the monasteries, fortresses, and dramatic landscapes that range from subtropical plains to steep mountains and valleys, it is a country that until recently had long been isolated from much of the rest of the world. Yet many of the same issues that our society faces—stress, isolation or loneliness, and suicide—have gradually seeped into their communities. Teachers, a crucial linchpin to children, were among those feeling the stress, and the primary target of this stage of the mindfulness campaign. Wangchuk viewed the program as a way of "future-proofing Bhutan"[58] by giving the teachers the mental habits that would help them adapt and be more resilient in this ever-changing world.

As part of the "future-proofing" of Bhutan, Norbu Wangchuk thought Bhutanese children should also be taught the mental and emotional intelligence skills he had learned when he went to the SIYLI program. Like the teachers, the children, too, could benefit from what SIYLI could bring to them, including the skill of empathy—the ability to put ourselves in others' shoes, and offer kindness. The values SIYLI teaches—tolerance and interdependence as well as empathy—are, as Norbu Wangchuk has said, part of a 2,500-year heritage that they now want to explore presenting in new ways. Adding the neuroscience perspective to Bhutan's still-vibrant tradition of meditation and mindfulness turned out to be very persuasive to the teachers who were trained.

Speaking of the pressures operating on the teachers, Tashi Namgyal, district education officer in the Ministry of Education and a former teacher himself, explained that "the social expectations are very high on the teacher and the kind of work that we do doesn't have a fixed time frame in a given day. Because it's an ongoing work you may at times feel overwhelmed—that you're unable to provide the service that you're there to provide. When you boil down and zoom into the needs of children that are directly impacted by you, you realize that some of your children are not able to improve or cope despite the fact that you are there 24/7 doing all that you can." The pressure "takes a toll on you," he said, "and can lead to burnout. It can lead to frustrations. Unhappy teachers will just give rise to unhappy children."[59]

The experience recounted by Wangmo, principal at Gelephu Middle School, illustrates all the points made by Tashi Namgyal. "I had gone through being stressed out almost into depression. I remember silently disappearing from the school saying that I need some time out. Crying over and over at night not realizing what's really happening—going through a lot of long sleepless nights." Unable to distance herself from her work—"I should say that I was hooked on the profession" and "I forgot to lead my personal life"— she said she was "in the job round-the-clock twenty-four hours. I was never out of school even on holidays."

Yizhao Zhang, the project manager who was invited in to direct the SIYLI program in Bhutan, couldn't have been more delighted with the opportunity Wangchuk offered her. A native of Beijing, China, Yizhao Zhang has been teaching mindfulness classes since she was fourteen years old. After attending over fifty meditation retreats and trainings around the world with renowned wisdom teachers, Zhang received guidance to keep sharing what was passed down to her. She spent eleven years in Europe, and then four years in Southeast Asia working for Google, where she taught mindfulness and emotional intelligence courses as part of the hugely popular "Search Inside Yourself" leadership program. When her flight landed in Bhutan in 2018, it was a dream come true for her. While working in Google's Singapore office, she had gone to Bhutan with other Googlers in 2013 to do volunteer work there. She worked with young children in an early childhood care and development center, where they shared stories about their different cultural backgrounds, made drawings, and sang together. It was such a transformative experience that she vowed to come back in five years to teach children the mindfulness program, which included how to pay attention, listen empathetically, and respond to triggers calmly (with steps like stopping, breathing, and reflecting before responding). Nearly five years to the day, it was as though her wish had been granted. Zhang was grateful for what she assumed would be another short stint there. Little did she know that the minister of education had hatched a grand scheme. The two-day program soon metamorphosed into an SIYLI program that had a goal of training all ten thousand of the country's teachers. Under Zhang's leadership, SIYLI first trained one hundred twenty-five Bhutanese teachers, who came from communities all across Bhutan. Their training began with five days of in-person training in Thimphu, the country's capital, after which they returned to their communities and over the course of nine months continued their coursework remotely, and then came back for additional in-person training.

Once the teachers completed their training over the course of about a year, from 2018 to 2019, they were sent out into the field to teach what they had learned to the rest of the country's teachers—teachings that will eventually be shared with young students in classrooms all over Bhutan. The most common feedback Zhang heard from the teachers was along the lines of "I wish I had this earlier. I wish we were taught emotional intelligence skills and mindfulness as children."

The data from nearly three thousand schoolteachers, who completed surveys before and after the program, with follow-up survey data collected one month after, showed a positive change across all the factors that were tracked. Those who participated in the program reported greater self-awareness, self-management, compassion, empathy, leadership, resilience, and satisfaction with life. Wangmo, for example, said that what she learned "manifested a lot of happiness in my life—made my life more meaningful and more wonderful." Another teacher described having a "mindful" conversation with a student who hadn't done her homework. Talking to her, he discovered that her parents had gotten divorced the day before, which of course explained why she had failed to do the work. "That gave me the realization that, as a teacher, we have so many multiple roles, not only to teach but really coming with the heart first."[60]

It didn't take long for excitement about the program to spread. About one year later Bhutan's leaders decided to offer the country's twenty-eight thousand civil servants mindfulness training. Zhang and SIYLI worked with ten ministries and seventy-one public agencies spanning healthcare, agriculture, forestry, and law enforcement to bring this work and this way of being to all civil servants in Bhutan.

Bhutan's leaders have continued to invest in the program, which is now given to new employees as they enter the civil service, and to those who, at the age of sixty, are retiring from it, as well. Many civil servant retirees, having served in the cities and towns of Bhutan during their work lives, return to their homes in the countryside when they leave their jobs. The program gives retirees tools they will need as they go through this major life transition.

Might other communities, with easier access, model a program like Bhutan's? There is certainly a lot of evidence for its benefits. Mindfulness can include training in how to be more attentive to one's breath, body, and surroundings; to listen with kindness and curiosity; to accept one's emotions and be compassionate to oneself; and to respond with empathy. Research indicates the benefits of mindfulness for altruism,[61] employee health,[62] engagement,[63] performance,[64] and leadership effectiveness.[65] Recent studies suggest that meditation reduces anxiety and depression and expands the ability to focus. Mindfulness training can result in a stronger immune system,[66] lower blood pressure,[67] and lower heart rate.[68] People sleep better[69] and feel less stressed.[70] Research found that a short daily mindfulness practice leads to changes in the structure and function of the brain that enhance self-awareness.[71] In a global IT company based in Silicon Valley, researchers found that just five weeks of ten-minute daily mindfulness sessions enhanced self-awareness up to 35 percent.

It's worth noting that some organizations have found that mindfulness and related programs generate cost savings as well as health benefits. Duke University School of Medicine found that practicing one hour of yoga a week decreased stress levels in Aetna's employees by a third, which reduced healthcare by an average of $2,000 per year.[72] In 2008, when he was president of Aetna, Mark Bertolini had a study done on the effects of mindfulness on employees. Mindfulness helped employees reduce stress, improve sleep, and better manage physical pain. In 2012, Aetna reduced its healthcare costs by 7 percent, which Bertolini credited to the stress relief achieved through meditation and yoga.[73]

After Aetna became part of CVS Health in 2018, it expanded its mindfulness program with a Mindfulness Challenge, a four-week series of mindfulness topics that attracted over eight thousand participants, who had no incentive to join it other than to improve their well-being. The results: an 18 percent reduction in stress, 4 percent increase in employee engagement as reported in the corporate survey, and an 87 percent employee recommendation rate.[74]

As a leader, you can do a lot to help promote recovery and prevent burnout. Watch for warning signs—tiredness, lack of focus, depressed mood, hostility, and expressions of hopelessness. Regularly check in with employees to gauge their physical, mental, and emotional energy. Set limits on workloads. Talk to your team about their capacity and deadlines. Shield employees from external pressures such as unreasonable or uncivil customers, patients, or clients. Insist on time for rest and renewal. Push employees to take vacation time—and to unplug and refuel during it.[75] In our study, Tony Schwartz and I found that a mere 20 percent of leaders encouraged sustainable work practices like these.

And again, remember that being a role model for the behaviors you are trying to promote is one of the most effective means of getting your message across. Tony refers to leaders as "chief energy officers" because their energy—for better or for worse—is so contagious. But we have found that fewer than 25 percent of leaders were seen by their employees to be modeling healthy, sustainable ways of working. Employees who worked for leaders who didn't model such practices were far more reluctant to adopt them for themselves, perhaps because they feared they would be judged as slacking off. Conversely, employees who reported to leaders who did model such practices felt empowered to follow suit. And those employees said they were 91 percent more likely to stay in the job, were 85 percent better able to focus and prioritize, and had a 71 percent higher level of health and well-being. They also had more than twice the level of trust in their supervisors.

When leaders do both—promote healthy work practices and role model them—the effect is even more powerful. Their employees reported being 1.2 times as likely to stay at the company as well as 55 percent more engaged by their work, and 53 percent more focused.

In short, there are a multitude of reasons to make wellness and well-being a priority in the workplace. As a leader you can have a big impact. When recovery practices are put into action in the context of a communal, collaborative effort, the effect is further amplified, as Jen Fisher, Tony Schwartz, and Leslie Perlow noted, speaking of their work with Deloitte, Ernst & Young, and Boston Consulting Group.

CHAPTER **10**

Mindset

I will not let anyone walk through my mind with their dirty feet.

—Gandhi

According to Mark Verstegen, our mindset is one of the four pillars of well-being. Verstegen defines mindset as "the reason you wake up each morning, the catalyst that keeps you going."[1] He views it as what connects you to your values, your aspirations, your game plan for becoming who you want to be. Our mindset affects how we face stress, challenges, and setbacks, and determines whether we will develop the passion and perseverance to pursue long-term goals in the face of those obstacles.

For an example of someone whose mindset certainly gave her that kind of passion and perseverance, and someone whose mindset was so contagious that it spread to all those who came in contact with her during her pursuit of a long-term goal, I cannot think of anyone more perfect than a woman I met a couple of years ago when I visited the University of Cincinnati Medical Center(UC Health) to present at its annual leadership event. Early that morning, the leaders seated at our Sharonville Convention Center table were absolutely bursting with excitement and anticipation as we awaited the arrival of someone named Jess Toews, whom I'd never heard of. They promised that I was in for a treat.

When she showed up, I saw a warm, bubbly woman with a wide grin that ends in dimples so deep they are like a permanent feature of her face. Jess grew up in a small town in Kentucky, a happy and healthy young girl who never missed a day of school. After graduating from Morehead State University and marrying her college boyfriend Tim, the Saturday after graduation, Jess got a job as a bank teller in Winchester, Kentucky. To hear her tell it, she was living the American dream, happy in her marriage, active in the volunteer work she and her husband did with children in their Baptist ministry, feeling fulfilled.

In 2009, however, she began having really bad headaches. It felt like a charley horse in her brain. But unlike a charley horse you might get in your leg, this was something she couldn't massage away. Each time she went to the doctor about it, she was told she had a sinus infection. At the same time, Jess began to notice that the hearing on her left side was affected—she felt as though she were hearing sounds through a barrel or underwater. Doctors treated her for an ear infection, but Jess had a feeling something else was wrong, and finally convinced one of the doctors to prescribe an MRI. The next day the doctor called and said, "You have to come to my office immediately, and don't come by yourself... I have your MRI results."

When Tim and Jess went to see the doctor, they learned she had bilateral acoustic neuromas—noncancerous tumors—growing on her auditory nerves. Jess was eventually diagnosed with NF2, a genetic disorder that causes tumors to grow at the site of nerve tissues. The tumors can grow anywhere in the body. If they grow on the auditory nerves, they have the potential to cause problems with balance, hearing, dizziness, facial numbness, and more. There is no cure for the disease, but the doctors she consulted in Kentucky all agreed that the tumor on her left side, which was pressing on both her auditory nerves and her brain stem, was life-threatening and had to come out.[2] But all the doctors she consulted thought the operation was too risky and were unwilling to do it.

Only twenty-five years old when she received her diagnosis, Jess recognized she "was a ticking time bomb," that she could go deaf—or even die—at any time. She took a day—only a day—and she cried a lot. She was mad and scared. The next day she woke up and said, "This is what I've been given, what are we going to do about it? How do I keep living like this?" She went back to work at the bank and to the children's ministry at her church.

Meanwhile her mother reached out to a top specialist in otolaryngology in Los Angeles, Dr. Derald Brackmann, who agreed to look at her case. Three weeks later he told her to fly to LA and he would remove the tumor on the left side—which Jess had named Bertha. Removing the tumor would leave her deaf in her left ear, but during the course of the same operation, he would do an auditory brainstem implant (ABI), which bypasses all the nerves in the ear and connects directly to the brain stem. The ABI would give her the ability to hear sounds on that side. There was just one problem. Jess didn't have the money to cover the operation. It was major surgery that would require a three-to-four-week hospital stay and extensive physical therapy afterward. The problem was solved—or so it seemed—when her church and other local organizations in the community pulled together to raise the required funds, and Jess headed to Los Angeles in November 2009.

As she was being wheeled to the operating room for the sixteen-hour procedure, however, she learned the game plan had changed. At the last moment the insurance company had denied the part of the procedure—the auditory brainstem implant—that would partially restore the hearing on her left side, because, since she still had hearing on her right side, it wasn't considered "medically necessary." Bertha would be removed, but nothing would be added to help her hearing. Knowing that the tumor had to be operated on, Jess was at peace with the choice to go ahead with the surgery. She kissed her husband, told him she loved him, and continued on to the OR.

Jess woke up in the ICU wired with determination. The staff couldn't believe she was talking and goofing off—or that she was walking in only two days. Because she did so well, Jess was released after four days. Though deaf on one side, she gratefully jumped back into life. She and Tim decided to become foster parents in 2011.

In the years that followed, the tumor on her right side grew larger, and the hearing in that ear declined, too. She learned to rely on lipreading and a little sign language to communicate with her children and her husband, but it was certainly a challenging time for her—a time when she began to wear crazy, fun-patterned socks every day because, she says, "In my opinion, you can't have a bad day when you're wearing fun socks.... For me the socks are just a visual [cue] that I can do hard things."[3]

Eventually Jess learned of a treatment trial at the National Institutes of Health (NIH) for pediatrics, and she was allowed to participate. Shuttling back and forth from Winchester, Kentucky, to Bethesda, Maryland, for treatments was well worth it, as her tumor shrank, and her hearing improved. However, when the trial ended, the tumor grew again. This time, Jess turned to Dr. Trent Hummel at Cincinnati Children's Hospital. She received twenty-eight doses of chemotherapy, all while wearing her "crazy fun socks." The tumor did shrink, but the long commutes meant she was missing out on a lot of time with her kids, so she decided to take a break from the treatments for a while—which unfortunately resulted in the tumor growing back once again and her going almost totally deaf.

At this point she was referred to Dr. Ravi N. Samy at UC Health. When Dr. Samy walked into his first appointment with her, Jess, without thinking, blurted out, "Could you please raise your pant legs so I can see your socks?" Dr. Samy obliged, and Jess was shocked to see he was wearing bright, colorful jelly bean socks (socks he later told her his eight-year-old twin daughters had given him). She knew she'd come to the right person. "After seeing those socks, nothing else mattered at all," she remembered thinking. "Whatever he says is what we're doing." His recommendation was that she do radiation treatment to shrink the tumor again and then get a cochlear implant—a small, surgically implanted electronic device that can restore hearing—on her right side. She agreed, on the condition that he promise to wear fun socks in the operating room. "Okay," he replied, "whatever you need, Jess." And this time, since she was virtually deaf by then, the operation would be covered by insurance.

On the day the implant was activated, the first words Jess heard were her daughter saying, "I love you, Mommy." Choking up as she recounted this to me, Jess said, "There are not words…that I can say that can explain to you what it feels like to be able to hear your kids. I had never heard their voices loud and clear."

Next Dr. Samy suggested she get an ABI on her left side, and since she trusted him, Jess again agreed—if he promised to wear crazy socks again. Six months later, as she was being wheeled into the operating room again, she said that she needed to show the surgical team something. She pulled up her operation gown to show off the chicken leg knee socks she was wearing, which made everyone laugh. Jess wanted to set the tone for the surgery—which went perfectly. Everyone in the operating room that day had crazy socks on (she had brought extra in case anyone didn't have them). She was able to go home a couple of days later.

Jess told me that the reason she went ahead with the ABI surgery was that she thought she was being helpful to the surgeons, who wanted her to try it because it was very likely that with tumor growth, the cochlear implant won't work forever. Jess became the first person ever to have two different implants (most people fit the criteria for one or the other). Deaf for eight years in her left ear, she didn't think it would actually work. She had to wait six weeks after surgery, "until everything had time to heal," to go back to the hospital for the activation. When the ABI was finally activated, she heard a beep in her left ear that scared her. She was so overcome with emotion at hearing the sound that she started crying, and soon there wasn't a dry eye in the room.

The day she gave her talk at our leadership conference, the message she gave us was this: "Life is hard and it's going to knock you down. Get back up. Refuse to quit. Enjoy every single second you have been given. And definitely wear fun socks, because they could change somebody's life." In fact, she brought a pair of crazy socks for me that day. (She'd already given them to everyone else at the table.) She's gifted many people with them over the years since her surgeries, always accompanied by the message about mindset.

By the end of her speech and the short video that accompanied it, the audience was visibly moved, with some people weeping. It was clear from what we saw on the video that the sock-wearing team of caregivers who had assisted her through her treatments and surgeries had been changed by her. As Dr. Samy said in the video, "Jess is one of those people that when you meet her, she becomes a part of your life. You just never forget her, and she brings a smile to your face. Jess is one of the most giving, kind people I've ever met in my life." The patient had energized the caregivers, inspired them, and provided meaning and joy and laughter through a high-stakes, challenging case. Her mindset mattered, both to her and to them, and the memory of it stayed with people long after the surgeries they'd performed.

Jess's story shows how your mindset can affect your community. And it also shows that you don't have to be leading the community to make a difference.

But if you *are* a leader, it's all the more important that you try to make that difference, especially if your team is going through something challenging.

For leaders who are having to manage their community in times of struggle, the challenge is to find a way both to acknowledge the fears of your members, and to let them know that you see a way forward—to project hope and confidence while not minimizing the pain that your tribe may have to endure. It's a mindset that is both positive and realistic. Remember that, as a leader, you are always being read by your people. Every nonverbal gesture is scrutinized, every word dissected, every show of emotion magnified. Your own mindset will be contagious, for better or worse. For leaders, this is gut check time. Will you cower before the ordeal, or will you soar? However you respond, your community is likely to follow. As you'll read in what follows, helpful mindsets are actually of several different, often overlapping kinds—positive mindset (which is how I'd describe Jess's), growth mindset, and what has been called neutral mindset. All of these are mindsets that will help you create what Mark Verstegen calls the "software"—the daily choices, habits, and rituals—that will keep you and your community moving ahead. This chapter reveals how your mindset matters, and what strategies you can employ to help you bring your best, mentally, to your communities—and to encourage your tribe to do so, too.

Neutral Mindset

Russell Wilson, quarterback of the Seattle Seahawks and Super Bowl champion, threw perhaps the most heartbreaking interception in Super Bowl history in 2015. It was when his team was down only four points, with a minute remaining on the clock, and the ball on the one-yard line, on the brink of victory, that he threw that interception.

The Seahawks had planned an epic postgame Super Bowl party (win or loss, as most teams do) at a nearby resort where they'd been staying. While the party went on as scheduled, some of the live music acts played "abbreviated sets and some acts failed to show. All the wind was out of the sails," is how Harrison "Harry" Wilson IV, Russell's older brother, described the mood to me. "You could feel the negative energy in the air as you walked around the campus of this resort. Players standing outside in little pods with family members, friends, cousins, teammates. I would imagine they were all talking about what happened at the end of the game...you just wanted to get to your room, and just disappear, not look at Twitter."

Meanwhile about fifteen of Wilson's family and close friends headed to his suite at the resort, where they huddled together waiting for him to arrive. "We just wanted to see Russ, and make sure he was okay. See his eyes and get a sense for where his head was at," Harry said. "The mood was somber and melancholy." Their mother pulled Harry aside, and asked, "How do you think he is? What do you think he's going to say?" Although Harry was sure his brother would be okay in the long run, he didn't expect him to be able to muster any show of good cheer in the immediate aftermath of the game. But when Russell showed up, he seemed to be in fine spirits. He hugged and thanked everyone, and told the group not to worry about him. "I was built for this. I was made for this," he said.

"What he meant by that," Harry explained, "was that he had been spending all these years engineering his adversity tolerance so that he could sustain body blows, so they wouldn't become 'knockout punches.' He knew this moment wouldn't define him, because he was built to recover from this devastating event."

The person who had helped Wilson "engineer his adversity tolerance" was Trevor Moawad, a mental conditioning coach Wilson had worked with very closely since before the NFL 2012 draft. To make sure that his athletes don't get derailed by the defeats that will inevitably come their way, Moawad stresses the importance of "neutral thinking"—a nonjudgmental, nonreactive way of assessing problems and analyzing crises. This includes staying in the moment, reacting to each moment as it unfolds, while also thinking ahead to how to accomplish your next move. You don't get sucked into analyzing past failures, and you also don't get hijacked by fears about the future. You just take one day and one play at a time.[4]

That's what Russell's training with Moawad had prepared him to do, and why Moawad could say this about him: "A lot of people catastrophize things and fall off the mountaintop. Russell doesn't."[5] After the Super Bowl, Russell spent the off-season with Moawad, following the plan Moawad devised to help him make both mental and physical improvements. The emphasis was always on moving forward. According to Moawad there was no lengthy discussion of why the Seattle Seahawks' season ended the way it did. "It was never really anything that needed to be re-framed," said Moawad. The interception "was an isolated play, and you're gonna have isolated great plays, and isolated bad plays. Ultimately you're gonna be measured by what you do next."[6]

To help Russell focus on the "great plays," Moawad put together clips of his long-standing history of successful fourth-quarter comebacks. "He knows that that's what he's about. It's...part of his DNA going back to high school, he's a finisher....He's always finished. He's a world-class finisher. It's who he is. It's how he's been able to do what he does."[7]

Wilson said the video session gave him chills. "You think about all the wins and all the things that have been...accomplished, it's a lot of hard work...but it also gives you that self-confidence that you can do it over and over again if you just keep preparing."[8]

The video wasn't just about reassuring Wilson that he could come back strong, however. It also served a diagnostic purpose, part of Moawad's commitment to neutral, analytic thinking. "We'll look at some of the best moments in his career where he's been able to perform at his highest levels and then just really try to understand specifically what he was doing at that time so he can continue to replicate those types of performances."

How well did Wilson bounce back? The following year he led the NFL in passer rating.

Negativity: The Enemy of Neutrality

What I've found in my research is that the number one thing that pulls people off track is getting mired in negativity. Moawad has certainly found that to be true in his work with athletes—hence his emphasis on the importance of maintaining a neutral mind. And he's found it to be true in his own life, too. His understanding of the destructive effects of negativity was shaped by his father, the late Bob Moawad, a world-renowned peak performance educator, who worked hard to instill self-esteem in Trevor and to protect him from negativity during his formative years. Growing up, Trevor wasn't allowed to watch national news, listen to country music or rhythm and blues, use the word *can't*, or complain. So it was natural to him to bring that message into his own coaching work.

But in late 2018, responding to a challenge from a former Navy SEAL, Moawad conducted a monthlong experiment on himself that was designed to test his long-held belief that managing your intake of negativity is crucial to negotiating life's challenges. To assess the impact of negative thinking, Moawad exposed himself to a diet of all the negative stuff he advises against. He wanted to know whether it would affect how he felt and how he interacted with people. He tuned in to three to four hours a day of external stimuli to drive negative noise into his mind. This included his least favorite news station for an hour each day (which he says often makes you mad, scared, or both), and to an hour and a half of heavy metal and an hour and a half of country music (both of which he hates) also. Moawad told me that the constant barrage of negativity created the most unfamiliar feelings in him—fearfulness, expectations of the worst, doubts about his ability to deal with anything unknown. He suddenly feared driving on the highway. He even canceled appointments with a doctor and a dentist because he believed that they would give him terrible news and he simply couldn't face it. In texts he sent to friends during this time he seemed so unlike himself that his friends got worried about him. Moawad tried to hold it together in his work and whenever he had to speak in public. But twenty-six days into the experiment, Moawad broke down. He was on a flight home from an event when he burst into tears. Back at home he woke up in the middle of the night, a mess. He felt like he was falling apart, physically and emotionally. The next day he decided the experiment was over. He was done.[9]

While Moawad's experience is particular to him and quite extreme, there's plenty of evidence of the toll negativity takes on people.

But unlike Moawad's experiment on himself, in which he basically manufactured the negativity he was exposed to and then made a decision to halt the experiment because it had such a terrible effect on him, our tendency toward negativity can be tough to shake. Our brains persist in their negative interpretations because they have what psychologists Paul Rozin and Edward

Royzman have described as a negativity bias, meaning that negative events are more memorable and powerful than positive events.[10] They quote a traditional Russian adage to illustrate the power of negativity: "A spoonful of tar can spoil a barrel of honey, but a spoonful of honey does nothing for a barrel of tar." The power of the negativity bias holds true across all sorts of events and experiences, ranging from the major to the everyday, and it can affect relationship outcomes, our social networks, even our learning processes. In *The Power of Bad*, journalist John Tierney and psychologist Roy Baumeister detail how negativity can destroy relationships and pollute communities.

Negative words, thoughts, and actions can be lethal. And they're not quickly offset by positive words, thoughts, or actions. The Rule of Four suggests that it takes four good things to overcome one bad thing.[11] Something along these lines is borne out by a study that measured the personalities of employees at several manufacturing companies, ranking them according to criteria like agreeableness, conscientiousness, and neuroticism. The researchers wanted to see how these characteristics affected the work the teams performed. What they found was that the team's performance wasn't driven by the average personality score of the team, as expected, but by the score of the worst person in the team. One disagreeable, lazy, or emotionally unstable member was enough to sink the team and its performance, and that person's effect couldn't be canceled out by a strong member.[12]

Rick Hanson, a psychologist and the author of *Hardwiring Happiness*, summarizes negativity bias as the brain's tendency to be like Velcro for bad experiences but Teflon for good experiences. And there's a reason for this, which relates to our survival mechanisms. The brain is designed through evolution to overlearn from painful experiences because that was how we managed to avoid life-threatening situations. "Our brain is designed to scan for bad news, overfocuses on it, overreacts to it, overlearns from it, and gradually, frankly, becomes sensitized to the negative along the way," Hanson says.[13] And because of this sensitization, we tend to become avoidant of anything that triggers memories of negative experiences in the past. The result, as Hanson explains, is that we may end up prone "to becoming kind of armored and inert when it comes to taking action and daring to change in any kind of way."[14] So what was once an adaptive mental strategy that prevented us from physical harm has turned into something counteradaptive in today's society, in which the ability to be flexible and open to new experiences and learnings is crucial. The negativity bias also makes us underreact to the positives we do notice; good experiences slip right through our brain, creating a "kind of bottleneck that makes it harder to get happiness into [our] brain."[15]

Granted, some of us are more sensitive to negativity than others, not only because of our past experiences but because our brains differ in their sensitivities to adrenaline, serotonin, and other stress modulators and neurotransmitters. A study reported in *Science* found that our genes largely determine whether stress in our lives will cause us to become depressed.[16] This gene also largely determines how we respond to threats, humiliation, loss, and defeat. In short, some of us just have a tougher time dealing with negative events than others do. But we all have some degree of this sensitivity to negativity, which affects us in many different ways, including even the ability to think clearly, as I discovered in some research I did.

In the study, with colleagues Amir Erez, Jake Gale, and Trevor Foulk, we tested what kind of effect exposure to negativity or rudeness might have on people's thought processes. We gathered 214 undergraduates and placed them in one of six groups. Depending on which group they were in, they saw video clips of media interviews that showed either uncivil or neutral behavior, in one of three different contexts—politics, sports, or celebrities. For example, the uncivil sports clip showed a head coach behaving rudely toward a journalist, while the control sports clip was of that same head coach behaving in a normal, or neutral, manner when answering a question about a basketball tournament.

After watching the clip, participants completed various tests of working memory. We found that those who witnessed rudeness had much more difficulty processing and recalling information. They recalled 12 percent less than those who had not witnessed rudeness.

In our next study, we randomly assigned groups of four or five undergraduates to the rudeness or control condition and asked each group to fill out a personality survey. While participants were completing this, an actor, playing the role of another student, arrived late and apologized. In both the control and the rudeness condition, the student was dismissed from the room and not allowed to participate in the study. But in the control condition, the experimenter dismissed the late student in a neutral tone. In the incivility condition, the experimenter dismissed the tardy student rudely, saying, "What is it with you? You arrive late...you're irresponsible...look at you...how do you expect to hold a job in the real world?"

In each of these situations, participants were then given various performance and creativity tasks to complete. We found that those who witnessed rudeness performed 24 percent worse on anagram tasks, and came up with 29 percent fewer creative ideas, which were also rated 23 percent lower on a scale of creativity, during a brainstorming task. In another study those who witnessed rudeness were 27 percent more likely to miss critical information than people who hadn't witnessed it.

We wondered what would happen if people simply read words associated with rudeness. First, we gave people combinations of words to use to make a sentence. Half the participants were provided with words on their lists that evoked rudeness—words like *aggressively*, *bother*, *obnoxious*, *annoying*, and *interrupt*. The other half of our participants were given a list of words that contained no rude associations. Those who read the rude words recalled 3.5 times fewer words than those who hadn't viewed the rude words. Moreover, their performance was 86 percent worse on the anagram tasks, they had 39 percent fewer ideas in the brainstorming task, and the ideas they did come up with were rated 33 percent less creative.

Finally, we found that those who read the rude words had to struggle to concentrate. It took them significantly longer to make decisions, and even to physically record their answers, as compared to those who hadn't seen the rude words. Negativity paralyzed people. Even if we're not supersizing our diet with negativity, as Trevor Moawad did, ingesting even modest amounts of negativity has adverse effects on our potential.

Negativity Is Infectious

Negativity is a virus. It's more destructive than we might think. Not only does it tank people's performance and lead to toxic interactions within the tribe, but, to make matters worse, like any virus, it's contagious, infecting those who are exposed to it. We've learned that even small doses of negativity get passed on to other tribe members.

Research I did with Alexandra Gerbasi found that negative emotions spread throughout social networks at work. People don't necessarily realize that their own negative feelings or energy can infect others, with costly consequence for the tribe and the organization, but the effects are real. For example, in a study I did with Christine Pearson, we analyzed the effects of negativity among 137 managers enrolled in an executive MBA program. Negative emotions led people to displace bad feelings onto their organization, which resulted in decreasing the effort or time they put into work, lowering their level of performance, and reducing their commitment to their organization. They also displaced their negative emotions onto their colleagues, bosses, customers, and clients. Negativity in the workplace led to communication breakdowns, lack of cooperation, failure to share information and knowledge, and decreased productivity.[17]

Poor mental well-being is also like an infectious disease. Researchers studied more than two hundred fifty thousand employees in over seventeen thousand firms over twelve years and found that negative mental health, in the form of anxiety, depression, and stress-related disorders, spreads. They found that newcomers who are diagnosed with these mental disorders or who leave unhealthy organizations (those with a higher prevalence of negative mental health) to start new jobs in other organizations serve as "carriers" of negative mental health and can "implant" depression, anxiety, and stress-related disorders into their people. Managers are particularly influential—they're "superspreaders" who spread low mental well-being more easily.[18]

And if all that's not enough to convince you of the killing effects of negativity, a recent study found that repetitive negative thinking in later life was linked to cognitive decline and greater deposits of two harmful proteins responsible for Alzheimer's disease.[19]

Consider what kind of negativity you might be taking in from your surroundings—the news you read, the social media you peruse, the conversations you overhear, the feedback you get from family, friends, colleagues, and bosses. Even more important, if you are a leader, what kind of negativity might you be dishing out?

How to Counter Negativity

Make it unacceptable in the workplace.

Be clear with your staff that rude, abusive, insulting, or demeaning language will not be tolerated. And to ensure that people know you mean what you say, let them know there will be consequences for such behavior.

Be careful what you verbalize.

Negative language is particularly insidious and potent. Be mindful of what you're thinking and particularly of what you are saying. What we say out loud carries significant weight. Based on research his father did years ago, Moawad revealed that it's ten times more damaging to our sense of thriving if we verbalize a negative thought than if we just think it.

Reframe and neutralize.

Think twice about how you frame a situation. Instead of saying, "This is the worst I've ever seen," or "It's terrible," tweak your language to be more neutral. You might say, "This situation is challenging," which recognizes both the difficulty and the opportunity for growth or learning. You can—and should—acknowledge the truth, while minimizing its power to drag you and your tribe down.

At Second City, if performers are shaking or sweating before an audition or a show, they're coached to say, out loud, "I'm excited" versus "I'm nervous." Second City also taps into community support. Performers have a mantra— "Pat each other on the back because I've got your back"—which they say before performing together.

Experiment. Try controlling your negative expressions for twenty-four hours. Yes, inevitably negative thoughts will cross your mind. Don't let yourself verbalize them. Be mindful of your language—choose it wisely. See how this affects you, your relationships, and your outcomes.[20]

Put the emphasis on progress.

Based on over a decade of research, which included a deep analysis of diaries kept by teammates on creative projects, psychologists Teresa Amabile at Harvard Business School and Steven Kramer, found that what motivates people on a day-to-day basis is the sense that they are making progress. Yet too often progress goes unnoticed in tribes.[21] Effective tribes often keep a scoreboard or find ways to celebrate small wins every day. At The Mighty's office, large whiteboards with numbers track various metrics, like number of readers of a story, or community members participating in an event. Employees update (and celebrate) the numbers throughout the day and week.

This approach is especially helpful during times of change. Rosabeth Moss Kanter, a world-renowned expert in leadership and change at Harvard, has found that change is hardest in the middle period. Inspired beginnings and successful endings fuel us. Everything can look harder and more like failure in the middle. Forecasts fall short, decision makers become stingy with resources, and there are often unexpected obstacles and hidden delays. The middle requires hard work—often harder than people thought it would be. Good leaders look for opportunities to point to progress, supporting and encouraging their communities during the "miserable middle" phase. If they can inch their people forward by helping them to see times like these as an opportunity to develop new skills and capabilities, their mindset will be contagious.[22]

Leaders need to find a way to help their tribes muscle through the hard times in the middle; but they may also, let's face it, have to help them deal with the defeats that sometimes occur at the end. Tina Sung, vice president at the nonprofit Partnership for Public Service, has decades of experience coaching colleagues through change, mergers and acquisitions, and challenges. She described sitting with her own team, with a box of Kleenex on the conference room table, mourning the loss of their company (to an acquisition). Sung recognized the importance of acknowledging loss, but also of getting her tribe unstuck. As she so aptly put it: "You can visit pity city, but you can't live there."

Use nostalgia and make memories to use as nostalgia.

Get your tribe unstuck by reminding them of positive events and accomplishments from the past. Relive your wins, as Wilson did. Use nostalgia to increase your resilience to current psychological threats.[23] When people engage in nostalgia for a few minutes before the start of their workday, they are better at coping with work stresses like a rude manager.[24]

Nostalgia helps counteract anxiety and loneliness. Couples who frequently reminisce about past happy events in their lives together enjoy better relationships.[25] Nostalgia encourages people to act more generously, which feeds and benefits relationships and community. Nostalgia helps people write more creatively. It helps us to finish tasks, overcome adversity, and strive toward goals.[26]

Consider social psychologist Constantine Sedikides, whose personal experiences including a move from Chapel Hill to the United Kingdom sparked innovative work on nostalgia. He has referred to it as the "perfect internal politician, connecting the past with the present, pointing optimistically to the future."[27] He encourages "anticipated nostalgia" by making good memories today that will make for positive thoughts in the future.[28] He's found that the more nostalgic memories that employees have of company events, the less likely they are to look for jobs elsewhere. Events and shared memories, from birthday dinners, anniversaries, to retreats or weekend trips endure and can be a wise investment for people—and communities.[29]

Growth Mindset

Carol Dweck, a pioneer researcher in the field of motivation and the author of *Mindset*, coined the term *growth mindset* while studying why children succeed (or don't) and how to foster success. Those who possess a growth mindset believe that their talents can be developed through hard work, smart strategies, and feedback from others. Those who have a fixed mindset tend to believe their talents, or lack thereof, are innate (and therefore not something they have a lot of power to change).[30]

Decades of research by Dweck and others reveal that the growth mindset is helpful for people and tribes.[31] It's positively related to the desire to work hard and the belief that greater effort leads to success.[32] A growth mindset is associated with persistence, self-determination, and willingness to seek help and feedback.[33] Those with a stronger growth mindset tend to show more initiative about developing themselves.

In 2010, Dweck and her team began collaborating with consulting firm Senn Delaney to learn more about how organizations might profit from a growth mindset. Surveying a diverse group of employees across seven different Fortune 1000 companies they found that companies—and their employees—tended to be characterized by either a growth or a fixed mindset. Employees at fixed-mindset companies felt like only a handful of stars were highly valued. They were less committed to their work, were worried more about failure, and pursued fewer innovative projects. They also tended to keep secrets, cut corners, and cheat to get ahead. Supervisors in growth-mindset companies rated their employees as more innovative and collaborative than supervisors in fixed-mindset companies did—and were more likely to believe that their employees had management potential. The positive feelings were mutual. Employees who worked in growth-mindset companies reported 47 percent higher trust in their company, were 34 percent more likely to feel a sense of ownership and commitment to the future of their company, and had 65 percent stronger agreement that their company supports risk-taking.[34]

How to Cultivate a Growth Mindset

TEACH THE GROWTH MINDSET TO OTHERS—AND MODEL IT.

Leaders and organizations can nudge people toward a growth mindset and reap the benefits.[35] We can see a vivid example of this in what happened at Microsoft. In 2014, when Satya Nadella became CEO, he made it his mission to revamp the leadership culture at Microsoft and to make growth mindset a critical focus of the company culture's transformation. For him, the C of CEO stood for "being the curator of culture." In his book, *Hit Refresh*, Nadella explains that mindsets, and growth mindset in particular, were his primary focus when revamping Microsoft and helping it rediscover its soul.

He spent his first few months on the job teaching people the value of a "learn it all" culture rather than a "know it all" culture. "I talked about these ideas every chance I got. And I looked for opportunities to change our practices and behaviors to make the growth mindset vivid and real."[36]

He led by example, sharing monthly videos where he discussed his top learnings and asked tribes across the company to discuss theirs, which they did. Microsoft created engaging interactive online modules with rich storytelling to teach employees more about growth mindset, and developed conversation guides to help managers facilitate meaningful conversations about what growth mindset looks like in team settings.

PUT THE GROWTH MINDSET INTO ACTION.

In 2014, as part of Nadella's commitment to changing the culture at Microsoft, making it once again a place where employees could take risks to change their world for the better, Microsoft launched an annual weeklong hackathon. Hacking is a long-standing tradition among computer programmers, who come together to use their coding skills to think up creative shortcuts to problem-solving. But under Nadella, the hackathon was something different. It was a company-wide event that invited employees and even interns from all divisions to contribute their skills and ideas to projects that were a break from their regular work responsibilities.

Although the hackathon was voluntary and Microsoft didn't know whether anyone would come, in the first year more than twelve thousand employees from eighty-three countries participated. They created more than three thousand hacks aimed at goals as diverse as ending sexism in video games, improving industrial supply-chain operations, and delivering better learning outcomes for kids with dyslexia. The winner of the hackathon that year was the Ability Eye Gaze, an interface that allows people with ALS and other disabilities to use eye movements to operate devices ranging from wheelchairs to their computers. The hackathon proved hugely popular and has become an annual event, attracting an ever-increasing number of employees. More than that, it has evolved into a way of working and thinking that embodies Nadella's ideas about a growth mindset.

RECOGNIZE A GROWTH MINDSET WHEN YOU SEE IT.

For Nadella, Phil Spencer, executive vice president of gaming at Microsoft, who leads the Xbox brand and the global creative and engineering teams for the gaming division, is a person who embodies his idea of a growth mindset. Some years ago Spencer and his team became interested in the Sweden-based company Mojang, because it had developed the hugely successful video game *Minecraft*. *Minecraft* holds great appeal for gamers but also for teachers, who love the way it encourages creativity, collaboration, and exploration. Before Nadella became CEO, Spencer pitched the idea of Microsoft acquiring *Minecraft*, but his boss at the time opted not to move forward. Spencer didn't fold. He believed that the game belonged at Microsoft, and continued to maintain a great relationship and build trust with Mojang. And then, not long after Nadella became CEO, Spencer received a text that Mojang was for sale, and brought the opportunity to Nadella. This time his pitch was successful. Microsoft spent $2.5 billion to acquire Mojang. Since the acquisition, Spencer and his team have managed to make it possible to play *Minecraft* on a number of different platforms, not just Xbox but Nintendo and PlayStation, among others, and it works on tablets, consoles, smartphones, and PCs. *Minecraft* is now one of the bestselling games of all time.[37]

Nadella views *Minecraft* as symbolic of a growth mindset because "it created new energy and engagement for people on our mobile and cloud technologies and opened up new opportunities in the education and software space," and he sees Spencer's story of pursuing *Minecraft* as indicative of what one person with a growth mindset can do against the odds.

The result of Nadella's focus on a growth mindset? From 2001 to 2014 the market capitalization and stock price at Microsoft stayed largely the same. Under Nadella's leadership, the company's market capitalization, stock capitalization, and stock price have more than tripled.[38]

INVEST IN YOUR TRIBE'S LEARNING.

Sarah Robb O'Hagan, CEO of EXOS whom you met in chapter 8, admitted that she always steered clear of finance. Actually, she "freakin' hated it."

However, once she became global president of Gatorade, she knew she had to be responsible for guiding all aspects of the business. So she asked her boss, Massimo d'Amore, if she could take a finance course. He one-upped her, and agreed to send her to Harvard Business School Executive Education. She remembered calling her husband most nights during the program, saying, "I think I'm becoming a total finance geek!" O'Hagan says the learning made her a far more experienced and balanced executive. She understands conversations tied to the financials of companies and is able to ask smart questions, which lead to answers that provide her with a deeper understanding of her company's needs. "Finance no longer feels like a foreign language," she says.[39]

Positive Mindset

Jess Toews exemplifies what it means to have a positive mindset. She's someone who's always able to see that there's a way to survive and thrive, whatever the circumstances she finds herself in, and she has a gift for inspiring a sense of purpose and joy in those around her. Another person who seems to me to have the same kind of spirit, and who has been able to bring it to a global company that employs hundreds of thousands of people, is David Rodriguez, the global chief human resource officer of Marriott, whom you met in chapter 6.

In May of 2014, Rodriguez was on vacation with his family. He had spent the morning on the beach, helping to clean it, when he broke for lunch and got a message that his doctor had been desperately trying to reach him. When Rodriguez returned the call, his doctor begged him to come into Johns Hopkins immediately. Once he arrived, he learned that he had a very serious cancer, and that if he hoped to survive it, the prescribed treatment would be extremely aggressive and tough to endure, and that it was necessary for him to start as soon as possible.

David Rodriguez could have crumbled. He could have pushed to savor the long-awaited days at the beach with his family and delayed taking action. He could have wallowed in indecision, fearful of learning about the specific challenges that lay ahead. Or he could have just decided that he wasn't up for undergoing such a difficult treatment regimen. Instead, following the advice of his doctor, he hurried home, showed up at the hospital the next day, and faced the negative news head-on.

During the difficult months that followed, he had to remain in the hospital for his treatment, enduring chemotherapy every three hours, twenty-four hours a day, every day. Because of his compromised immunity during this time, he was allowed very few visitors and felt like he was "living in a bubble."

His medical team warned that he might have to spend a year in the hospital, but David hoped that eventually he could go home and receive treatment on an outpatient basis. And that hope was the catalyst for some changes he made. "One day, after my body had adjusted to treatment...a thought came to me." He realized that "the doctors were more likely to accelerate my transition to outpatient chemotherapy if I was not just physically strong enough, but also mentally and spiritually ready." To strengthen himself physically, he embarked on an energetic walking program, taking laps down the hospital corridors. Soon he began tracking his laps, keeping a scoreboard in his room. "It wasn't long after that I was christened 'Lap King' by a staff member who noticed I was keeping a daily log of my whirls around the ward."

At a time when his visitors were so restricted, he realized that isolation was taking a toll on him, and that making himself mentally ready would require him to reach out to those people whom he did have regular contact with—in other words, his medical team.

Rodriguez has a terrific sense of humor, so he mustered the energy to crack jokes and deliver one-liners to those who were caring for him. He said, "Soon, I had staff members laughing. I got to know more of them as I walked and then race-walked around the ward with my I.V. in tow." Rodriguez began to see his moments of positivity and humor as a gift he could give to the devoted staff members who nursed him back to health.[40] And gradually his feelings of social isolation lessened. He told me, "I wanted to draw in community with me." Small daily actions "made the walls between us melt a bit."

On the day that a decision was to be made about whether he was ready for an early release to outpatient status, Rodriguez staged "a performance that was Oscar-worthy." Awake early that morning, he set up shop at the table in his room, with an IV machine on his side, and laptop on the table. He propped up his iPad to write emails while his Bluetooth speaker blared favorite songs. As the doctors and hospital staff came in for the morning round, Pharrell Williams's "Happy" was blaring and Rodriguez was laughing with a friend on his iPhone. Later that day came the news that the staff had determined that he was now ready to go home. And just as he had thought was the case, "A nurse confirmed that my performance was a factor in their 'parole' decision."[41]

What Rodriguez learned during those three months in the hospital, and the nine months of chemotherapy twice a week that followed, has served him well ever since, both personally and in his career. He's aware that negativity—anxiety, depression, and stress, and other aspects of poor mental health—can be contagious, and he's careful not to spread it. He went one step further, hoping that his positive spirit would help to buffer what the nurses, staff, and physicians caught daily—the cries and groaning from suffering patients, the negative diagnoses, and the yellow tape across rooms, which indicated a patient death.

When he returned to Marriott, he encouraged people to think of their TakeCare program more holistically. His time in the hospital had taught him that true well-being has to encompass the social—your ties to those you work, interact, and live with, and beyond that to the broader society. And forging those connections makes you feel empowered, as he did when he felt he could bring moments of humor to the nurses.

Rodriguez learned that it's "not about big bangs, but the smaller behaviors." "There is a lot in life we cannot control," he adds. "But there are also important choices that we can make. We can choose to be positive. We can choose to see the humor in things and enjoy a healing laugh every day. We can choose to turn personal adversity into a gift of hope to offer someone else."[42] He knows from experience that it's always possible to make a difference in someone else's life, even if it's just something as simple as enjoying a shared moment of laughter in the midst of a dark time.

Saying "it's all in your mind" used to be a way of dismissing the importance of our thoughts and feelings in favor of some notion of an inalterable reality.

But we now know a lot more about how the inner workings of the mind can effect changes in that reality, for both the better and the worse. The stories I've told in this chapter are about people who have the kinds of mindsets that have made a positive difference for themselves and their communities.

Consider how your mindset is affecting your teams, families, organizations, and communities. Your mindset can help lift people up or pull them down. Adopting a neutral mindset can guide them through losses and disappointments by showing them how to learn from the past and move forward into a better future. Adopting a growth mindset helps people to become their best selves, and to bring those selves to their communities. Having a basically positive mindset is a gift that makes facing challenges easier and inspires those who come in contact with it—because while negativity is a virus that is contagious, positivity is infectious, too.

David Rodriguez, Russell Wilson, Jess Toews, Satya Nadella, and Trevor Moawad are all examples of how to use mindset not just to lift ourselves up, but to make life better for those around us. We can improve our tribe's resilience, we can help them get unstuck, we can show them how to move from emotions to actions. And while you may not be able to stop the flow of negativity in your life, you can resist its toxic effects by making smart choices about whom and what you surround yourself with, the mindset you adapt, and the information you consume. Not only will you be better off because of these choices, but those around you will, too. Like these people, you can be an energizer in your community through your mindset. "The best is yet to come" (BYTC)— is a saying Russell Wilson lives by and shares with his tribe often. Your actions are more contagious than you might think. We are carriers, potentially affecting others' mindset, mental health, and potential, for better or worse.

Finding Ubuntu

> One of the sayings in our country is Ubuntu—the essence of being human. Ubuntu speaks particularly about the fact that you can't exist as a human being in isolation. It speaks about our interconnectedness. You can't be human all by yourself, and when you have this quality—Ubuntu—you are known for your generosity... When you do well, it spreads out; it is for the whole of humanity.
>
> —Desmond Tutu

It was early fall of 2007. There was a meeting of the Marquette University board of directors and when they broke for lunch, two members of the board, former classmates, had a chance to chat with each other. One was Stephanie Russell, head of the school's Office of Mission and Identity. The other was Doc Rivers, then coach of the NBA's Boston Celtics.

The Celtics were coming off a dismal season with twenty-four wins and fifty-eight losses. Training camp was just a few weeks away, and nine of the fifteen players who would be showing up at training camp were new to the team. "I thought we really needed something to connect us to each other," Rivers recalled.

And that's when it happened. Out of Russell's mouth came a word that spoke to Rivers: Ubuntu. "Right when she said that, I said, 'That's it. That's the word. That's the philosophy. That's what I need.'"

Once Rivers taught it to the team, egos fell to the wayside. Players embraced whatever roles they were given. The team truly united behind a goal and on the means to get there. "Without that word our season could've been different," Rivers says. "It was a perfect philosophy for our team."

In 2008, the Celtics went on to win the NBA championship with the greatest turnaround season in history, from a record of 24–58 to 66–16, a forty-two-game swing.

Many of the players credit their turnaround to the word that became their rallying cry. They wore it on bracelets and T-shirts, posted it in their locker room, and broke every huddle by shouting it.[1]

Ubuntu, as described by Desmond Tutu, was the magical rallying cry, the motto that encapsulated everything they wanted to stand for that season.

Pronounced Ooh-BOON-too, the word comes from the African Bantu language and describes a philosophy that loosely translates to "I am what I am because of who we all are."

Could Ubuntu be a game-changing philosophy for your workplace or community? Ubuntu means so many things:

- Working toward the same goal
- Understanding each other's roles on the team
- Setting each other up to succeed
- Treating each other with respect
- Coaching each other by providing feedback
- Supporting each other through the highs and lows
- Celebrating victories
- Learning from defeats

How can we have Ubuntu in our lives? Start small. Look for opportunities to connect. Unplug for periods of time and fully tune in to others in your tribe. Take a hike in nature with someone. Volunteer to help a neighbor or member of your community. Send a thank-you note. Visit family and friends. Cook together. Host a gathering. Prioritize people.

In 2017, Carla Piñeyro Sublett, a twenty-year veteran of the technology industry (whom you met in part 2), had spent two and a half years as chief marketing officer at Rackspace, a period during which the company was positioning itself to be sold. It did sell, but those were the hardest years in her career. "I sat in my kitchen one morning, looked up, and saw my kids packing their lunches, and my husband making his breakfast, and no one speaking to each other," Carla told me. "I felt like a ghost in my own home. It wasn't the sort of life I wanted. I felt lost and disconnected."

That moment in her kitchen impelled her to the realization that she needed to reconnect with what was most important in her life—mainly her children, then ages fourteen and eleven, and her husband. She quit her job, vowing to take a full year off to find her way back to them, and to herself.

She wasn't quite sure what she wanted to do, but about a month later she attended an Aspen Institute seminar on global leadership—part of her Henry Crown Fellowship, which seeks to develop the next generation of community-spirited leaders. They were learning about Nelson Mandela's and Desmond Tutu's philosophy of Ubuntu, which was "all about connection."[2] The week she spent there gave her the idea that the most meaningful thing she could do with her year would be to take her kids out into the world in an effort to "pop their bubble"—the bubble that prevents all of us from seeing our connections to each other, and not just to the people in our immediate communities, but to people in the community at large, the global community. Her family decided to take four long trips, spending time in India, Bhutan, Mexico, Croatia, France, Italy, and Japan. The trips spanned different cultures during their respective holy weeks. She called it "Finding Ubuntu" and decided that her family would travel virtually device-free during their time abroad, taking only one notebook computer to upload journal entries just "to tell family we're alive and okay."

For Carla her year off allowed her "to figure out who I was without work. I realized that when people had asked me how I was doing, I'd answer based on how things were going that quarter. I also realized that I had become extremely disconnected from my heart. I was functioning from brain and gut only (not heart). I had developed two personas...work and home...and they were very distinct. Over the course of this year, those two personas merged."

What most struck Carla about her children's experience during that year was the connections she saw them making, both with each other and with those they encountered on the road, regardless of culture or age. They were able to see community everywhere, sometimes in ways to which she herself had been blind. One evening at dinner, she asked her son how he felt about what they had seen in the streets of Old Delhi and Agra, India. When he told her that he saw community, she probed further, and asked: "What about when we saw those men bathing in the alley?" He said, "So? It works for them." Carla realized that where she felt pity and shame, he saw people coming together in a meaningful communal act. "And he's right. We have witnessed the role of family, friendship, work, food, fun, religion and how universal it all is."

Although Carla's journey back to herself, and into a deeper understanding of her place in the world, came during a year of travels, one of the lessons she and her tribe learned is that you don't need to go to the ends of the earth to find connection. You can do it in your own backyard and it doesn't cost a dime. It does take discipline, however, like making a conscious decision to disconnect from technology and tune in to one another—listening, talking, sharing a meal together, and talking about your day, Carla said.

While she was away, a good friend wrote to Carla: "From all my retreats and travels, what strikes me most is that all of the lessons I keep learning are available to me right here at home...the connection and love we're all seeking is right here in us, and the opportunities for deeper growth are right across the street, or maybe even in the mirror."[3]

Yet, Ubuntu—that sense of belonging and interconnectedness—feels elusive for many of us. One way to find it is to plug into tribes and organizations that seem to have mastered it. Carla had expected to look for a CEO role when she came off her year of Finding Ubuntu. Instead she ended up taking a chief marketing role with a company she admired for its values. "What I realized with this time away is that the people I work with and for are the most important thing in making career decisions," she told me. When she considered her options, she prioritized organizations that valued connection and that made a difference in their communities.

Organizations and communities, if approached with the right perspective, can be bright spots for people, and society. They can be the place where we practice coming together to unite and support one another, the place where we learn that even the smallest actions can make a difference for someone else in our community.

In the end it is up to each of us to see what we can do to make our tribes—family, friends, religious, work—and our community a place where we find Ubuntu.

ACKNOWLEDGMENTS

I've been blessed with family, friends, teachers, churches, and communities that have lifted me up and taught me about thriving tribes and communities. My experiences at Gilmour, College of the Holy Cross, and University of North Carolina at Chapel Hill shaped my future and interests. I'm also grateful to The Mighty community for inspiring this work.

The insights here were brought to life by thousands of individuals who described their work experiences to me. I am grateful for their candor, which has educated and inspired me for more than two decades. In particular, I'm grateful to Sara Ray, Marshall Goldsmith, Dorie Clark, Alisa Cohn, Marianne Sumego, Tawny Jones, Adrienne Boissy, Fran Katsoudas, Kim Scott, Ralph Boyd, Becky Kanis Margiotta, Joe McCannon, Rosanne Haggerty, Ryan Martinez, Gary Kelly, Whitney Eichinger, Raquel Daniels, Michael Nixon, Aman Bhutani, Jen O'Twomney, Karen Tillman, Rebecca Onie, Jeremy Andrus, Jane Walters, Jordan Pack, Chris Lu, Stuart Price, Matt Dailey, Kelly Leonard, Christa Quarles, Chris O'Neill, Alan Friedman, Amy D'Ambra, Ellie D'Ambra, Kim Malek, Jean Sharon Abbott, David Rodriguez, Leah Evert, Minh Tam Quang Thi, DeeAnn Hobbs, Jozsef Ladanyi, Julian Lowry, Jehan Suanico, Tom Gardner, David Gardner, Lee Burbage, Kara Chambers, Sanjay Amin, Eric Dickson, Tod Wiesman, Laura Flynn, Jena Adams, Carol Flynn, Tasha Eurich, Peter Sims, Susan David, Anson Dorrance, Mark Verstegen, Amy Verstegen, Sarah Robb O'Hagan, Allison Schoop, Amanda Carlson-Phillips, Michael Forman, Alexandra Wicksell, Jen Fisher, Dan Helfrich, Yizhao Zhang, Jess Toews, Ravi Samy, Anya Sanchez, Rick Lofgren, Russell Wilson, Harry Wilson, Trevor Moawad, D. J. Edison, Tina Sung,

ACKNOWLEDGMENTS

Nina Vaca, Carla Piñeyro Sublett, Ya-Ting Leaf, Jeff McHenry, Mimi Weber, Matthew Davis, Mary Mulligan Thorne, Jo Solet, Barbara Reynolds, and Tina Quinn. Thanks to Laszlo Bock, Jennifer Kurkoski, and Google for its re:Work conferences and Global People Ops meeting.

I'm grateful to the team at Fletcher & Company. I appreciate the wonderful guidance of literary agents Grainne Fox and Christy Fletcher. You helped me navigate the entire publication process while keeping my spirits up, providing unwavering support along the way. Thanks for leading me to Beth Rashbaum, an extraordinary editor whose suggestions consistently added tremendous value. She provided radical candor and thoughtful editing.

I appreciate valuable feedback from Seth Schulman and Rachel Gostenhofer in the early conception of the book. I'm grateful for Christine Pearson's mentorship, and the opportunity to collaborate with her over decades. I've learned so much from her. Thanks also to Jane Dutton, Tom Bateman, and Ed Lawler for your mentoring.

I am deeply grateful to Gretchen Young and Grand Central Publishing for believing in me and championing the project, as well as providing exceptional feedback and edits. My thanks go to Carolyn Levin for her review, and Angelina Krahn for her excellent copyediting. Thanks to Haley Weaver and others at Grand Central Publishing. I appreciate all the work you've done!

I appreciate collaborations with Tony Schwartz, Amir Erez, Alexandra Gerbasi, Gretchen Spreitzer, Cristina Gibson, Robert Cross, Kristin Cullen-Lester, Andrew Parker, and other colleagues. Many thanks to Ryan Kaps for your strong encouragement and support. I'm grateful to Bob Sutton for his support and wisdom. I appreciate Sanoop Luke's ideas and thoughts about our inner tribe and thriving. Thanks to Dan Pink, Mark Kennedy, Adam Grant, Kimberly Perttula, Amy Wrzesniewski, Amy Gallo, Heather Knight Ahearn, Lauren George, Bailey O'Donnell, and Laura Hastings Faith for your helpful assistance and encouragement.

I am incredibly grateful to my family—my parents, Mark Porath, Carrie and Tripp Cherry, Mike and Sarah Porath, my niece, and nephews—and close friends for their support. They are always lifting me up and making me smile!

INDEX

TK—16 pages

INDEX

INDEX

INDEX

INDEX

INDEX

INDEX

INDEX

INDEX

INDEX

INDEX

INDEX

INDEX

NOTES

INTRODUCTION

1 McPherson, M., Smith-Lovin, L., & Brashears, M. E. (2006). Social Isolation in America: Changes in Core Discussion Networks over Two Decades. *American Sociological Review*, *71*(3), 353–75. https://doi.org/10.1177/000312240607100301.

2 Fox, M. (2018, May 10). Major Depression on the Rise Among Everyone, New Data Show. NBC News. https://www.nbcnews.com/health/health-news/major-depression-rise-among-everyone-new-data-shows-n873146.

3 Hadley, C. N., & Mortensen, M. (2021, Winter). Are Your Teammates Lonely? *MIT Sloan Management Review*. https://sloanreview.mit.edu/article/are-your-team-members-lonely/.

4 Twaronite, K. (2019, February 28). The Surprising Power of Simply Asking Coworkers How They're Doing. *Harvard Business Review*. https://hbr.org/2019/02/the-surprising-power-of-simply-asking-coworkers-how-theyre-doing.

5 Achor, S., Kellerman, G. R., Reece, A., & Robichaux, A. (2018, March 19). America's Loneliest Workers, According to Research. *Harvard Business Review*.

6 Ozcelik, H., & Barsade, S. (2018). No Employee on an Island: Workplace Loneliness and Job Performance. *Academy of Management Journal*, *61*(6), 2

343–66. https://doi.org/10.5465/amj.2015.1066; Barsade, S., & Ozcelik, H. (2018, April 24). The Painful Cycle of Employee Loneliness, and How It Hurts Companies. *Harvard Business Review*. https://hbr.org/2018/04 /the-painful-cycle-of-employee-loneliness-and-how-it-hurts-companies.

7 Murthy, V. (2017, September 26). Work and the Loneliness Epidemic. *Harvard Business Review*. https://hbr.org/2017/09/work-and-the-loneliness -epidemic.

8 Spreitzer, G., & Porath, C. L. (2012, January–February). Creating Sustainable Performance. *Harvard Business Review*, 92–99. https://hbr.org/2012/0 1/creating-sustainable-performance.

9 Ryan, R. M., & Deci, E. L. (2000). Self-Determination Theory and the Facilitation of Intrinsic Motivation, Social Development, and Well-Being. *American Psychologist*, 55(1), 68–78. https://doi.org/10.1037/0003-066X. 55.1.68; and Deci, E. L., Connell J. P., & Ryan, R. M. (1989). Self-Determination in a Work Organization. *Journal of Applied Psychology*, 74(4), 58 0–90. https://doi.org/10.1037/0021-9010.74.4.580.

10 Totterdell, P. (1999). Mood Scores: Mood and Performance in Professional Cricketers. *British Journal of Psychology*, 90(3), 317–32. https://doi.org/10. 1348/000712699161422; Christakis, N., & Fowler, J. (2009). *Connected: The Surprising Power of Our Social Networks and How They Shape Our Lives* . New York: Little, Brown; and Kensbock, J. M., Alkærsig L., & Lomberg, C. (2021, May 18). The Epidemic of Mental Disorders in Business—How Depression, Anxiety, and Stress Spread Across Organizations Through Employee Mobility. *Administrative Science Quarterly*. https://doi:10.1177/000 18392211014819.

CHAPTER ONE: CREATE A TRIBE THROUGH SHARING INFORMATION

11 Kerr, S., & Carroll, P. (2020, April 28). NFL Draft Recap, Handling a Championship Loss, and Vulnerability in Sports with Brené Brown. *Flying Coach with Steve Kerr and Pete Carroll* [Audio podcast]. https://www .theringer.com/2020/4/28/21239564/nfl-draft-recap-handling-a-champi-

onship-loss-and-vulnerability-in-sports-with-brene-brown.

12   Jackson, P., & Delehanty, H. (2006). *Sacred Hoops: Spiritual Lessons of a Hardwood Warrior*. New York: Hyperion.

13   Kerr, S., & Carroll, P. NFL Draft Recap, Handling a Championship Loss, and Vulnerability in Sports with Brené Brown. *Flying Coach with Steve Kerr and Pete Carroll* [Audio podcast].

14   Hoffer, R. (1996, May 27). Sitting Bull. *Sports Illustrated*. https://vault.si .com/vault/1996/05/27/sitting-bull-phil-jackson-may-invoke-sioux-lore -and-zen-mysticism-in-coaching-michael-jordan-co-but-the-real-message -is-play-smart-basketball.

15   Ibid.

16   Shelburne, R. (2020, April 26). How Phil Jackson Is Influencing Today's NBA Coaches. ESPN. https://www.espn.com/nba/story/_/id/29101166 /how-phil-jackson-coaching-legacy-influencing-nba.

17   Hoffer, Sitting Bull.

18   Jackson & Delehanty. *Sacred Hoops*.

19   Jackson & Delehanty. *Sacred Hoops*.

20   Hoffer, Sitting Bull.

21   Jackson & Delehanty. *Sacred Hoops*.

22   Ibid.

23   Kerr & Carroll. NFL Draft Recap.

24   Geller, J. (2019, April 19). Group Visit Series Part 1: Lessons from Two Decades of Group Visits. *Evolution of Medicine* [Audio podcast]. https: //functionalforum.com/podcasts/podcast-group-visit-series-part-1-lessons -from-two-decades-of-group-visits.

25   Hyman, M. The Love Diet: Healing Through Community, with James Maskell & Tawny Jones. *The Doctor's Farmacy* [Audio podcast]. https: //drhyman.com/blog/2019/11/13/podcast-ep80/.

26   Jones, T. (2019, May 19). Group Visit Series Part 3: The Cleveland Clinic Is "Functioning for Life." *Evolution of Medicine* [Audio podcast]. https: //functionalforum.com/podcasts/podcast-group-visit-series-part-3-the -clevelandclinic-is-functioning-for-life.

27   Hyman. The Love Diet.

28   Shibuya, K., Pantalone, K., & Burguera, B. (2018, December 14). Obesity:

Are Shared Medical Appointments Part of the Answer? Consult QD . https://consultqd.clevelandclinic.org/obesity-are-shared-medical-appointments-part-of-the-answer/.

29 Cleveland Clinic. (2021, April 13). Cleveland Clinic Study Finds Functional Medicine's Shared Medical Appointments Deliver Improved Patient Outcomes at Less Cost. https://newsroom.clevelandclinic.org/2021/04/13/cleveland-clinic-study-finds-functional-medicines-shared-medical-appointments-deliver-improved-patient-outcomes-at-less-cost/.

30 Hyman. The Love Diet.

31 Lavoie, J.G., Wong, S.T., Chongo, M. et al. (2013). Group Medical Visits Can Deliver on Patient-centered Care Objectives: Results from a Qualitative Study. *BMC Health Services Research, 13,* 155.

32 Hyman. The Love Diet.

33 Wylie, M. (2016, March 10). Cisco's Chief People Officer Is "Breaking HR ." Bizwomen, https://www.bizjournals.com/bizwomen/news/profiles-strategies/2016/03/san-jose-cisco-s-chief-people-officer-is-breaking.html?page=all.

34 For All Summit. (2019). In Conversation: Executive Leadership Team at Cisco [Video and transcript]. https://www.greatplacetowork.com/forall-summit/keynotes/in-conversation-executive-leadership-team-at-cisco.

35 Wylie. Cisco's Chief People Officer Is "Breaking HR"; and Moorhead, P. (2018, August 8). Cisco's "People Deal" Exemplifies Its Cutting Edge Commitment to Employees. *Forbes.* https://www.forbes.com/sites/patrickmoorhead/2018/08/08/ciscos-people-deal-exemplifies-its-cutting-edge-commitment-to-employees/?sh=21d2fe087ff7.

36 Moorhead. Cisco's "People Deal" Exemplifies Its Cutting Edge Commitment.

37 In Conversation: Executive Leadership Team at Cisco.

38 Ibid.

39 Segal, G. Z. (2019, April 3). This Self-Made Billionaire Failed the LSAT Twice, Then Sold Fax Machines for 7 Years Before Hitting Big—Here's How She Got There. Make It. CNBC. https://www.cnbc.com/2019/04/03/self-made-billionaire-spanx-founder-sara-blakely-sold-fax-machines-before-making-it-big.html.

40 Briody, B. (2018, June 21). Sara Blakely: Start Small, Think Big, Scale Fast
    . Insights by Stanford Business. https://www.gsb.stanford.edu/insights/sara
    -blakely-start-small-think-big-scale-fast.

41 MasterClass, Sara Blakely. https://www.masterclass.com/classes/sara
    -blakely-teaches-self-made-entrepreneurship.

42 Lardinois, F. (2020, February 18). Alphabet Takes the Wind out of Its
    Makani Energy Kits. TechCrunch, https://techcrunch.com/2020/02/18
    /alphabet-takes-the-wind-out-of-its-makani-energy-kits/.

43 Teller, A. (2020, February 12). Tips for Unleashing Radical Creativity. X
    blog. https://blog.x.company/tips-for-unleashing-radical-creativity-f4ba55
    602e17.

44 Teller, A. (2016, April 20). Celebrating Failure Fuels Moonshots [Entire
    Talk] Astro Teller. Stanford eCorner. https://ecorner.stanford.edu/videos
    /celebrating-failure-fuels-moonshots-entire-talk/attachment/4208/https:
    //www.google.com/url?sa=t.

CHAPTER TWO: UNLEASH

45 Carnegie Foundation. (2017). *Becky Margiotta and Joe McCannon's 2017
    Summit Keynote Video.* https://www.carnegiefoundation.org/resources/vid-
    eos/becky-margiotta-and-joe-mccannons-2017-summit-keynote-video/.

46 Drabkin, D., Jamieson, J., Rao, H., Soule, S., & Sutton, B. (2016). L-30
    The 100,000 Homes Campaign. https://stanford.edu/dept/gsb-ds/Inkling/
    100.html.

47 Ibid.

48 Ibid.

49 Foderaro, L. (1994, December 28). A Rare Mix of Tenants: Working Resi-
    dents Create a New Model for Welfare Hotels. *New York Times.* https:
    //www.nytimes.com/1994/12/28/nyregion/a-rare-mix-of-tenants-working
    -residents-create-a-new-model-for-welfare-hotels.html; Moore, J. (2009,
    September 7). Taking the homeless beyond shelters. *The Christian Science
    Monitor.* https://www.csmonitor.com/The-Culture/2009/0907/p02s03

-lign.html.

50   Carnegie Foundation. *Becky Margiotta and Joe McCannon's 2017 Summit Keynote Video*.

51   Drabkin et al. L-30 The 100,000 Homes Campaign.

52   Becky Margiotta (2020, August 18). Building a Fear Free Army. *Unleashing Social Change* [Audio podcast]. http://www.unleashingsocialchange.com/2 020/08/18/27-joe-mccannon-building-a-fear-free-army/.

53   Carnegie Foundation. Becky Margiotta and Joe McCannon's 2017 Summit Keynote Video.

54   Carnegie Foundation. Becky Margiotta and Joe McCannon's 2017 Summit Keynote Video.

55   Community Solutions. (2014, July 5). Campaign Reaches Goal as 100,00 0th Homeless American Housed. https://community.solutions/campaign -reaches-goal-as-100000th-homeless-american-housed/.

56   Carchidi, S. (2012, February 28). Herb Kelleher Shows No Fear of Flying. *Jersey Man Magazine*.

57   Fletcher, M. (2018, January 11). Ginger Hardage on How Southwest Airlines Built a Legendary Company Culture. *Game Changers with Molly Fletcher* [Audio podcast]. https://mollyfletcher.com/podcasts/ginger -hardage-southwest-airlines-culture/.

58   Freiberg, K., & Freiberg, J. (2019, January 4). 20 Reasons Why Herb Kelleher Was One of the Most Beloved Leaders of Our Time. *Forbes*. https: //www.forbes.com/sites/kevinandjackiefreiberg/2019/01/04/20-reasons -why-herb-kelleher-was-one-of-the-most-beloved-leaders-of-our-time.

59   Glynn, M. (2014, May 19). Ex-Southwest Airlines CEO Offers Lessons in Leadership from Post-9/11 Crisis. *Buffalo News*. https://buffalonews.com /business/local/ex-southwest-airlines-ceo-offers-lessons-in-leadership-from -post-9-11-crisis/article_059aa2c5-381c-57e7-8471-eab9c149437c.html.

60   Gwynne, S. C. (2012, March). Luv and War at 30,000 Feet. *TexasMonthly*. https://www.texasmonthly.com/articles/luv-and-war-at-30000-feet/.

61   Sutton, R. I. (2010). *Good Boss, Bad Boss: How to Be the Best…and Learn from the Worst*. New York: Business Plus.

62   Gwynne, S. C. Luv and War at 30,000 Feet.

63   Freiberg & Freiberg. 20 Reasons Why Herb Kelleher Was One of the Most

Beloved Leaders.

64 Ballard, J. (2019, August 31). Where Will Southwest Airlines Be in 10 Years? Motley Fool. https://www.fool.com/investing/2019/08/31/where -will-southwest-airlines-be-in-10-years.aspx.

65 Bishop, T. (2015, June 30). Expedia Has a President Again: Tech Leader Aman Bhutani Elevated to Big Role at Online Travel Giant. GeekWire. https://www.geekwire.com/2015/expedia-has-a-president-again-tech -leader-aman-bhutani-elevated-to-big-role-at-online-travel-giant/.

66 Tan, C. L. (2020, December 18). GoDaddy's New CEO on Leadership Now: "Change Is a Tiger." YahooNews (Reuters). https://news.yahoo.com /godaddys-ceo-leadership-now-change-100000900.html.

67 Ibid.

68 Heath, D. (2020). *Upstream: The Quest to Solve Problems before They Happen*. New York: Avid Reader Press.

69 Harden, G. (2020, January). Unstoppable Cultures Newsletter. https://un-stoppablecultures.com/newsletters/january-2020/.

70 Lunney, J., Lueder, S., & O'Connor, G. (2018, April 24). Postmortem Culture: How You Can Learn from Failure. re:Work. https://rework.with-google.com/blog/postmortem-culture-how-you-can-learn-from-failure/.

71 Ancona, D., & Isaacs, K. (2019, July 11). How to Give Your Team the Right Amount of Autonomy. *Harvard Business Review*. https://hbr.org/20 19/07/how-to-give-your-team-the-right-amount-of-autonomy.

72 MacArthur Foundation. (2021, April 7). Community Solutions Awarded $100 Million to End Homelessness [Press release]. https://www.macfound .org/press/article/community-solutions-awarded-$100-million-to-end -homelessness.

CHAPTER THREE: RESPECT

73 Andrus, J. (2019, March–April). Traeger's CEO on Cleaning Up a Toxic Culture. *Harvard Business Review*. https://hbr.org/2019/03/traegers-ceo-on -cleaning-up-a-toxic-culture; Feldman, A. (2017, October 22). Jeremy An-

drus Found Success with Skullcandy. Now He Hopes to Do It Again with Traeger Grills. *Forbes.* https://www.forbes.com/sites/forbestreptalks/2017/10/22/jeremy-andrus-found-success-with-skullcandy-now-he-hopes-to-do-it-again-with-traeger-grills/?sh=3bf17fa417ea; and AFT Construction. (2020, July 6). *AFT PODCAST: Developing a Winning Culture* [Video]. YouTube. https://www.youtube.com/watch?v=4QpUyY8_Sr4.

74   Johnson, W. (2020, February 11). Jeremy Andrus: Building Something of Value. *Disrupt Yourself Podcast.* https://whitneyjohnson.com/jeremy-andrus/.

75   Ibid.

76   Andrus, J. Traeger's CEO on Cleaning Up a Toxic Culture.

77   Johnson, W. Jeremy Andrus: Building Something of Value.

78   Ibid.

79   Ibid.

80   Ibid.

81   Ibid.

82   Ibid.

83   Ibid.

84   Rosenstein, A. H., & O'Daniel, M. (2008). A Survey of the Impact of Disruptive Behaviors and Communication Defects on Patient Safety. *Joint Commission Journal on Quality and Patient Safety, 34*(8), 464–71. https://doi.org/10.1016/s1553-7250(08)34058-6.

85   Cooper, B., Giordano, C. R., Erez, A., Foulk, T. A., Reed, H., & Berg, K. B. (In Press). Trapped by A First Hypothesis: How Rudeness Leads to Anchoring. *Journal of Applied Psychology.* http://doi.org/10.1037/apl0000914.

86   Riskin, A., Erez, A., Foulk, T. A., Kugelman, A., Gover, A., Shoris, I., Riskin, K. S., & Bamberger, P. A. (2015). The Impact of Rudeness on Medical Team Performance: A Randomized Trial. *Pediatrics, 136*(3), 487–95. https://doi.org/10.1542/peds.2015-1385.

87   Porath, C. (2015, December 7). How Civility Matters for You and Your Network. *Google re:Work.* https://rework.withgoogle.com/blog/how-civility-matters-for-you-and-your-network/.

88   Hathaway, B. (2016, January 11). Do the Math: Why Some People Are

Jerks yet Others Are Even Nice to Strangers. YaleNews. http://news.yale.edu/2016/01/11/research-news-do-math-why-some-people-are-jerks-yet-others-are-even-nice-strangers; and Bear A., & Rand, D. G. (2016). Intuition, Deliberation, and the Evolution of Cooperation, *Proceedings of the National Academy of Sciences, 113*(4), 936–41. https://doi.org/10.1073/pnas.1517780113.

89   Parker, A., Gerbasi, A., & Porath, C. L. (2013). The Effects of De-energizing Ties in Organizations and How to Manage Them. *Organizational Dynamics, 42*(2), 110–18, https://doi.org/10.1016/j.orgdyn.2013.03.004.

90   Ibid.

91   Kennedy, J., Porath, C., & Gerbasi, A. (n.d.). When Do Jerks Get Ahead? Testing and Bounding the Moral Virtue of Status Attainment [Unpublished paper]. Vanderbilt University; and Kennedy, J., Porath, C., & Gerbasi, A. (2019, July 8). Do Jerks Get Ahead? The Consequences of Incivility for Social Rank. International Association of Conflict Management Conference. Dublin, Ireland.

92   Porath, C. L. (2014, November 19). Half of Employees Don't Feel Respected by Their Bosses. *Harvard Business Review.* https://hbr.org/2014/11/half-of-employees-dont-feel-respected-by-their-bosses; Porath, C. L. (2016). *Mastering Civility: A Manifesto for the Workplace.* New York: Grand Central Publishing.

93   Porath, C., Gerbasi, A., & Schorch, S. (2015, September). The Effects of Civility on Advice, Leadership, and Performance. *Journal of Applied Psychology, 100*(5), 1527–41. https://doi.org/10.1037/apl0000016; and Porath, C., Gerbasi, A. (2015, October–December). Does Civility Pay? *Organizational Dynamics, 44*(4), 281–86. https://doi.org/10.1016/j.orgdyn.2015.09.005.

94   Rozovsky, J. (2015, November 17). The Five Keys to a Successful Google Team. *The Water Cooler.* re:Work. https://rework.withgoogle.com/blog/five-keys-to-a-successful-google-team/.

95   Nazar, J. & Bhutani, A. GoDaddy CEO Shares How to Build Your Brand In a New Era of Innovation & Growth. *Entrepreneur.* https://www.entrepreneur.com/page/godaddy-ceo-shares-how-to-build-your-brand?p=486101957.

96   Author interview with Ryan Martinez, September 21, 2020.

97   Porath. *Mastering Civility*.

98   Haman, K. (2015, July 27). "One Firm" Approach Treats Colleagues like Clients. *Orange County Business Journal*, https://www.ocbj.com/news/2015/jul/27/one-firm-approach-treats-colleagues-clients/; and 2015 Best Places to Work in Orange County. Orange County Business Journal Best Places to Work. https://bestplacestoworkoc.com/2015-best-places-to-work-in-orange-county-rankings.

99   Appold, K. (2015, September). Rise of the Chief Patient Experience Officer. *The Hospitalist*. https://www.the-hospitalist.org/hospitalist/article/122188/rise-chief-patient-experience-officer.

100 Garcia, L. C., Shanafelt, T. D., West, C. P., et al. (2020, August 7). Burnout, Depression, Career Satisfaction, and Work-Life Integration by Physician Race/Ethnicity. *JAMA Network Open*, 3(8), e2012762. https://doi:10.1001/jamanetworkopen.2020.12762.

101 Han, S., Shanafelt, T. D., Sinsky, C. A., Awad, K. M., Dyrbye, L. N., Fiscus, L. C., Trockel, M., & Goh, J. (2019, June 4). Estimating the Attributable Cost of Physician Burnout in the United States. *Annals of Internal Medicine*, *170*, 784–90. https://doi.org/10.7326/M18-1422.

102 Boissy, A., & Lee, T. H. (2017, October 12). Better Communication Makes Better Physicians. *NEJM Catalyst*. https://catalyst.nejm.org/doi/full/10.1056/CAT.17.0377.

103 Grant, A. (2020, May). Burnout Is Everyone's Problem. *WorkLife with Adam Grant* [Audio podcast]. https://podcasts.apple.com/us/podcast/burnout-is-everyones-problem/id1346314086?i=1000468645838.

104 Ibid.

105 Ibid.

106 Ibid.

107 Boissy, A., Windover, A. K., Bokar, D., Karafa, M., Neuendorf, K., Frankel, R. M., Merlino, J., & Rothberg M. B. (2016). Communication Skills Training for Physicians Improves Patient Satisfaction. *Journal of General Internal Medicine*, *31*, 755–61. https://doi.org/10.1007/s11606-016-3597-2.

108 Boissy, A. (2018, October 24). How—and—Why to Listen Until Some-

one Feels Heard. *Stanford Social Innovation Review*. https://ssir.org/articles/entry/howandwhy_to_listen_until_someone_feels_heard.

109   Porath & Gerbasi. Does Civility Pay?

110   Porath, C. L. (2016, February 3). How to Avoid Hiring a Toxic Employee. *Harvard Business Review*. https://hbr.org/2016/02/how-to-avoid-hiring-a-toxic-employee.

111   Ibid.

112   Pennington, B. (2018, February 15). The Ski Team That Sleeps Together Wins a Lot of Gold Medals Together. *New York Times*. https://www.nytimes.com/2018/02/15/sports/olympics/norway-skiing-olympics.html.

113   Leavitt, B. Developing a Winning Culture.

CHAPTER FOUR: RADICAL CANDOR

114   Scott, K. Radical Candor. Talk at Qualtrics.

115   Scott, K., & Spar, D. Kim Scott & Debora Spar Discuss the Intersection of Technology and Human Relationships. *Radical Candor* [Audio podcast]. https://www.radicalcandor.com/podcast/kim-scott-debora-spar/.

116   Ibid.

117   Hart, H. (2015, February 26). Yes, and...5 More Lessons in Improv-ing Collaboration and Creativity from Second City. *Fast Company*. https://www.fastcompany.com/3042080/yes-and-5-more-lessons-in-improv-ing-collaboration-and-creativity-from-second-city.

118   Scott, K. Leading with Kindness & Clarity During a Crisis. *Radical Candor* [Audio podcast]. https://www.radicalcandor.com/podcast/podcast2-ep1-leading-during-a-crisis/.

119   Mosley, E., & Irvine, D. (2020). *Making Work Human: How Human-Centered Companies Are Changing the Future of Work and the World*. New York: McGraw Hill.

120   Buckingham, M., & Goodall, A. (2019). *Nine Lies About Work: A Freethinking Leader's Guide to the Real World*. Boston: Harvard Business Review Press, 117–18.

121 Cook C. R., Fiat A., Larson M., Daikos, C., Slemrod, T., Holland, E. A., Thayer, A. J., & Renshaw, T. (2018, February 19). Positive Greetings at the Door: Evaluation of a Low-Cost, High-Yield Proactive Classroom Management Strategy. *Journal of Positive Behavior Interventions*. *20*(3), 149–59. https://doi:10.1177/1098300717753831.

122 Kraus, M. W., Huang, C., & Keltner, D. (2010). Tactile Communication, Cooperation, and Performance: An Ethological Study of the NBA. *Emotion*, *10*(5), 745–49. https://doi: 10.1037/a0019382.

123 Ibid.

124 Fonseca, T. (2017, October 27). High Fives Correlation with Team Bonding and Success. Fox Sports Stories. http://foxsportsstories.com/2017/10/27/high-fives-correlation-with-team-bonding-and-success/. http://foxsportsstories.com/2017/10/27/high-fives-correlation-with-team-bonding-and-success/.

125 Ibid.

126 Ibid.

127 See for a review Forer, B. (2011, June 9). Winning Touch: NBA Teams That Touch the Most Win the Most, Study Says. ABC News. https://abcnews.go.com/Health/winning-touch-nba-teams-touch-win-study/story?id=13801567; and Keltner, D. (2010, September 29). Hands On Research: The Science of Touch. *Greater Good*. https://greatergood.berkeley.edu/article/item/hands_on_research.

128 Grossman, E. (2016, October 7). The Suns Are Tracking High-Fives This Season and Sports Psychologists Are Giving Them Dap for Decision. *New York Daily News*. https://www.nydailynews.com/sports/basketball/suns-tracking-high-fives-article-1.2821334.

129 Ryan, R. M., & Deci, E. L. (2000). Self-Determination Theory and the Facilitation of Intrinsic Motivation, Social Development, and Well-Being. *American Psychologist*, *55*(1), 68–78. https://doi.org/10.1037/0003-066X.55.1.68; Deci, E. L., Connell, J. P., & Ryan, R. M. (1989). Self-Determination in a Work Organization. *Journal of Applied Psychology*, *74*(4), 580–90. https://doi.org/10.1037/0021-9010.74.4.580.

130 Ibid.

131 Grant, A. (2016, May 4.). Stop Serving the Feedback Sandwich. Medium.

https://medium.com/@AdamMGrant/stop-serving-the-feedback-sand-wich-bc1202686f4e.

132 Ibid.

133 Yeager, D. S., Purdie-Vaughns, V., Garcia, J., Apfel, N., Brzustoski, P., Master, A., Hessert, W. T., Williams, M. E., & Cohen, G. L. (2014). Breaking the cycle of mistrust: Wise interventions to provide critical feed-back across the racial divide. *Journal of Experimental Psychology: General, 1 43*(2), 804–824. https://doi.org/10.1037/a0033906.

134 Hallowell, E. M. (2010, December). What Brain Science Tells Us About How to Excel. *Harvard Business Review*. https://hbr.org/2010/12/manag-ing-yourself-what-brain-science-tells-us-about-how-to-excel.

135 Grant, A. Stop Serving the Feedback Sandwich.

136 Ibid.

137 Spreitzer, G., & Porath, C. L. (2014). Self-Determination as a Nutriment for Thriving: Building an Integrative Model of Human Growth at Work. In M. Gagné (Ed.), *The Oxford Handbook of Work Engagement, Motivation, and Self-Determination Theory*, 245–58. Oxford: Oxford University Press.

138 Workhuman (2019, March) conference, Nashville, TN (and email corre-spondence).

139 Vallance, D. (2019, April 24). Kim Scott on Why Most Work Communi-cation Fails and How to Fix It. *Work Culture* [Blog]. DropBox. https://blog.dropbox.com/topics/work-culture/kim-scott-interview.

140 National championships won by UNC under Dorrance. The first came in 1981, in a twelve-team tournament sanctioned by the Association for In-tercollegiate Athletics for Women. The remaining twenty-one are NCAA championships.

141 What Drives Winning. (2015, October 11). *Anson Dorrance: Grading Character* [Video of presentation at the What Drives Winning Conference, July 11, 2015, St. Louis, Missouri]. YouTube. https://www.youtube.com/watch?v=IpHFVu3dPGs; and author interview with Anson Dorrance, July 2021.

142 Author conversation (via Zoom) with Kelly Leonard. April 6, 2020.

CHAPTER FIVE: PROVIDE A SENSE OF MEANING

143 Buchanan, R. (2018, July 22). Faces of Marketing Podcast: Kim Malek, Founder of Salt + Straw Ice Cream [Transcript]. Medium. https://medium.com/@ryanbuchanan_39941/faces-of-marketing-with-kim-malek-founder-of-salt-straw-70a73f02d06e.

144 Bloom, L. B. (2017, May 16). This Disruptor Left a 6-Figure Job to Scoop Ice Cream and Built a Sweet Success Story. *Forbes*. https://www.forbes.com/sites/laurabegleybloom/2017/05/16/this-woman-left-a-6-figure-job-to-scoop-ice-cream-and-built-a-massive-success-story/#102673b11825.

145 Ibid.

146 Malek, K. (2015, September 25). Thank You Tribe Salt & Straw. Salt & Straw. https://saltandstraw.com/blogs/news/thank-you-tribe-salt-straw.

147 Salt & Straw. (n.d.). About Us. https://saltandstraw.com/pages/about.

148 Bloom. This Disruptor Left a 6-Figure Job to Scoop Ice Cream and Built a Sweet Success Story.

149 Malek, K. Thank You Tribe Salt & Straw.

150 Ibid.

151 Ibid.

152 Mosley, E., & Irvine, D. (2020). *Making Work Human: How Human-Centered Companies Are Changing the Future of Work and the World*. New York: McGraw Hill.

153 Net Impact. (2012, May 23). Job Security and Meaningful Work in High Demand for Today's Workforce. https://www.netimpact.org/about/press-releases/job-security-and-meaningful-work-in-high-demand-for-todays-workforce.

154 Fosslien, L. (2019, June 20). Author and Professor Barry Schwartz on Meaning and Work. *Insights* [Blog]. Humu. https://www.humu.com/blog/author-and-professor-barry-schwartz-on-meaning-and-work.

155 Blue Zones Project. (n.d.). The Blue Zones Story. https://info.bluezonesproject.com/origins.

156 Beheshti, N. (2019, July 13). What Is the Happiest Profession in America? The Answer May Surprise You. *Forbes*. https://www.forbes.com/sites

/nazbeheshti/2019/07/31/what-is-the-happiest-profession-in-america-the
-answer-may-surprise-you/#113d2e77430b.

157 Harter, J. (2020, February 4). 4 Factors Driving Record-High Employee
Engagement in U.S. Workplace. Gallup. https://www.gallup.com/work-
place/284180/factors-driving-record-high-employee-engagement.aspx.

158 Schwartz, T., & Porath, C. L. (2014, June 30). The Power of Meeting Your
Employees' Needs. *Harvard Business Review*. https://hbr.org/2014/06/the
-power-of-meeting-your-employees-needs.

159 Wrzesniewski, A., Dutton, J. E., & Debebe, G. (2003). Interpersonal
Sensemaking and the Meaning of Work. In R. Kramer & B. Staw (Eds.),
*Research in Organizational Behavior: An Annual Series of Analytical Essays
and Critical Reviews*, vol. 25, Oxford: Elsevier, 93–135; and re:Work with
Google. (2014, November 10). *Job Crafting—Amy Wrzesniewski on Creating Meaning in Your Own Work* [Video]. YouTube. https://www.youtube
.com/watch?v=C_igfnctYjA.

160 Dutton, J. E., & Berg, J. M. (2009). Job Crafting at Burt's Bees, Global
Lens Case 1-428-854.; and Wrzesniewski, A. (2014). Engage in Job Craft-
ing. In J. E. Dutton & and G. M. Spreitzer (Eds.), *How to Be a Positive
Leader: Small Actions, Big Impact* (pp. 65–75). San Francisco: Berrett
-Koehler.

161 Zayan, L. V. (2017, January 18). How Starbucks, Honest Co., and TOMS
Have Made Purpose a Vital Part of Their Culture (and You Can Too). *Talent Blog*. LinkedIn. https://business.linkedin.com/talent-solutions/blog
/company-culture/2017/how-starbucks-honest-co-and-toms-have-made
-purpose-a-vital-part-of-their-culture-and-you-can-too.

162 re:Work. (n.d.). KPMG: Motivating Employees Through a Deeper Sense
of Purpose [Case study]. https://rework.withgoogle.com/case-studies
/KPMG-purpose/.

163 Ibid.

164 KPMG Advisory. (n.d.). KPMG Purpose. https://advisory.kpmg.us/in-
sights/future-hr/future-hr-purpose-culture/kpmg-purpose.html.

165 re:Work. KPMG: Motivating Employees Through a Deeper Sense of Purpose.

166 re:Work. KPMG: Motivating Employees Through a Deeper Sense of Pur-

pose; and Pfau, B. (2015, October 6). How an Accounting Firm Convinced Its Employees They Could Change the World. *Harvard Business Review*. https://hbr.org/2015/10/how-an-accounting-firm-convinced-its-employees-they-could-change-the-world.

167 Pfau, B. How an Accounting Firm Convinced Its Employees They Could Change the World.

168 Grant, A. (2014). Outsourcing Inspiration. In J. Dutton & G. Spreitzer (Eds.), *How to Be a Positive Leader: Small Actions, Big Impact.* San Francisco: Berrett-Koehler.

169 Grant, A. M. (2008). The Significance of Task Significance: Job Performance Effects, Relational Mechanisms, and Boundary Conditions. *Journal of Applied Psychology, 93*(1), 108–24. https://doi.org/10.1037/0021-9010.93.1.108; Bellé, N. (2013). Experimental Evidence on the Relationship Between Public Service Motivation and Job Performance. *Public Administration Review, 73*(1), 143–53. https://doi.org/10.1111/j.1540-6210.2012.02621.x; Turner, Y. N., Hadas-Halpern, I., & Raveh, D. (2008). Patient Photos Spur Radiologist Empathy and Eye for Detail [Paper presented at the annual meeting of the Radiological Society of North America, Chicago]; Grant, A. M., & Hoffman, D. A. (2011). It's Not All about Me: Motivating Hospital Hand Hygiene by Focusing on Patients, *Psychological Science, 22*(12), 1494–99. https://doi.org/10.1177/0956797611419172.

170 [1]Mycoskie, B. (2016, January–February). The Founder of TOMS on Reimagining the Company's Mission. *Harvard Business Review.* https://hbr.org/2016/01/the-founder-of-toms-on-reimagining-the-companys-mission.

171 Chochrek, E. (2020, November 19). As Toms' Challenges Continue, Brand Reveals It Has Donated Almost 100M Pairs of Shoes. *Footwear News*. https://footwearnews.com/2019/business/financial-news/toms-shoe-donations-impact-report-1202876080/.

172 For All Summit. (2019). In Conversation: Executive Leadership Team at Cisco [Video and transcript]. https://www.greatplacetowork.com/forall-summit/keynotes/in-conversation-executive-leadership-team-at-cisco.

173 Ibid.

CHAPTER SIX: BOOST WELL-BEING

174 Gelfand, M., Gordon, S., Li, C. Choi, V., & Prokopowicz, P. (2018, October 2). One Reason Mergers Fail: The Two Cultures Aren't Compatible. *Harvard Business Review*. https://hbr.org/2018/10/one-reason-mergers-fail-the-two-cultures-arent-compatible.

175 Schoolov, K. (2019, August 22). How Amazon is fighting back against efforts to unionize. CNBC. https://www.cnbc.com/2019/08/22/how-amazon-is-fighting-back-against-workers-efforts-to-unionize.html; Haddon, H. (2018, September 6). Whole Foods Workers Push to Unionize. *Wall Street Journal*. https://www.wsj.com/articles/whole-foods-workers-push-to-unionize-1536235201; Campbell, A.F. 2018. Whole Foods employees are worried about new owner Amazon—so they're trying to unionize. Vox, Sept. 17. https://www.vox.com/2018/9/7/17831462/amazon-whole-foods-employees-unionize

176 Blanding, M. (2018, May 14). Amazon vs. Whole Foods: When Cultures Collide. Harvard Business School Working Knowledge. https://hbswk.hbs.edu/item/amazon-vs-whole-foods-when-cultures-collide.

177 CNBC. (2016, September 23). Marriott Buys Starwood Becoming World's Largest Hotel Chain. https://www.cnbc.com/2016/09/23/marriott-buys-starwood-becoming-worlds-largest-hotel-chain.html.

178 McIlvaine, A. R. (2019, September 22). Marriott CHRO Makes Employee Wellbeing the Company's Cornerstone. *Human Resources Executive*. https://hrexecutive.com/marriotts-chro-makes-employee-wellbeing-the-companys-cornerstone/

179 Ibid.

180 Marriott Culture Guide (2020). (Working paper)

181 Email correspondence with Michael Bush, CEO of Great Place to Work, March 15, 2001.

182 Tkaczyk, C. (2019, May 9). Inclusion from Top to Bottom. Great Place to Work. https://www.greatplacetowork.com/resources/blog/inclusion-from-top-to-bottom.

183 Hilton, J. (2019, October 31). Marriott International Is a People-First

Company. *Human Resources Director* (New Zealand). https://www.hcamag
.com/nz/specialisation/employee-engagement/marriott-international-is-a
-people-first-company/190123.

184 Clemence, S., Frauenheim, E., & Tkaczyk, C. *Marriott International—A
New Marriott for All and by All.* Marriott International and Great Place to
Work. https://www.greatplacetowork.com/resources/reports/a-new-mar-
riott-for-all-and-by-all.

185 Tkaczyk, C. Inclusion from Top to Bottom.

186 Ibid.

187 Clemence, Frauenheim, & Tkaczyk. *Marriott International—A New Marriott for All and by All.*

188 Ibid.

189 Marriott International News Center. (2020, May 6). Marriott International Ranks #1 On DiversityInc Top 50 List. https://news.marriott.com
/news/2020/05/06/marriott-international-ranks-1-on-diversityinc-top-50
-list; Marriott International News Center. (n.d.). Recognition. https:
//news.marriott.com/p/awards-and-recognition.

190 RedWeek. (2010, November 29). How Marriott Phuket Resorts Aid Sea
Turtle Conservation. https://www.redweek.com/blog/2010/11/29/how
-marriott-phuket-resorts-aid-sea.

191 Clemence, Frauenheim, & Tkaczyk. *Marriott International—A New Marriott for All and By All.*

192 Durbin, D. (2020, September). Marriott to Lay Off 17 percent of Corporate Staff Next Month. AP News. https://apnews.com/article/maryland
-archive-ac90f91534bcd404e4ebc6605d20adfc; and Change, S. (2021,
January 16). Marriott Marquis Workers Rally for Severance and Rehire
Rights Following Layoff Announcement. *Gothamist.* https://gothamist
.com/news/marriott-marquis-workers-rally-severance-and-rehire-rights
-following-layoff-announcement.

193 Marriott International. Arne Sorenson video (emailed to author).

194 Hougaard, R., & Carter, J. (2018). *The Mind of the Leader: How to Lead
Yourself, Your People, and Your Organization for Extraordinary Results.* Boston: Harvard Business Review Press.

195 McIlvaine, A. R. Marriott CHRO Makes Employee Wellbeing the Com-

pany's Cornerstone.

196　Gardner, D. (2021, May 5). Company Culture Tips, Vol. 8: The New Normal. *Rule Breaker Investing* [Audio podcast]. https://www.fool.com /podcasts/rule-breaker-investing/2021-05-05-company-culture-tips-vol-8 -the-new.

197　Southwick, A. (2020, May 8). Here's How the Motley Fool Landed on Inc .'s Best Workplaces List. *Workplace Culture Blog*. Motley Fool. https://cul-ture.fool.com/2020/05/heres-how-the-motley-fool-landed-on-inc-s-best -workplaces-list/.

198　Southwick. A. (2017, October 19). Heroes of Conscious Capitalism. *Work-place Culture Blog*. Motley Fool. https://culture.fool.com/2017/10/heroes -of-conscious-capitalism/. Conscious Capitalism. https://www.conscious-capitalism.org/philosophy.

199　Gardner, T. (2014, May 29). 6 Ways to Save Your Life—and Your Com-pany. LinkedIn. https://www.linkedin.com/pulse/20140529152729-4217 0371-6-ways-to-save-your-life-and-your-company/.

200　Gardner, T. (2014, November 26). Time for a New Sick Policy. LinkedIn. https://www.linkedin.com/pulse/20141126204152-42170371-time-for-a -new-sick-policy/.

201　Ibid.

202　Insidemotleyfool. (2013, September 26). Core Value #4: Fun – Revel in Your Work. *Workplace Culture Blog*. Motley Fool. https://culture.fool.com/ 2013/09/core-value-4-fun-revel-in-your-work/.

203　The Motley Fool. (2012, September 3). A Culture of Trust. https://culture .fool.com/2012/09/a-culture-of-trust/.

204　Zak, P. (2018, May 15). Creating a High-Trust, High-Performance Cul-ture. re:Work. https://rework.withgoogle.com/blog/creating-a-high-trust -performance-culture/.

205　Ibid.

206　Cash, K. (2017, September/October 2017). The Motley Fool: Definitely *Not* Your Cookie Cutter Wellness Program. *Well-Being Practitioner*. https: //foolculture-wpengine.netdna-ssl.com/wp-content/uploads/2017/10 /WellBeingPractitioner-SepOct-2017.pdf.

207　Ibid.

208 Gardner, T. 6 Ways to Save Your Life—and Your Company.

209 Southwick, A. (2015, July 14). Foolientation Secrets from a Recruiter. *Workplace Culture Blog.* Motley Fool. https://culture.fool.com/2015/07/jobs-foolientation-newhire-employee-orientation-onboarding-hiring/.

210 Insidemotleyfool. (2012, July 16). Foolish First Day. *Workplace Culture Blog.* The Motley Fool. https://culture.fool.com/tag/foolientation/.

211 Ibid.

212 Waldman, K. (2014, March 17). Negotiation While Female: Sometimes It Does Hurt to Ask. *Slate.* https://slate.com/human-interest/2014/03/should-women-negotiate-for-more-pay-a-female-academic-leans-in-and-allegedly-loses-her-job-offer.html.

213 Lagorio-Chafkin, C. (2018, September 24). This Company Offered All of Its Employees $200 to Ask for a Raise. *Inc.* https://www.inc.com/christine-lagorio/motley-fool-employees-paid-to-ask-for-raises.html.

214 Ibid.

215 Barsade, S. G., & O'Neill, O. A. (2014, May 24). What's Love Got to Do with It? A Longitudinal Study of the Culture of Companionate Love and Employee and Client Outcomes in a Long-Term Care Setting. *Administrative Science Quarterly, 59*(4), 551–98. https://doi.org/10.1177/0001839214538636.

216 Ibid.

217 Barsade, S., & O'Neill, O. A. (2014, January 13). Employees Who Feel Love Perform Better. *Harvard Business Review.* https://hbr.org/2014/01/employees-who-feel-love-perform-better.

218 Totterdell, P. Mood Scores: Mood and Performance in Professional Cricketers. *British Journal of Psychology, 90*(3), 317–32. https://doi.org/10.1348/000712699161422.

219 Kuhl, P. K., Tsao, F.-M., & Liu, H.-M. (2003). Foreign-Language Experience in Infancy: Effects of Short-Term Exposure and Social Interaction on Phonetic Learning. *Proceedings of the National Academy of Sciences, 100*(15) 9096–101; https://doi.org/10.1073/pnas.1532872100.

220 Pinker, S. (2020, April 2). The Science of Staying Connected. *Wall Street Journal.* https://www.wsj.com/articles/the-science-of-staying-connected-11585835999.

221 Ibid.

222 Ibid.

223 Twaronite, K. (2019, February 28). The Surprising Power of Simply Asking Coworkers How They're Doing. *Harvard Business Review*. https://hbr.org/2019/02/the-surprising-power-of-simply-asking-coworkers-how-theyre-doing.

224 Rath, T. (2006). *Vital Friends: The People You Can't Afford to Live Without*. Washington, DC: Gallup Press.

225 Burkus, D. (2016, June 8). Some companies are banning email and getting more done. *Harvard Business Review*.

226 Belkin, L. Y., Becker, W. J., & Conroy, S. A. (2017, November 30). Exhausted, but Unable to Disconnect: After-Hours Email, Work-Family Balance and Identification. *Academy of Management Proceedings*, (1), https://doi.org/10.5465/ambpp.2016.10353abstract.

227 Burkus, D. (2017, July 26). Why Banning Email Works (Even When It Doesn't). *Inc.* https://www.inc.com/david-burkus/why-you-should-outlaw-email-even-if-you-dont-succe.html.

228 Ibid.

229 Rogelberg, S. G. (2019). *The Surprising Science of Meetings*. New York: Oxford University Press.

230 Ibid.

231 Tonieto, G. N., Malkoc, S. A., & Nowlis, S. M. (2019, February). When an Hour Feels Shorter: Future Boundary Tasks Alter Consumption by Contracting Time. *Journal of Consumer Research*, 45(5), 1085–102. https://doi.org/10.1093/jcr/ucy043.

232 Rogelberg. *The Surprising Science of Meetings*.

PART TWO: THE CHALLENGE—IT STARTS WITH YOU

233 Vaca, N. Lean In. https://leanin.org/stories/nina-vaca.

234 Vaca, N. How Treating Yourself like a Corporate Athlete Drives Stronger Performance. Nina Vaca. https://www.ninavaca.com/blog/how-treating

-yourself-like-a-corporate-athlete-drives-stronger-performance/.

235   Ibid.

236   Ibid.

<h2 style="text-align:center">CHAPTER SEVEN: SELF-AWARENESS</h2>

237   George, B., & Sims, P. (2007). *True North: Discover Your Authentic Leadership*. San Francisco: Jossey-Bass; and Hougaard, R., Carter, J., & Afton, M . (2018, January 12). Self-Awareness Can Help Leaders More Than an MBA Can. *Harvard Business Review.* https://hbr.org/2018/01/self-awareness-can-help-leaders-more-than-an-mba-can.

238   Eurich, T. (2017). *Insight: Why We're Not as Self-Aware as We Think, and How Seeing Ourselves Clearly Helps Us Succeed at Work and in Life*. New York: Currency.

239   Ibid.

240   David, S. (2016). *Emotional Agility: Get Unstuck, Embrace Change, and Thrive in Work and Life*. New York: Avery.

241   Ibid.

242   Ibid.

243   Eurich, *Insight*; Sutton, A., Williams, H. M., & Allinson, C. W. (2015). A Longitudinal, Mixed Method Evaluation of Self-Awareness Training in the Workplace. *European Journal of Training and Development, 39*(7), 610–27. https://doi.org/10.1108/EJTD-04-2015-0031; Ridley, D. S., Schutz, P. A ., Glanz, R. S., & Weinstein, C. E. (1992). Self-Regulated Learning: The Interactive Influence of Metacognitive Awareness and Goal-Setting. *Journal of Experimental Education, 60*(4), 293–306. https://doi.org/10.1080/0022 0973.1992.9943867; Franzoi, S. L., Davis, M. H., & Young, R. D. (1985 , June). The Effects of Private Self-Consciousness and Perspective Taking on Satisfaction in Close Relationships, *Journal of Personality and Social Psychology, 48*(6), 1584–94. https://doi.org/10.1037/0022-3514.48.6.1584; Fletcher, C., & Bailey, C. (2003). Assessing Self-Awareness: Some Issues and Methods. *Journal of Managerial Psychology, 18*(5), 395–404. https:

//doi.org/10.1108/02683940310484008; Sosik, J. J., & Megerian, L. E. (1 999). Understanding Leader Emotional Intelligence and Performance: The Role of Self-Other Agreement on Transformational Leadership Perceptions . *Group and Organization Management, 24*(3), 367–90. https://doi.org/10. 1177/1059601199243006; Warren, H. K., & Stifter, C. A. (2008). Maternal Emotion-Related Socialization and Preschoolers' Developing Emotion Self-Awareness. *Social Development, 17*(2), 239–258. https://doi.org/10.1 111/j.1467-9507.2007.00423.x; Franzoi, Davis, & Young. The Effects of Private Self-Consciousness and Perspective Taking on Satisfaction in Close Relationships; Burpee, L. C., & Langer, E. J. (2005, January). Mindfulness and Marital Satisfaction. *Journal of Adult Development, 12*(1), 43–51 . https://doi.org/10.1007/s10804-005-1281-6; and Hart, D., & Sussman, R. W. (2005). *Man the Hunted: Primates, Predators, and Human Evolution* . Basic Books, 159–64.

244   Eurich. *Insight.*

245   Ibid.

246   Parker, A., Gerbasi, A., & Porath, C. L. (2013, April–June). The Effects of De-energizing Ties in Organizations and How to Manage Them. *Organizational Dynamics, 42*(2), 110–18.

247   Sala, F. (2003). Executive Blind Spots: Discrepancies Between Self- and Other-Ratings. *Consulting Psychology Journal: Practice and Research, 55*(4), 222–29. https://doi.org/10.1037/1061-4087.55.4.222.

248   What Drives Winning. (2015, October 11). *Anson Dorrance: Grading Character* [Video of presentation at the What Drives Winning Conference, July 11, 2015, St. Louis, Missouri]. YouTube. https://www.youtube.com /watch?v=IpHFVu3dPGs; and author interview with Anson Dorrance July 2021.

249   Gawande, A. (2011, September 6). Personal Best: Top Athletes and Singers Have Coaches. Should You? *New Yorker.* https://www.newyorker.com /magazine/2011/10/03/personal-best.

250   Ibid.

251   Ibid.

252   Ibid.

253   Ibid.

254 Harbinger, J. Tasha Eurich: The Surprising Truth About Insight. *The Jordan Harbinger Show*. [Audio podcast]. https://www.jordanharbinger.com/tasha-eurich-the-surprising-truth-about-insight/.

255 Mogill, M. Kim Scott—Radical Candor: How to be a Kickass Boss. *The Game Changing Attorney Podcast with Michael Mogill*. https://www.crispvideo.com/podcast/episode-25-kim-scott/.

256 Lublin, J. S. (2003, January 7). Job Candidates Get Manual from Boss: "How to Handle me." *Wall Street Journal*. https://www.wsj.com/articles/SB1041881615563021064.

257 Ibid.

258 Goldsmith, M., & Reiter, M. (2007). *What Got You Here Won't Get You There: How Successful People Become Even More Successful*. New York: Hyperion.

CHAPTER EIGHT: PHYSICAL WELL-BEING

259 Chance, Z., Dhar, R., Bakker, M. (2016, March 3). How Google Optimized Healthy Office Snacks. *Harvard Business Review*. https://hbr.org/2016/03/how-google-uses-behavioral-economics-to-make-its-employees-healthier.

260 Heil, N. (2018, November 8). Mark Verstegen, the Smartest Man in Fitness, Wants to Solve the Obesity Crisis. *Men's Health*. https://www.menshealth.com/fitness/a24789523/mark-verstegen-interview/.

261 EXOS. (n.d.). Improving How One Firm Supports Employees in a High Performance Culture. Case Study: FS Investments.

262 Greenfield, R. (2017, September 12). An Extreme Wellness Plan That Feeds You Three Meals a Day. *Benefits Pro*. https://www.benefitspro.com/2017/09/12/an-extreme-wellness-plan-that-feeds-you-three-meal/?slreturn=20210226142255.

263 Rosenblum, J., & Carlson-Phillips, A. (2016, September 27). Personal Return on Investment: Creating an environment to support transformational change in the workplace. HERO Forum, Atlanta, GA.

264 EXOS. Improving How One Firm Supports Employees in a High Performance Culture.

265 Ibid.

266 EXOS. Case Study: Game Changing Results. Changing Stakeholder Behaviors to Give More and Cost Less.

267 re:Work. (n.d.). Understanding How Employees Value Their Benefits. https://rework.withgoogle.com/case-studies/Wegmans-conjoint-analysis/.

268 Berman, J. (2017, December 6). Wegmans Improves Its Bottom Line by Helping Employees Shrink Their Waistlines. *Huffington Post*. https://www.huffpost.com/entry/wegmans-wellness_n_3696411.

269 Orgel, D. (2013, February 4). Danny Wegman's Urgent Message on Health Initiatives. *Supermarket News*. https://www.supermarketnews.com/blog/danny-wegmans-urgent-message-health-initiatives.

270 Friends of the Genesee Valley Greenway. (n.d.). The Genesee Valley Greenway Passport to Family Wellness Program. http://fogvg.org/wegmans-passport-program/.

271 Wegmans. (2020, February 18). Great Place to Work and Fortune Names Wegmans One of the 2020 Fortune 100 Best Companies to Work For, Ranking #3. https://www.wegmans.com/news-media/press-releases/great-place-to-work-and-fortune-name-wegmans-one-of-the-2020-fortune-100-best-companies-to-work-for-ranking/.

272 Johnson, H., & Taylor, K. (2019, March 6). We visited the regional grocery chain that beat out Amazon and Costco to become the most beloved brand in America. Here's what it's like to shop there. *Business Insider*. https://www.businessinsider.com/review-of-wegmans-the-best-grocery-chain-in-the-us-2017-6#wegmans-features-spacious-aisles-full-of-everything-from-paper-goods-to-champagne-6.

273 Gregory, J. Best Practices in Employee Relations: Wegmans. *ProjectHR Podcast*. https://projectionsinc.com/employee-relations-best-practices-wegmans/.

274 Ratey, J. J. (2008). *Spark: The Revolutionary New Science of Exercise and the Brain*. New York: Little, Brown.

275 Ibid.

276 McGonigal. K. (2020). *The Joy of Movement: How Exercise Helps Us Find*

Happiness, Hope, Connection, and Courage. New York: Avery.

277 Ibid.

278 Ibid.

279 Harris, D. (2020, January). Making and Breaking Habits, Sanely: Kelly McGonigal. *Ten Percent Happier with Dan Harris* [Audio podcast]; and McGonigal. *The Joy of Movement.*

280 McGonigal. *The Joy of Movement.*

281 Yemiscigil, A., Vlaev, I. (2021, April 23). The Bidirectional Relationship Between Sense of Purpose in Life and Physical Activity: A Longitudinal Study. *Journal of Behavioral Medicine.* https://doi.org/10.1007/s10865-021-00220-2.

282 O'Hagan, S. R. (2017). *Extreme You: Step Up. Stand Out. Kick Ass. Repeat.* New York: Harper Collins.

283 Trezza V., Baarendse, P. J. J., & Vanderschuren, L. J. M. J. (2010, October). The Pleasures of Play: Pharmacological Insights into Social Reward Mechanisms. *Trends in Pharmacological Sciences, 31*(10), 463–69. https://doi.org/10.1016/j.tips.2010.06.008.

284 Yorgason, J. B., Johnson, L. N., Hill, M.S. & Selland, B. (2018). Marital Benefits of Daily Individual and Conjoint Exercise Among Older Couples . *Family Relations, 67*(2), 227–39. https://doi.org/10.1111/fare.12307.

285 Young, K. C., Machell, K. A., Kashdan, T. B., & Westwater, M. L. (2018, January). The Cascade of Positive Events: Does Exercise on a Given Day Increase the Frequency of Additional Positive Events? *Personality and Individual Differences, 120,* 299–303. https://doi.org/10.1016/j.paid.2017.03.032.

286 Federation of American Societies for Experimental Biology (FASEB). (2015, March 29). Highly Processed Foods Dominate U. S. Grocery Purchases . *ScienceDaily.* www.sciencedaily.com/releases/2015/03/150329141017.htm.

287 Chance, Dhar, Hutzis, & Bakker. How Google Optimized Healthy Office Snacks.

288 Gardner, T. (2014, May 29). 6 Ways to Save Your Life—and Your Company. LinkedIn. https://www.linkedin.com/pulse/20140529152729-42170371-6-ways-to-save-your-life-and-your-company/.

289 Kniffin, K. M., Wansink, B., Devine, C. M., & Sobal, J. (2015). Eating Together at the Firehouse: How Workplace Commensality Relates to the Performance of Firefighters. *Human Performance*, *28*(4), 281–306. https://doi.org/10.1080/08959285.2015.1021049.

290 Fisher, J. Humanity in the Workplace: A WorkWell Podcast with Erica Keswin. *WorkWell*. Deloitte. https://www2.deloitte.com/us/en/pages/about-deloitte/articles/humanity-in-the-workplace.html.

291 Team Building in the Cafeteria. (2015, December). *Harvard Business Review*.

292 Chance, Dhar, & Bakker. How Google Optimized Healthy Office Snacks.

293 Kelley, S. (2015, November 19). Groups That Eat Together Perform Better Together. *Cornell Chronicle*. https://news.cornell.edu/stories/2015/11/groups-eat-together-perform-better-together.

294 Merchant, N. (2013, February). Got a Meeting? Take a Walk [Video]. TED. https://www.ted.com/talks/nilofer_merchant_got_a_meeting_take_a_walk?language=en.

295 Oppezzo, M., & Schwartz, D. L. (2014). Give Your Ideas Some Legs: The Positive Effect of Walking on Creative Thinking. *Journal of Experimental Psychology: Learning, Memory, and Cognition*, *40*(4), 1142–52. https://doi.org/10.1037/a0036577; Wong, M. (2014, April 24). Stanford Study Finds Walking Improves Creativity. Stanford News. https://news.stanford.edu/2014/04/24/walking-vs-sitting-042414/.

296 Leberecht, T. (2015, September 18). In the Age of Loneliness, Connections at Work Matter. *Harvard Business Review*. https://hbr.org/2015/09/in-the-age-of-loneliness-connections-at-work-matter.

297 Gardner. 6 Ways to Save Your Life—and Your Company.

CHAPTER NINE: RECOVERY

298 Cohen, D. (2019, June 3). How Deloitte's Jen Fischer Became Its First Chief Well-Being Officer. *Adweek*. https://www.adweek.com/agencies/how-deloittes-jen-fisher-became-its-first-chief-well-being-officer/.

299 McHugh, A. When You Deny You're Burning Out with Jen Fisher. *Work Life Play: Hosted by Aaron McHugh* [Audio podcast]. https://www.aaronmchugh.com/podcast/when-you-deny-youre-burning-out-with-jen-fisher-169/.

300 Ibid.

301 Ibid.

302 Ibid.

303 Panwar, P. (2020, October 16). Deloitte Chief Well-being Officer Jen Fisher: 5 Ways That Businesses Can Help Promote the Mental Wellness of Their Employees. *Authority Magazine.* https://medium.com/authority-magazine/deloitte-chief-well-being-officer-jen-fisher-5-ways-that-businesses-can-help-promote-the-mental-1877866250e8.

304 Hopler, W. (2017, December 17). Deloitte's Jen Fisher Creates a Corporate Culture of Well-Being. Center for the Advancement of Well-Being. https://wellbeing.gmu.edu/articles/11428.

305 Reilly, C. (2020, October 6). Chief Well-Being Officer Takes a Collective Approach to Solve Burnout. *Forbes.* https://www.forbes.com/sites/colleenreilly/2020/10/06/chief-well-being-officer-takes-a-collective-approach-to-solve-burnout/.

306 Ibid.

307 Gonzalez, F. (2021, March). Deloitte's Jen Fisher on How Wellness Is a Work in Progress. American Way. https://www.americanway.com/articles/wellness-is-a-work-in-progress/.

308 Hopler. Deloitte's Jen Fisher Creates a Corporate Culture of Well-Being.

309 McHugh, A. When You Deny You're Burning Out with Jen Fisher.

310 UMA. (n.d.). UMA Talks with Jen Fisher, Deloitte's Managing Director of Well-Being. (n.d.). https://beboldbeuma.com/uma-talks-with-jen-fisher-deloittes-managing-director-of-well-being/.

311 Gervais, M. (2019, July 10). Dr. Matthew Walker, Professor and Sleep Expert. *Finding Mastery* [Audio podcast]. https://findingmastery.net/matthew-walker/.

312 Luckhaupt, S. E., Tak, S., & Calvert, G. M. (2010, February). The Prevalence of Short Sleep Duration by Industry and Occupation in the National Health Interview Survey. *Sleep, 33*(2), 149–59. https://doi.org/10.1093

/sleep/33.2.149.

313 Park, S., Cho, M. J., Chang, S. M., Bae, J. N., Jeon, H. J., Cho, S.-J., Kim, B.-S., Chung, I.-W., Joon, H. A., Lee, H. W., & Hong, J. P. (2010, December). Relationships of Sleep Duration with Sociodemographic and Health-Related Factors, Psychiatric Disorders and Sleep Disturbances in a Community Sample of Korean Adults. *Journal of Sleep Research*, *19*(4), 56 7–77. https://doi.org/10.1111/j.1365-2869.2010.00841.x; Ravan, A. R., Bengtsson, C., Lissner, L., Lapidus, L., & Björkelund, C. (2010, September). Thirty-Six-Year Secular Trends in Sleep Duration and Sleep Satisfaction, and Associations with Mental Stress and Socioeconomic Factors—Results of the Population Study of Women in Gothenburg, Sweden. *Journal of Sleep Research*, *19*(3), 496–503. https://doi.org/10.1111/j.1 365-2869.2009.00815.x; Salminen, S., Oksanen, T., Vahtera, J., Sallinen, M., Härmä, M., Salo, P., Virtanen, M., & Kivimäki, M. (2010). Sleep Disturbances as a Predictor of Occupational Injuries Among Public Sector Workers. *Journal of Sleep Research*, *19*(1): 207–13. https://doi.org/10.1111 /j.1365-2869.2009.00780.x; and Westerlund, H., Alexanderson, K., Åkerstedt, T., Hanson, L. M., Theorell, T., & Kivimäki, M. (2008). Work -Related Sleep Disturbances and Sickness Absence in the Swedish Working Population, 1993–1999. *Sleep*, *31*(8), 1169–77.

314 Ibid.

315 Kessler, R. C., Berglund, P. A., Coulouvrat, C., Hajak, G., Roth, T., Shahly, V., Shillington, A. C., Stephenson, J. J., & Walsh, J. K. (2011). Insomnia and the performance of US workers: results from the America insomnia survey. *Sleep*, *34*(9), 1161–1171. https://doi.org/10.5665 /SLEEP.1230.

316 Hafner, M., Stepanek, M., Taylor, J., Troxel, W. M., & Van Stolk, C. (201 6). Why Sleep Matters — the Economic Costs of Insufficient Sleep: A Cross-Country Comparative Analysis. https://www.rand.org/pubs/research_reports/RR1791.html.

317 Scott, B. A., & Judge, T. A. (2006, October). Insomnia, Emotions, and Job Satisfaction: A Multilevel Study. *Journal of Management*, *32*(5), 622–4 5. https://doi.org/10.1177/0149206306289762.

318 Baranski, J. V., Cian, C., Esquivié, D., Pigeau, R. A., & Raphel, C. (1998

). Modafinil During 64 Hr of Sleep Deprivation: Dose-Related Effects on Fatigue, Alertness, and Cognitive Performance. *Military Psychology*, *10*(3), 173–93. https://doi.org/10.1207/s15327876mp1003_3.

319 Nilsson, J. P., Söderström, M., Karlsson, A. U., Lekander, M., Åkerstedt, T., Lindroth, N. E., & Axelsson, J. (2005, March). Less Effective Executive Functioning After One Night's Sleep Deprivation. *Journal of Sleep Research*, *14*(1), 1–6. https://doi.org/10.1111/j.1365-2869.2005.00442.x.

320 Harrison, Y., & Horne, J. A. (1999). One Night of Sleep Loss Impairs Innovative Thinking and Flexible Decision Making. *Organizational Behavior and Human Decision Processes*, *78*(2), 128–45. https://doi.org/10.1006/obhd.1999.2827; and Pilcher, J. J., & Huffcutt, A. I. (1996, June). Effects of Sleep Deprivation on Performance: A Meta-analysis. *Sleep*, *19*(4), 318–26. https://doi.org/10.1093/sleep/19.4.318.

321 Kessler, R. C., Berglund, P. A., Coulouvrat, C., Hajak, G., Roth, T., Shahly, V., Shillington, A. C., Stephenson, J. J., & Walsh, J. K. (2011). Insomnia and the Performance of U.S. Workers: Results from the America Insomnia Survey. *Sleep*, *34*(11), 1161–71. https://doi.org/10.5665/sleep.1408.

322 Barnes, C. M., & Wagner, D. T. (2009). Changing to Daylight Saving Time Cuts into Sleep and Increases Workplace Injuries. *Journal of Applied Psychology*, *94*(5), 1305–17. https://doi.org/10.1037/a0015320; Kling, R. N., McLeod, C. B., & Koehoorn, M. (2010). Sleep Problems and Workplace Injuries in Canada. *Sleep*, *33*(5) 611–18. https://doi.org/10.1093/sleep/33.5.611; Salminen et al. Sleep Disturbances as a Predictor of Occupational Injuries Among Public Sector Workers; and Salo, P., Oksanen, T., Sivertsen, B., Hall, M., Pentti, J., Virtanen, M., Vaherta, J., & Kivimäki, M. (2010). Sleep Disturbances as a Predictor of Cause-Specific Work Disability and Delayed Return to Work. *Sleep*, *33*(10), 1323–31. https://doi.org/10.1093/sleep/33.10.1323.

323 Salo et al. Sleep Disturbances as a Predictor of Cause-Specific Work Disability and Delayed Return to Work.

324 Wagner, D. T., Barnes, C. M., Lim, V. K. G., & Ferris, D. L. (2012). Lost Sleep and Cyberloafing: Evidence from the Laboratory and a Daylight Saving Time Quasi-experiment. *Journal of Applied Psychology*, *97*(5), 1068–76

. https://doi.org/10.1037/a0027557.

325 Christian, M. S., & Ellis, A. P. J. (2011). Examining the Effects of Sleep Deprivation on Workplace Deviance: A Self-Regulatory Perspective. *Academy of Management Journal*, *54*(5), 913–34. https://doi.org/10.5465/amj.2 010.0179.

326 Barnes, C. M., Schaubroeck, J. M., Huth, M., & Ghumman, S. (2011, July). Lack of Sleep and Unethical Conduct. *Organizational Behavior and Human Decision Processes*, *115*(2), 169–80. https://doi.org/10.1016/j.ob-hdp.2011.01.009.

327 Ibid.

328 Walker, M. (2019, April). Sleep Is Your Superpower [Video]. TED. https://www.ted.com/talks/matt_walker_sleep_is_your_superpower?language =en.

329 Ibid.

330 Gross, T. (2018, July 20). Sleep Scientist Warns Against Walking Through Life "In an Underslept State." NPR. https://www.npr.org/2018/07/20/63 0792401/sleep-scientist-warns-against-walking-through-life-in-an-under-slept-state; and Vedantam, S. (2018, September 21). Eyes Wide Open. *Hidden Brain*. NPR. https://www.npr.org/2018/09/20/650114225/radio -replay-eyes-wide-open.

331 Cohut, M. (2019, March 12). Sleep Loss Can Turn Us into Social Outcasts . Medical News Today. https://www.medicalnewstoday.com/articles/3246 78#Alienation-is-contagious.

332 Anwar, Y. (2018, August 14). Poor Sleep Triggers Viral Loneliness and Social Rejection. Berkeley News. https://news.berkeley.edu/2018/08/14 /sleep-viral-loneliness/.

333 Ibid.

334 Chuah, L. Y. M., Dolcos, F., Chen, A. K., Zheng, H., Parimal, S., & Chee, M. W. L. (2010). Sleep Deprivation and Interference by Emotional Distracters. *Sleep*, *33*(10), 1305–13. https://doi.org/10.1093/sleep/33.10.130 5; Lim, V. K. G. (2002, August). The IT Way of Loafing on the Job: Cyberloafing, Neutralizing and Organizational Justice. *Journal of Organizational Behavior*, *23*(5), 675–94. https://doi.org/10.1002/job.161.

335 Guarana, C. L., & Barnes, C. M. (2017, July). Lack of Sleep and the De-

velopment of Leader-Follower Relationships over Time. *Organizational Behavior and Human Decision Processes, 141*, 57–73. https://doi.org/10.10 16/j.obhdp.2017.04.003.

336 Walker, M. (2018). *Why We Sleep: Unlocking the Power of Sleep and Dreams* . New York: Scribner.

337 Schwartz, T. (2013, February 9). Relax! You'll Be More Productive. *New York Times.*

338 Mejia, Z. (2018, August 30). New Research Finds Taking a Vacation Could Help You Live Longer. Make It. CNBC. https://www.cnbc.com/2018/08/ 30/new-study-finds-taking-your-vacation-could-help-you-live-longer.html .

339 Schwartz, T., Polizzi, R., Gruber, K., & Pines, E. (2019). What Happens When Teams Fight Burnout Together. *Harvard Business Review*, September 30.

340 Ibid.

341 Dean, M. (2016, June 4). Would You Pay Bonuses to Employees for Getting a Good Night's Sleep? Peakon Post. https://peakon.com/us/blog /growth-development/would-you-pay-bonuses-to-employees-for-getting-a -good-nights-sleep/.

342 Hougaard, R., & Carter, J. (2018, February 28). Senior Executives Get More Sleep Than Everyone Else, *Harvard Business Review*. https://hbr.org /product/senior-executives-get-more-sleep-than-everyone-else/H046XF -PDF-ENG.

343 Martin, E. (2017, November 9). Jeff Bezos, Sheryl Sandberg and 5 Other Business Leaders All Prioritize the Same Habit. CNBC. https://www.cnbc .com/2017/11/09/jeff-bezos-sheryl-sandberg-and-other-leaders-who-pri- oritize-sleep.html.

344 Gervais, M. Dr. Matthew Walker, Professor and Sleep Expert.

345 Goldhaler, S. Z. (2009, May). Do Take That Break. *Harvard Business Review.*

346 Haviland, D. (n.d.). Aetna's Mindfulness Initiative Leads to Unique Employee Engagement. Customer Strategist. https://www.ttec.com/articles /aetnas-mindfulness-initiative-leads-unique-employee-engagement.

347 Davidson, O. B., Eden, D., Westman, M., Cohen-Charash, Y., Hammer,

L. B., Kluger, A. N., Krausz, M., Maslach, C., O'Driscoll, M., Perrewé, P. L., Quick, J. C., Rosenblatt, Z., & Spector, P. E. (2010). Sabbatical Leave: Who Gains and How Much? *Journal of Applied Psychology, 95*(5), 953–64. https://doi.org/10.1037/a0020068.

348   Bawden, D., & Robinson, L. (2009). The Dark Side of Information: Overload, Anxiety, and Other Paradoxes and Pathologies, *Journal of Information Science, 25*(2), 180–91. https://doi.org/10.1177/0165551508095781.

349   Ward A. F., Duke, K., Gneezy, A., Bos, M. W. (2017, April). Brain Drain: The Mere Presence of One's Own Smartphone Reduces Available Cognitive Capacity. *Journal of the Association for Consumer Research, 2*(2). https://doi.org/10.1086/691462; and Bergland, C. (2017, June 25). Are Smartphones Making Us Stupid? *Psychology Today.* https://www.psychologytoday.com/us/blog/the-athletes-way/201706/are-smartphones-making-us-stupid.

350   Ibid.

351   Perlow, L. A. (2012, May 14). Breaking the Smartphone Addiction. Harvard Business School, Working Knowledge. https://hbswk.hbs.edu/item/breaking-the-smartphone-addiction.

352   Carter, J., Hougaard, R. (2018). *The Mind of the Leader: How to Lead Yourself, Your People, and Your Organization for Extraordinary Results.* Boston: Harvard Business Review Press.

353   Mendler, A. (n.d.). Thirty Minute Mentors Podcast Transcript: Interview with Deloitte Consulting CEO Dan Helfrich. Adam Mendler. https://www.adammendler.com/blog/deloitte-consulting-ceo-dan-helfrich.

354   Fernandez, R. (2020, January 7). Search Inside Yourself: SIY Field Report. https://www.garrisoninstitute.org/news/search-inside-yourself-siy-field-report/; and author interview with Yizhao Zhang, May 2021.

355   Search Inside Yourself Leadership Institute. (2019, August 7). *Bringing Search Inside Yourself to All Teachers and Government Employees in Bhutan* [Video]. YouTube. https://www.youtube.com/watch?v=u-6qA_LW_pY.

356   Ibid.

357   Ibid.

358   Iwamoto, S. K., Alexander, M., Torres, M., Irwin, M. K., Christakis, N. A., & Nishi, A. (2020). Mindfulness Meditation Activates Altruism. *Scien-*

tific Reports, *10*, 6511. https://doi.org/10.1038/s41598-020-62652-1.

359   Allen, T. D., & Kiburz, K. M. (2012). Trait Mindfulness and Work-Family Balance Among Working Parents: The Mediating Effects of Vitality and Sleep Quality. *Journal of Vocational Behavior*, *80*, 372–79. https://doi.org/10.1016/j.jvb.2011.09.002; Glomb, T. M., Duffy, M. K., Bono, J. E., & Yang, T. (2011). Mindfulness at Work. In J. Martocchio, H. Liao, & A. Joshi (Eds.), *Research in Personnel and Human Resource Management*. Bingley, UK: Emerald Group. https://doi.org/10.1108/S0742-7301(2011)0000030005; Hülsheger, U. R., Alberts, H. J. E. M., Feinholdt, A., & Lang, J . W. B. (2013, March). Benefits of Mindfulness at Work: The Role of Mindfulness in Emotion Regulation, Emotional Exhaustion, and Job Satisfaction. *Journal of Applied Psychology*, *98*(2), 310–25. https://doi.org/10.1037/a0031313; and Marzuq, N., & Drach-Zahavy, A. (2012). Recovery During a Short Period of Respite: The Interactive Roles of Mindfulness and Respite Experiences. *Work & Stress*, *26*(2), 175–94. https://doi.org/10.1080/02678373.2012.683574.

360   Leroy, H., Anseel, F., Dimitrova, N. G., & Sels, L. (2013). Mindfulness, Authentic Functioning, and Work Engagement: A Growth Modeling Approach. *Journal of Vocational Behavior*, *82*(3), 238–47. https://doi.org/10.1016/j.jvb.2013.01.012.

361   Dane, E., & Brummel, B. J. (2014). Examining Workplace Mindfulness and Its Relations to Job Performance and Turnover Intention. *Human Relations*, *67*(1), 105–28. https://doi.org/10.1177/0018726713487753; Reb, J., Narayanan, J., & Ho, Z. W. (2015). Mindfulness at Work: Antecedents and Consequences of Employee Awareness and Absentmindedness. *Mindfulness*, *6*(1), 111–22. https://doi.org/10.1007/s12671-013-0236-4; and Zhang, J., Ding, W., Li, Y., & Wu, C. (2013). Task Complexity Matters: The Influence of Trait Mindfulness on Task and Safety Performance of Nuclear Power Plant Operators. *Personality and Individual Differences*, *55*(4), 433-39. https://doi.org/10.1016/j.paid.2013.04.004.

362   Reb, J., Narayanan, J., & Chaturvedi, S. (2014). Leading Mindfully: Two Studies on the Influence of Supervisor Trait Mindfulness on Employee Well-Being and Performance. *Mindfulness*, *5*(1), 36–45. https://doi.org/10.1007/s12671-012-0144-z.

363   Davidson, R. J. Kabat-Zinn, J., Schumacher, J., Rosenkranz, M., Muller, D., Santorelli, S. F., Urbanowski, F., Harrington, A., Bonus, K., & Sheridan, J. F. (2003). Alterations in Brain and Immune Function Produced by Mindfulness Meditation. *Psychosomatic Medicine*, *65*(4), 564–70. https://doi.org/10.1097/01.psy.0000077505.67574.e3.

364   Rosenzweig, S., Reibel, D. K., Greeson, J. M., Edman, J. S., Jasser, S. A., McMearty, K. D., & Goldstein, B. J. (2007). Mindfulness-Based Stress Reduction Is Associated with Improved Glycemic Control in Type 2 Diabetes Mellitus, *Alternative Therapies in Health and Medicine*, *13*(5), 36–38.

365   Zeidan, F., Johnson, S. K., Gordon, N. S., & Goolkasian, P. (2010). Effects of Brief and Sham Mindfulness Meditation on Mood and Cardiovascular Variables. *Journal of Alternative and Complementary Medicine*, *16*(8), 867–73. https://doi.org/10.1089/acm.2009.0321.

366   Carlson, L. E., & Garland, S. N. (2005, December). Impact of Mindfulness Based Stress Reduction (MBSR) on Sleep, Mood, Stress and Fatigue Symptoms in Cancer Outpatients. *International Journal of Behavioral Medicine*, *12*(4), 278–85. https://doi.org/10.1207/s15327558ijbm1204_9.

367   Jensen, C. G. Corporate-Based Mindfulness Training in Denmark—Three Validation Studies [Forthcoming]. Neurobiological Research Unit, Copenhagen University Hospital.

368   Tang, Y.-Y., Hölzel, B. K., & Posner, M. I. (2015). The Neuroscience of Mindfulness Meditation. *Nature Reviews Neuroscience*, *16*, 213–25. https://doi.org/10.1038/nrn3916.

369   Ibid.

370   Goodman, P. S. (2013, July 11). Why Companies Are Turning to Meditation and Yoga to Boost the Bottom Line. *Huffington Post*. http://www.huffingtonpost.com/2013/07/11/mindfulness-capitalism_n_3572952.html.

371   Accenture (with Marriott International). (2020). *Elevate Your People. Lift Your Business: How Modern HR Mindset Can Leave Your People and Organization Net Better Off.*.

372   Valcour, M. (2016, November). Beating Burnout. *Harvard Business Review*. https://hbr.org/2016/11/beating-burnout.

CHAPTER TEN: MINDSET

373 Nokkonen, M. (2017, May 2). 4 Tips for Peak Performance. Gameplan A. https://www.gameplan-a.com/2017/05/4-tips-peak-productivity-work/.

374 Chertok, B. L. (2019, January/February). Hearing with the Brain and the Brainstem—Jessica's Unique Dual Implants. *Hearing Life*. https://www.hearingloss.org/wp-content/uploads/HL_2019_1_Chertok.pdf.

375 Ibid.

376 Moawad, T., & Staples, A. (2020). *It Takes What It Takes: How to Think Neutrally and Gain Control of Your Life*. New York: HarperOne.

377 Rodrick, S. (2015, August 26). Russell Wilson: The Chosen One. *Rolling Stone*, Aug. 26. https://www.rollingstone.com/culture/culture-sports/russell-wilson-the-chosen-one-50937/.

378 Kapadia, S. (2016, June 28). Russell Wilson Benefits from Working with a Mental Conditioning Coach. *NFL Nation* [Blog]. ESPN. https://www.espn.com/blog/seattle-seahawks/post/_/id/20547/how-russell-wilson-benefits-from-working-with-a-mental-conditioning-coach.

379 Ibid.

380 Ibid.

381 Moawad & Staples. *It Takes What It Takes*.

382 Rozin, P., & Royzman, E. B. (2001). Negativity Bias, Negativity Dominance, and Contagion, *Personality and Social Psychology Review*, 5(4), 296–320. https://doi.org/10.1207/S15327957PSPR0504_2.

383 Tierney, J., & Baumeister, R. (2019). *The Power of Bad: How the Negativity Effect Rules Us and How We Can Rule It*. New York: Penguin Books.

384 Barrick. M. R., Stewart, G. L., Neubert, M. J., & Mount, M. K. (1998). Relating Member Ability and Personality on Work-Team Processes and Team Effectiveness. *Journal of Applied Psychology*, 83(3), 377–91. https://doi.org/10.1037/0021-9010.83.3.377.

385 Hanson, R. (2021, May 26). Life After COVID [Webinar].

386 Hanson. Life After COVID [Webinar]; Hanson, R. (2013). *Hardwiring Happiness: The New Brain Science of Contentment, Calm, and Confidence*. New York: Harmony.

387   Hanson. *Hardwiring Happiness*.

388   Caspi, A., Sugden, K., Moffitt, T. E., Taylor, A., Craig, I. W., Harrington, H., McClay, J., Mill, J., Martin, J., Braithwaite, A., & Poulton. (2003). Influence of Life Stress on Depression: Moderation by a Polymorphism in the 5-HTT Gene. *Science, 301*(5621), 386–89. https://doi.org/10.1126/science.1083968.

389   Porath, C. L. (2016). *Mastering Civility: A Manifesto for the Workplace*. New York: Grand Central; Porath, C. L., & Pearson, C. M. (2012, December). Emotional and Behavioral Responses to Workplace Incivility and the Impact of Hierarchical Status. *Journal of Applied Social Psychology, 42*(Suppl. 1), E326–57. https://doi.org/10.1111/j.1559-1816.2012.01020.x.

390   Kensbock J. M., Alkærsig L., & Lomberg C. (2021, May 18). The Epidemic of Mental Disorders in Business—How Depression, Anxiety, and Stress Spread Across Organizations Through Employee Mobility. *Administrative Science Quarterly*. doi:10.1177/00018392211014819.

391   Marchant, N. L., Lovland, L. R., Jones R., Binette, A. P., Gonneaud, J., Arenaza-Urquijo, E. M., Chételat, G., & Villeneuve, S. (2020, July). Repetitive Negative Thinking Is Associated with Amyloid, Tau, and Cognitive Decline. *Alzheimer's & Dementia, 16*(7), 1054–64. https://doi.org/10.1002/alz.12116.

392   Moawad. *It Takes What It Takes*.

393   Amabile, T., & Kramer, S. (2011). *The Progress Principle: Using Small Wins to Ignite Joy, Engagement, and Creativity at Work*. Boston: Harvard Business Review Press.

394   Kanter, R. M. (2009, August 12). Change Is Hardest in the Middle. *Harvard Business Review*. https://hbr.org/2009/08/change-is-hardest-in-the-middl.

395   Davis, F. (1977). Nostalgia, Identity and the Current Nostalgia Wave. *Journal of Popular Culture, 11*(2), 414–24. https://doi.org/10.1111/j.0022-3840.1977.00414.x.

396   Van Dijke, M., Leunissen, J. M., Wildschut, T. & Sedikides, C. (2019, January). Nostalgia Promotes Intrinsic Motivation and Effort in the Presence of Low Interactional Justice. *Organizational Behavior and Human Decision Processes, 150*, 46–61. https://doi.org/10.1016/j.obhdp.2018.12.0

03.

397   Zhou, X., Wildschut, T., Sedikides, C., Chen, X., & Vingerhoets, A. J. J. M. (2012). Heartwarming Memories: Nostalgia Maintains Physiological Comfort. *Emotion*, *12*(4), 678–84. https://doi.org/10.1037/a0027236.

398   Sedikides, C., Cheung, W.-Y., Wildschut, T., Hepper, E. G., Baldursson, E., & Pedersen, B. (2018). Nostalgia Motivates Pursuit of Important Goals by Increasing Meaning in Life. *European Journal of Social Psychology*, *48*(2), 209–16. https://doi.org/10.1002/ejsp.2318; Van Dijke et al. Nostalgia Promotes Intrinsic Motivation and Effort in the Presence of Low Interactional Justice; van Tilburg, W.A.P., Sedikides, C., Wildschut, T., & Vingerhoets, A. J. J. M. (2019, April). How Nostalgia Infuses Life with Meaning: From Social Connectedness to Self-Continuity. *European Journal of Social Psychology*, *49*(3): 521–32. https://doi.org/10.1002/ejsp.2519; and Sedikides, C., & Wildschut, T. (2018). Finding Meaning in Nostalgia, *Review of General Psychology*, *22*(2), 48–61. https://doi.org/10.1037/gpr00 00109.

399   Adams, T. (2014, November 9). Look Back in Joy: The Power of Nostalgia. *Guardian*. https://www.theguardian.com/society/2014/nov/09/look-back -in-joy-the-power-of-nostalgia.

400   Cheung, W.-Y., Hepper, E. G., Reid, C. A., Green, J. D., Wildschut, T., & Sedikides, C. (2020). Anticipated Nostalgia: Looking Forward to Looking Back. *Cognition and Emotion*, *34*(3), 511–25, https://doi.org/10.1080/02699931.2019.1649247.

401   See Adams, Look Back in Joy: The Power of Nostalgia (and as discussed in Tierney and Baumeister, *The Power of Bad*).

402   Dweck. C. (2008). *Mindset: The New Psychology of Success*. New York: Ballantine Books.

403   Dweck. C. (2016, January 13). What Having a "Growth Mindset" Actually Means. *Harvard Business Review*.

404   Helmreich, R. L., & Spence, J. T. (1978). The Work and Family Orientation Questionnaire: An Objective Instrument to Assess Components on Achievement Motivation and Attitudes Toward Family and Career. *JSAS Catalog of Selected Documents in Psychology*, *8*, 35; and Ames, C. (1992). Classrooms: Goals, Structures, and Student Motivation. *Journal of Educa-*

tional Psychology, *84*(3), 261–71. https://doi.org/10.1037/0022-0663.84 .3.261.

405 Elliot, A. J., & Harackiewicz, J. M. (1996). Approach and Avoidance Achievement Goals and Intrinsic Motivation: A Mediational Analysis. *Journal of Personality and Social Psychology*, *70*(3), 461–75. https://doi.org/10.1 037/0022-3514.70.3.461; Elliot, A. J., & McGregor, H. A. (1999). Test Anxiety and the Hierarchical Model of Approach and Avoidance Achievement Motivation. *Journal of Personality and Social Psychology*, *76*(4), 628–4 4. https://doi.org/10.1037/0022-3514.76.4.628; Elliot, A. J., McGregor, H. A., & Gable, S. (1999). Achievement Goals, Study Strategies, and Exam Performance: A Mediational Analysis. *Journal of Educational Psychology*, *91* (3), 549–63. https://doi.org/10.1037/0022-0663.91.3.549; Elliot, A. J., & Sheldon, K. M. (1997). Avoidance Achievement Motivation: A Personal Goals Analysis. *Journal of Personality and Social Psychology*, *73*(1), 171–85. https://doi.org/10.1037/0022-3514.73.1.171; and VandeWalle, D., Brown, S. P., Cron, W. L., & Slocum, J. W., Jr. (1999). The Influence of Goal Orientation and Self-Regulation Tactics on Sales Performance: A Longitudinal Field Test. *Journal of Applied Psychology*, *84*(2), 249–59. https://doi.org/10.1037/0021-9010.84.2.249.

406 How Companies Can Profit from a "Growth Mindset." (2014, November) . *Harvard Business Review*. https://hbr.org/2014/11/how-companies-can -profit-from-a-growth-mindset.

407 Porath, C. L., & Bateman, T. S. (2006). Self-Regulation: From Goal Orientation to Job Performance. *Journal of Applied Psychology*, *91*(1), 185–92. https://doi.org/10.1037/0021-9010.91.1.185; and Kozlowski, S. W. J., Gully, S. M., Brown, K. G., Salas, E., Smith, E. M., & Nason, E. R. (200 1, May). Effects of Training Goals and Goal Orientation Traits on Multidimensional Training Outcomes and Performance Adaptability. *Organizational Behavior and Human Decision Processes*, *85*(1), 1–31. https: //doi.org/ 10.1006/obhd.2000.2930.

408 Nadella, S., Shaw, G., & Nichols, J. T. (2017). *Hit Refresh: The Quest to Rediscover Microsoft's Soul and Imagine a Better Future for Everyone*. New York: Harper Business.

409 Ibid.

NOTES

410 Ibid.

411 O'Hagan, S. R. (2017). *Extreme You: Step Up. Stand Out. Kick Ass. Repeat.* New York: HarperCollins.

412 Rodriguez, D. (2015, June 18). Laugh Your Way Out. LinkedIn. https://www.linkedin.com/pulse/laugh-your-way-out-david-rodriguez/.

413 Ibid.

414 Ibid.

CONCLUSION

415 CelticsLife. "I Am Because of Who We Are"—Flashback on UBUNTU. https://www.celticslife.com/2010/07/i-am-because-we-are-flashback-on-ubuntu.html.

416 Salesforce. (2021, June 22). *How IBM Hopes to Win an Oscar by Modernizing Its Marketing.* [Video]. You Tube. https://www.youtube.com/watch?v=5I3iLMRamoc.

417 [2]Piñeyro Sublett, C. (2018, November 14). Finding Ubuntu. It's Been a Minute. https://www.findingubuntu.com/.